upper-intermediate

second edition

coursebook

Innovations

a course in natural English

Hugh Dellar and Darryl Hocking
with Andrew Walkley

THOMSON
✶
TM
HEINLE

United Kingdom • United States • Australia • Canada • Mexico • Singapore • Spain

THOMSON

HEINLE

Innovations Upper-Intermediate Coursebook, Second Edition
Dellar/Hocking/Walkley

Publisher: *Christopher Wenger*
Series Editor: *Jimmie Hill*
Editorial Manager: *Howard Middle/HM ELT Services*
Director of Development, ESL/ELT: *Anita Raducanu*
Director of Marketing, ESL/ELT: *Amy Mabley*
Developmental Editor: *Paul MacIntyre*
Editorial Assistant: *Lisa Geraghty*
Sr. Production Editor: *Sally Cogliano*
Sr. Print Buyer: *Mary Beth Hennebury*
Associate Marketing Manager: *Laura Needham*

Compositor: *Process ELT (www.process-elt.com)*
Production Management: *Process ELT*
Illustrator: *Peter Standley*
Photography Manager: *Sheri Blaney*
Photo Researcher: *Process ELT*
Copyeditor: *Process ELT*
Cover/Text Designer: *Studio Image & Photographic Art*
(www.studio-image.com)

Printer: *Seng Lee Press*

Cover Images: Kandinsky: © *2003 Artists Rights Society (ARS), New York/ADAGP, Paris;* Da Vinci: © *Bettmann/CORBIS;*
Guggenheim Museum: *Tim Hursley/SuperStock*

For permission to use material from this text or
product, submit a request online at:
www.thomsonrights.com

**ISBN: 0-7593-9847-X
(Coursebook)**

Photo Credits

Photos on pages 8 (middle left, middle right and right), 11 (left column), 12,
20 (top and middle), 21, 22, 24, 31, 36, 40, 42, 44, 48, 50, 51, 55, 64 (top right
and bottom left), 71 (top left and bottom left), 77, 82, 92, 94, 104, 108, 109,
120 (top), 124 (right column), 126, 129 (bottom), 138, 140 (top, upper
middle and lower middle) and 141 by Anna Macleod.

Photos from other sources:
Page 8 (left) © ThinkStock LL Index Stock Imagery, page 11 (right column)
Allstar Picture Library, page 15 © Photonews/Topham/The Image Works,
page 17 © Roy Morsch/Corbis, page 18 (top) © AP Photo/Ben Margot, page
18 (middle) © AP Photo/Russell MacPhedran, page 18 (bottom) © AP
Photo/James A. Finley, page 19 © AP Photo/Rob Griffith, page 25 (left, middle
and right) © Heinle, page 27 (bottom) © AP Photo/Czarek Sokolowski, page
29 © AP Photo/Jim Rogash, page 30 (top) © AP Photo/Michael Sohn, page 38
(top left) © Mark Peterson/Corbis, page 38 (top middle) © Tomas del
Amos/Index Stock Imagery, page 38 (top right, bottom left and bottom
right) © Photofusion, page 47 © AP Photo/Phil Noble/WPA, pool, page 53
(left, middle and right) © Graham Burns/Photofusion, page 56 © Scott
Huston/Corbis, page 57 (top) © AP Photo/Alastair Grant, page 57 (bottom)
© David Bartuff/Index Stock Imagery, page 58 © AP Photo/Charles
Dharapak, page 59 (top left) © AP Photo/Laurent Rebours, page 59 (top
right) © AP Photo/Susan Walsh, page 59 (middle) © AP Photo/Charles Rex
Arbogast, page 59 (bottom) © AP Photo/Rune Petter Ness/NTB, page 64
(top left) © Heinle, page 67 (bottom) © Henryk Kaiser/Index Stock Imagery,
page 69 © AP Photo/Richard Lewis, page 73 © Royalty-Free/Corbis, page 79
© Lynda Richardson/Corbis, page 84 © Corbis Sygma, page 98 (top) © AP
Photo/Laurent Rebours, page 98 (bottom) © AP Photo/J. Paul Getty

Museum, ho, page 100 © AP Photo/Dan Chung/pool, page 101 © AP
Photo/Richard Lewis, page 102 © AP Photo/ho, page 103 © AP
Photo/Czarek Sokolowski, page 106 © 20th Century Fox/The Kobal
Collection/Sebastian, Lorey, page 110 (top) © 20th Century
Fox/Paramount/The Kobal Collection, page 110 (bottom left) ©
Poygram/Channel 4/Working Title/The Kobal Collection/Morey, Stephen,
page 110 (bottom right) © Icon/Ladd Co/Paramount/The Kobal Collection,
page 113 © Orion/The Kobal Collection, page 115 (first row left) © AP
Photo, page 115 (first row right) © AP Photo, page 115 (second row left) ©
AP Photo/Eric Risberg, page 115 (second row right) © AP Photo, page 115
(third row left) © AP Photo, page 115 (third row right) © AP
Photo/Menahem Kahana, pool, page 115 (fourth row left) © AP Photo, page
115 (fourth row right) © AP Photo/Gianni Foggia , page 120 (bottom) ©
Annebicque Bernard/Corbis Sygma, page 123 © AP Photo/Antonio Calanni,
page 127 (top left) © Cornelius Hog/Index Stock Imagery, page 127 (top
right) © Heinle, page 127 (bottom left) © Alan Schein Photography/Corbis,
page 127 (bottom right) © Owen Franken/Corbis, page 129 (top left) ©
Henry Diltz, page 129 (top middle) © Hulton/Archive by Getty Images,
page 129 (top right) © Lynn Goldsmith/Corbis, page 130 © AP
Photo/Nikolas Giakoumidis, page 131 (top left) © AP Photo/Thanassis
Stavrakis, page 131 (top right) © Heinle, page 131 (bottom left) © Heinle,
page 131 (bottom right) © Heinle, page 132 © AP Photo/Ann Johnsson,
page 135 (middle) © Hoa Qui/Index Stock Imagery, page 135 (bottom) ©
AP Photo/Mark Lennihan, page 136 © Peter Ciresa/Index Stock Imagery,
page 137 © AP Photo/Lynne Sladky, page 139 (left) © AP Photo/Jaime
Puebla, page 139 (right) © AP Photo/Stephen Chernin, page 140 (bottom) ©
William Swartz/Index Stock Imagery, page 142 © AP Photo/BBC

All other photos are by Painet Inc.

To the student

How do you learn a language? There is no easy answer to this question. People learn languages in many different ways. The **Innovations** series starts from the basis of natural conversations people have every day, then teaches you the language you need to have similar conversations in English.

To make this process as interesting, motivating, and productive as possible, the **Innovations** series:

*   contains numerous examples of the way grammar and vocabulary are naturally used. You can learn a lot of useful vocabulary from good grammar exercises, and good vocabulary activities will give you practice with the grammar of English.
*   introduces you to many new features of spoken grammar and useful idiomatic language, followed by opportunities to practise them in meaningful contexts.
*   includes reading texts that are intriguing and challenging, giving you plenty to talk – and think – about.
*   features 'Learner advice' pages, which will help you study better.

We hope you find **Innovations** as fun and interesting to learn from as we did to write!

Acknowledgements

The authors and publishers would like to thank the following teachers for their valuable input on this material at various stages during production:

David Frank Barnes, The British Institute of Florence; Richard Booker, School of Professional and Continuing Education, University of Hong Kong; Michael Bowles, The British Council; John Cargill, The British Council; Alex Chevrolle, EF English First; José Olavo de Amorim, Colégio Bandeirantes; Audrey Don, Universidad Latina de América; John Eaglesham, British School of Milan; Frank Farmer, Universidad de Quintana Roo, Unidad Cozumel; Kirsten Holt, St Giles Eastbourne; Pamela Humphreys, The British Council; Maria Helena Primon Iema, Sociedade Brasileira de Cultura Inglesa São Paulo; Belgin Ogrek, Ozel Florya Koleji; Guy Perring, The British Council; Mark Rendell, EF English First; Mark Rossiter, American University of Dubai; Andre Joao Rypl, Cultura Inglesa Porto Alegre.

In addition to those at Thomson, and in particular Jimmie, Andrew would like to thank Harry and Shirley Walkley for being great parents and true internationalists, Macu for her love and support, and Harry Dancey – a good friend made through teaching.

Hugh Dellar has taught EFL, ESP and EAP in Indonesia and Britain, where he is now a teacher and teacher-trainer at the University of Westminster, London. He trains both native-speaker and non-native speaker teachers. He has also given papers and teacher development workshops all over the world. He would like to thank the following people: Lisa – for just being there; his mum and dad, Julian Savage, Maud Dunkeld, Andy Fairhurst, Nick Groom, Carole Patilla, Sally Dalzell, Nick Barrett, Darryl Hocking, Andrew Walkley, Rob Batstone, Ivor Timmis, Scott Thornbury, Chris Wenger, Howard Middle, Stuart Tipping, Michael Lewis and Jimmie Hill for their help, support, inspiration and enthusiasm over the years and Thierry Henry, Patrick Viera, Robert Pires, Curtis Mayfield, Pharoah Sanders, Iain Sinclair and Wong Kar-Wei for bringing beauty and joy to my rare moments of free time and for helping me get through!!

Darryl Hocking is a teacher and teacher-trainer in both ESOL and EAP, as well as a lecturer in art and design, at Auckland University of Technology, New Zealand. He specialises in developing academic literacies programmes in art and design and has also worked in this area at Goldsmiths, University of London. He would like to thank Rosemary, Lucia and Isaac.

Andrew Walkley has taught mainly in Spain and Britain over the past twelve years. He currently divides his time between teaching general English, writing materials and maintaining a family life. He also does teacher training and regularly gives talks and workshops to teachers from all over the world. He would like to thank Macu, Rebeca and Santiago. Much love, and sorry for spending so much time in front of the computer!

Contents

What's she like? • Yes, but what's she really like? • A bit on the thin side. • No, I wouldn't go so far as to say that! • Well, he does take after his father. • He's very laid-back. • I've never met anyone else like him. • She's a real laugh. • I think she's a bottle blonde. • I know it's not very PC of me to say so. • She's a really lovely person. • Do you fancy him? • She wouldn't say boo to a goose. • You'd never think it. • He's got a really sexy voice. • I've always thought of myself as a very creative person. • It's his aftershave. • No, I don't really go for redheads. • She can be really cheeky sometimes. • He's fifty if he's a day. • Oh, I just heard it on the grapevine. • She's a friend of a friend of mine. • He's an absolute hoot.

1 Talking about people

Using vocabulary

1 | Describing people

Think of three people you know – friends or family. Write their initials beside three of the adjectives or expressions below. Then tell a partner about your choices.

Tick the six adjectives or expressions which best describe you. Then describe yourself to your partner.

Age	Hair	Height	Personality
young	fair	quite tall	amusing
in his/her twenties	darkish	a bit on the short side	a bit dull
quite elderly	completely white		conservative
younger than (s)he looks	going grey	**Other**	warm
older than (s)he looks	losing his hair	lazy	narrow-minded
	almost bald	hard-working	independent
Looks		bad-tempered	fun
good-looking	**Weight**	easy-going	a bit of a workaholic
not very good-looking	a bit thin	friendly	religious
	overweight	moody	musical
	on the plump side	energetic	sporty
		a bit of a fitness fanatic	creative
			very political
			a good sense of humour

2 | Speaking

Discuss these questions with a partner.

1. When you're speaking your own language, which adjectives do you use most to describe people?

2. What features of a person's appearance do you usually notice first?

3. Are you happy with your own appearance? Why/why not?

3 | Who's who?

Listen to the descriptions of Jenny, Nick, Matt, and Kirsty. Decide who's who. Then work in pairs, trying to remember as much as you can from the descriptions you heard.

1. ....   2. ....   3. ....   4. ....

Using grammar

1 | Modifiers

The words used before adjectives or nouns to make a comment stronger, weaker, or more acceptable are called modifiers. Add adjectives in the spaces to talk about people you know.

1. *very/really* + adjective
   She's very nice.   He's really bossy.
   I've got a friend who can be very . . . . at times,
   but usually she's really . . . .

2. *quite* + adjective
   He's quite creative – he paints and draws.
   My father's quite . . . .
   My teacher can be quite . . . . sometimes.

3. *a bit* + negative adjective
   He's a bit boring.   She's a bit immature.
   I have to admit, I can be a bit . . . . sometimes.

4. *a bit of a* + negative noun
   She's a bit of a moaner. He's a bit of a workaholic.
   My mum/dad is a bit of a . . . .

5. *a bit too* + positive adjective
   She's a bit too nice, if you know what I mean.
   I've got a friend who's very . . . .
   In fact, I think he's a bit too . . . .

Tell your partner as much as you can about what you have written.

▶ For more information on modifiers, see G1.

2 | Pronunciation

🎧 **Listen to the stress and intonation of these examples.**

It's <u>quite</u> expensive.
(This means it's expensive, but not too expensive.)

It's quite ex<u>pen</u>sive.
(This means you think it really *is* expensive.)

🎧 **Listen to these examples. Each is said in two different ways. Then try saying them yourself, so that the difference is clear.**

1. I live quite near the office.
2. She's quite nice.
3. He's quite a good cook.
4. We're quite happy with the colour.
5. He's quite friendly.
6. I think they're quite conservative.
7. The weather was quite good.
8. It's quite interesting.

3 | Speaking

Do you agree with these statements?

1. Jeans are a bit old-fashioned nowadays.
2. Tattoos are really cool.
3. Body-piercing is a bit too risky for me!
4. Surfing the net can be a bit of a bore.
5. Long hair is very attractive.
6. Vegetarians can be a bit of a pain in the neck.
7. Alcohol is very dangerous.
8. Parents can be a bit too protective.

> **Real English:** a pain in the neck
>
> If someone is a pain in the neck, they are very annoying. You can also use it about a situation. *Parking's become absolutely impossible in the town centre. It's a real pain in the neck.*

4 | Friends and relatives

Do you say the following in your language?

A friend of a friend is a friend.
A friend of an enemy is an enemy.
An enemy of a friend is an enemy.
An enemy of an enemy is a friend.

Check you understand these useful expressions for talking about your friends and relatives.

1. I don't really know John Baker. I only know him by sight.
2. Mary's an old girlfriend of mine.
3. We're old schoolfriends.
4. He's her ex.
5. This is my partner, Jean.
6. Bill's just an acquaintance. I don't really know him that well.
7. She's my sister-in-law.
8. I don't know them, but I know of them.
9. I'm his godson.
10. My sister and I are really close.

Are there people in your life who fit the above descriptions? Who and what are they? Tell a partner about them.

Listening

1 | Before you listen

Tell a partner as much as you can about your family.

2 | While you listen

🎧 **Simon and Melanie work in the same office. Simon's popped in to Melanie's house after work for a cup of tea. As you listen to their conversation, try to answer these questions.**

1. Do Melanie and Simon have any brothers and sisters?
2. Do Melanie and Simon get on well with the other members of their families?

Listen again and try to fill in the gaps in the conversation in the next column.

3 | Speaking

Discuss these questions with a partner.

1. Melanie thinks her mum is a bit too nice. Is it possible to be too nice? Do you know anyone like that?
2. Melanie is an only child. Do you know any only children? Which would you prefer: to be an only child or to be one of ten or eleven?
3. Do you know anyone who comes from a really big family? How many brothers and sisters did your parents have? What about their parents?

The Brother from Hell!

Melanie: I can't remember. Do you take milk?

Simon: Please, but no sugar. Thanks. It's weird, you know, but I've been to your house (1) ...., and I still haven't met your parents.

Melanie: Yes, they're out a lot. My dad works for the BBC and my mum's a, she does sort of (2) .... work for a company. You know, like an advertising agency. They're both really busy.

Simon: Oh, they sound really interesting.

Melanie: Do you think so? I find my dad (3) .... dull, to be honest. He works late every day, even works some weekends, doesn't read, doesn't go out. I mean, don't (4) ...., he's (5) .... nice, but I don't know, I just don't have anything to say to him. I think (6) ...., we just don't spend enough time together.

Simon: How old is he, then?

Melanie: About fifty-five, I think. I can never really remember.

Simon: Oh, yeah.

Melanie: But my mum's lovely. She's (7) ...., a bit too nice though, sometimes, always trying to look after me. She worries about me leaving home. She's (8) .... over-protective, if you know what I mean. I'm an (9) ...., so...

Simon: Oh, I didn't know that.

Melanie: What? You mean you can't tell!

Simon: I don't know. I've never thought about it, I suppose.

Melanie: So, what about you? Have you got any brothers or sisters yourself?

Simon: Yes, I've got one of each, (10) ....

Melanie: Oh right. Older or younger?

Simon: My sister's two or three years younger than me, but my brother's (11) .... older. He's about forty now.

Melanie: Do you get on with them all right? You haven't really talked about them very much.

Simon: Well, my brother, not (12) .... well, actually. He's different from me, (13) .... old-fashioned, (14) .... traditional. Well, actually, he's a bit, how can I (15) ...., right-wing. You know – things aren't what they used to be, more police, death penalty – that kind of thing. He's (16) .... fool, actually.

Melanie: Oh, well, it takes all sorts, I suppose.

Simon: But my sister, she's great. We (17) .... We've got the same kind of (18) ....

Melanie: Just a pity about the brother from hell, eh?

Simon: Yes. Oh, but he's not that bad. We get on all right, as long as you steer (19) .... of certain topics. Anyway, you were telling me about your parents.

Melanie: Oh, there's not much to tell, actually.

> **Real English:** the brother from hell
> This means that he is not a very pleasant person. In fact, he is rather unpleasant. The kind of neighbours who play loud music in the middle of the night are the neighbours from hell! Other people's children can be the children from hell!

Using vocabulary

1 | Adjectives

Mark each of the adjectives below P or N, depending on whether you think they are positive or negative. Use your dictionary if necessary. Then discuss your answers with your partner.

1. religious	9. strict
2. traditional	10. business-minded
3. quiet	11. nice
4. talkative	12. individual
5. tidy	13. messy
6. laid-back	14. liberal
7. conservative	15. hard-working
8. ambitious	16. sensible

Underline the main stressed syllable in each adjective. Look back at the adjectives used to describe people on page 8. Which is the most positive for you? Which is the most negative?

Make a list of the four most positive adjectives and the four most negative adjectives you can use about someone.

Positive	Negative
1.	1. ....
2.	2. ....
3.	3. ....
4.	4. ....

Compare your lists with a partner.

2 | Judging by appearances

Work with a partner. Decide what you think these people are like. Use more than one adjective for each person. Begin: *He/she looks ... .*

3 | Emphasising

We often use more than one adjective to describe things or people. These adjectives are often emphasised by using the same adverb before each adjective.

It was really cold and really windy.
She's very nice, very interesting.
It was extremely long and extremely boring.

We can use two *different* adjectives with a similar meaning.

He's a bit strange, a bit weird.
He's a bit old-fashioned, a bit traditional.
It was really scary, really frightening.

🎧 **Listen to the six sentences above, and practise saying them.**

Now talk about the pictures below using two adjectives and the same adverb. For example:

What a bike! It's really big and really fast.

Underline the adjectives and adverbs which make this dialogue sound interesting.

A: Didn't you go to Turkey last summer?

B: No, we went to Thailand. It was really nice, really interesting.

A: Whereabouts did you go?

B: Well, first we went to Bangkok, which was a bit too crowded, a bit too mad for me, so we went off to the islands instead, which were really beautiful, really relaxing.

Now describe the following to your partner in a similar way.

1. your last holiday
2. the best place you've ever been to
3. food from your country
4. your best friend
5. your home town

Reading

1 | Before you read

Discuss these questions with a partner.

1. Do you have any kids? If so, how many?
2. If not, do you want any? Why/why not?
3. What's the best number of children to have?
4. What's the best age to have them at?

2 | While you read

Now read this text about a family with more children than any of your parents – the Pridhams. As you read, underline anything that surprises you.

FULL-TIME JOB!

Every English-speaking child knows the nursery rhyme about the old woman with lots of children:

There was an old woman who lived in a shoe.
She had so many children she didn't know what to do.

Nicola Pridham must understand the old woman's predicament very well. She's expecting her twentieth child and she's only forty! She and her husband Kevin already have twelve sons and seven daughters.

Kevin Pridham is a self-employed builder, but what he earns is not enough to feed and clothe their large family. Every week their grocery bill comes to £400. They go through thirty-five loaves of bread and twenty-five boxes of breakfast cereal per week.

If you have a child in Britain today, researchers have shown that it will cost you almost £100 per week when you take into consideration food, clothes, pocket money and all the other expenses involved in bringing up children.

Before they are eighteen you will have spent almost £100,000 per child. This means that Nicola and Kevin will have to find two million pounds! You can be fairly sure that the Pridham children will be handing clothes down to each other and doing odd jobs to provide themselves with pocket money.

3 | Speaking

Tell a partner what surprised you about the article above. Then discuss these questions.

1. Do you know anyone who's expecting a child at the moment?
2. Do you know anyone who's self-employed? What do they do?
3. Did you ever get clothes handed down to you?
4. Do you think housewives should be paid by the state? Why/why not?

Using grammar

1 | Present tenses

Here are four ways of talking about what you do for a living.

I'm	a journalist / a civil servant / out of work.
I work	in a factory / in IT / as a DJ.
I run	a guest house / a restaurant.
I do	cleaning jobs / a lot of work for the BBC.

Complete these sentences with a suitable verb. The first two are done for you.

1. I .... am ... self-employed.
2. He ... works .. in advertising.
3. She .... an architect.
4. You .... for the government, don't you?
5. He .... as a waiter at weekends.
6. I .... in a bank.
7. She .... a businesswoman.
8. My dad .... unemployed at the moment.
9. My brother .... in the army.
10. I sometimes .... bar work.
11. He .... the occasional design job.
12. My mother .... a retired teacher.
13. I .... on a boat.
14. She .... her own business.

2 | Speaking

Ask some other students in the class about their jobs and/or their parents' jobs. Who has the most interesting job? The most stressful? The most unusual?

3 | Grammar discussion

With a partner, discuss the difference in meaning between the verb forms in these sentences.

1a. My dad works for the BBC as a cameraman.
1b. My dad's working in Manchester this month.

2a. I find my dad a bit dull. He's only interested in making money.
2b. I'm finding my job a bit boring at the moment.

3a. He even works some weekends.
3b. He's working this weekend. He's finishing off a special report.

4a. My mum is a really nice person.
4b. She's being really nice at the moment. I wonder why!

5a. Do you get on with them all right?
5b. Are you getting on with them OK again?

In the examples above, underline the time expressions used with the present continuous.

4 | Grammar in context

Complete these sentences using the present simple or present continuous.

1. He usually .... (work) in the centre of town, but this week he .... (work) from home because he .... (try) out a new computer link-up for the company. It could be the thing of the future.
2. Don't you think John .... (act) pretty strangely at the moment? I mean, he .... (not be) normally that quiet. Do you think he's OK?
3. My dad .... (run) his own business, but he's sick at the moment, so my older brother .... (look after) it for a while. I think they want him to take it over eventually.
4. You .... (not talk) about your parents a lot. .... (you not get on) with them very well?
5. He .... (be) very left-wing. I think he .... (still / wait) for the socialist revolution!
6. We .... (not talk) to each other just now, actually. He .... (be / still) annoyed with me for forgetting his birthday last year.

Now complete these pairs of sentences with information which is true.

7. My .... works ....
   My .... is working .... at the moment.
8. I get on very well with ....
   I'm not getting on very well with .... at the moment.
9. My .... lives in ....
   My .... is living in .... at the moment.

> For more information on the present simple and present continuous, see G2.

> **Real English: pretty**
>
> The adjective pretty means beautiful or attractive.
> As an adverb it means fairly.
> I'm pretty good at badminton.
> He's acting pretty strangely.
>
> Is there anything you're pretty good at?

5 | Famous present tenses

These two famous quotations use the present simple. Which is your favourite?

1. Freedom is the right to tell people what they do not want to hear.
2. Foreigners have sex lives; the English have hot water bottles.

Here are some famous sayings. When would you say them?

3. What goes up must come down.
4. An elephant never forgets.
5. It never rains, but it pours.
6. You're making a mountain out of a molehill.

He's a bit strange. • He's a bit of an oddball. • What a nose! • I think she had it done in America. • He's brighter than yo[u] think. • She's not really my type. • I wouldn't like to meet him on a dark night! • We get on like a house on fire. • I've bee[n] meaning to write for ages. • Men with beards usually have weak chins. • Too spotty for my taste. • An old head on your shoulders, as they say. • There's no insanity in my family. • She's really easy to talk to. • Didn't you hear he's passed away? • She's one in a million. • She's got her head screwed on. • I wish he'd pull his socks up a bit! • No, I'm not with anyone at th[e] moment. • I think they've split up, gone the[ir] separate ways. • Like father, like son!

2 Friends and relatives

Reading

1 Before you read

Discuss these questions with a partner.

1. Who are the most infamous criminals in your country? Tell your partner as much as you can about them.

2. Can you think of any examples of an infamous kidnapping? An infamous murder? An infamous robbery? An infamous terrorist act?

3. How would you feel if your parents were involved in crime?

2 While you read

🎧 **You are now going to read about a son being reunited with his infamous father. When you have read the text, answer these questions.**

1. Why has Bronson spent so long in prison?

2. How did his son feel about meeting him?

3. How realistic are their plans for their future?

Surprise for Jailbird Dad

There are many happy stories about children being reunited with the famous parents they did not know they had, but perhaps one of the most unusual is that of a twenty-five-year-old chef from Liverpool, who was recently informed of the fact that the father he had never known was actually one of Britain's most dangerous men.

Originally jailed for robbery and burglary, Charles Bronson has spent twenty-two of the last twenty-six years in prison. Much of this is because he has repeatedly taken hostages in jail and attacked fellow inmates. He is a man of incredible physical strength and has a terrible temper. He has already caused over half a million pounds' worth of damage to prison property and has had to be moved to a special secure unit, costing the taxpayer over £60,000 a year.

Twenty-five years ago, he became a father, when his son, Michael, was born. However, he split up with the boy's mother when he began a prison sentence three years later. Last year, though, an old friend managed to track down Bronson's son in Liverpool. The news that his father was the infamous 'most dangerous man in Britain' obviously came as a total shock to the son, who nevertheless decided to get in touch with his father. When Bronson first heard from Michael, he said: 'I was on a mission of madness, now I'm on a mission of peace. All I want to do now is get home and have a pint with my boy.'

When the two men finally met in prison, Michael said that he got on like a house on fire with his father. 'I gave him a great big hug. It was very nice to finally meet him after all these years. People get the wrong impression of him from the media. He's not as bad as they make out. He's actually a very sensitive and talented guy.' Interestingly, the facts do back up this claim, because as well as having a reputation for violence, Bronson also has a reputation for his cartoons and poetry. He's been attempting to have his work published, but the prison authorities have stood in the way of any such plan, because they don't want him to profit from his crimes.

Michael also commented on the fact that he and his father looked very similar, except for his dad's large bushy beard. Bronson himself said: 'I'm delighted to be back in touch with my son. It's taken twenty-two years to get him back into my life.'

When Charles Bronson is eventually released, father and son want to open up a restaurant. Mike plans to be the chef – while Bronson intends to be the security on the door! These plans, however, may have to be put on hold – it seems that old habits die hard. Only last week, Bronson was involved in yet another violent incident and an early release looks increasingly unlikely. If you would like to know more about Charles Bronson's amazing life, a biography is currently being written about him. You can read it with a clear conscience because any profits will be going to charity.

14

3 | Speaking

Discuss these questions with a partner.

1. Would you be interested in reading a biography of Charles Bronson? Why/why not?

2. Do you think locking people up for a long time is a good idea?

3. What effect does prison have on people? What about their families?

4. Can you think of any alternatives to prison?

4 | Vocabulary check

Complete these sentences with words from the text.

1. If you haven't met someone for fifty years, it can be a very emotional occasion when you are
    . . . .

2. If you are found guilty of breaking into someone's home and stealing from them, you are guilty of
    . . . .

3. Sometimes one country tries to put pressure on another country by taking some of its citizens
    . . . . Sometimes these . . . .
    are killed; sometimes money has to be paid for their release.

4. If you are famous for something bad or evil, you are
    . . . .

5. If you put your arms round someone, you are giving them a . . . .

6. If a beard is . . . ., it means that it is large and very thick – like a bush!

7. If you can't carry out a plan immediately because of some problem, you have to put the plan on
    . . . .

8. If you give away the money you make from something to a good cause, the profits go to . . . .

Using vocabulary

1 | Idioms focus

> Michael said he got on like a house on fire with his father.

Complete the idioms in these sentences with moment, eye, wavelength and close.

1. We argue about everything. We simply don't see eye to . . . . on anything.

2. There's never a dull . . . . in our house. There's always something going on!

3. I get on really well with my mum. We're really . . . .

4. It's incredible. Although my gran is in her seventies, we really are on the same . . . .

Use two of the idioms to tell a partner about two people in your life.

2 | Body idioms

The Real English note on page 9 explained a pain in the neck. Circle the correct word in the body idioms in these sentences.

1. My car's on its last feet / legs. I've already started looking for a new one.

2. Have you seen Paula's new laptop? I bet it cost her an arm and a leg / hand.

3. I'm under a lot of pressure at work. My boss is breathing down my back / neck all the time.

4. I'm afraid I've just put my foot / mouth in it. I've just said something to Kate without realising she and Pete have split up.

5. When Frank slipped on that banana skin, I nearly laughed my legs / head off.

6. Yes, it was funny, wasn't it? I tried to keep a straight mouth / face, but it was impossible.

7. If you're worried about something, tell me – it's far better to get it off your chest / back.

8. I can't even have a morning off. I'm up to my eyes / nose in work.

Can you translate the eight idioms above into your language?

3 | Speaking

When was the last time you ...

*   **put your foot in it? Why? What did you say?**
*   **found it impossible to keep a straight face?**
*   **bought something that cost an arm and a leg?**

Charles Bronson

Using grammar

1 | Comparatives: *not as ... as ...*

In the article that you read about Charles Bronson, his son, Michael, said that his dad is **not as bad as** the media make out.

Make six more examples of sentences that use this structure. Match the sentence beginnings 1–6 to the endings a–f.

1. I don't see my mum ☐
2. I'm not as close to my older brother ☐
3. I don't get on as well with my sister ☐
4. He's not as serious ☐
5. She's not as old ☐
6. We don't get on with them now as well ☐

a. as she looks.
b. as I do with my brother.
c. as I am to my younger.
d. as often as I see my dad.
e. as we used to.
f. as he seems when you first meet him.

Now complete these sentences in ways that are true for you.

7. I'm not as close to my . . . . as I am to
   . . . .
8. I'm not as . . . . as some people think.
9. I don't see . . . . as often as I used to.
10. My dad's not as . . . . as he might seem.
11. . . . . isn't as old as he/she looks.

Now explain what you have written to your partner.

Have you ever got the wrong impression of someone when you first met them?

2 | Comparing the present with the past

We often compare the present with the past. For example, we often compare recent experiences with past ones. Look at these examples:

A: How's the new car?
B: Great! Honestly, it's much easier to park than the old one, now we've got power steering.

A: How was the holiday? Was the weather OK?
B: Yeah, it was great. It was much better going in May. It wasn't as hot as the last time and there were fewer tourists about.

Complete these dialogues using the adjectives in brackets in the comparative form.

1. A: Did I hear you say you've got a new bike? What's it like?
   B: Brilliant! It's 1100cc, so it's much . . . . than my old one. I'll take you out on it next week sometime, if you like. (powerful)

2. A: What's their new flat like? Is it nice?
   B: Lovely, it's much . . . . than their old one and it's not nearly . . . . (big, dark)

3. A: What's your new teacher like? Is he all right?
   B: Yeah, he's OK but he's not . . . . as our last one, Jane. I mean, he's clear and everything, but he's . . . . than Jane. We used to have a laugh with her. It was just . . . . with her. (good, serious, fun)

4. A: How was your journey? Was there much traffic?
   B: Yeah, it was awful! We thought it would be . . . . taking the motorway than the way we came last time, but it was much . . . . We were stuck in this terrible traffic jam for about an hour. (quick, slow)

5. A: You went to Lake Como again, didn't you? Was it nice?
   B: Yeah, it was OK, but it was a bit . . . . than I remember it being. (touristy)

What do you think touristy means?

3 | Pronunciation: the schwa sound

The sound we call 'schwa' /ə/ is used for most
unstressed vowel sounds. In the sentences below,
the stressed words or syllables are underlined.
Most of the other syllables are unstressed. Try to
say this sentence stressing the underlined words.

It's <u>much</u> better than it <u>used</u> to be.

Now practise saying these sentences.

1. It's <u>bet</u>ter than my <u>old</u> one.
2. It's <u>bet</u>ter than it <u>was</u> be<u>fore</u>.
3. It's <u>big</u>ger than the <u>last</u> one.
4. It's <u>much</u> <u>more</u> <u>tou</u>risty than it <u>used</u> to be.
5. It's <u>much</u> <u>cheap</u>er than it <u>used</u> to be.
6. It was <u>quick</u>er than <u>last</u> time.
7. It wasn't as <u>good</u> as the <u>last</u> <u>time</u> we <u>went</u>.
8. It wasn't as <u>good</u> as I re<u>mem</u>bered.
9. It's <u>not</u> as <u>good</u> as it <u>used</u> to be.

🎧 **Now listen and check your pronunciation.
Then listen again and repeat the sentences.**

**What do you think it means in each of the
sentences above?**

**How many of the sentences above can you use to
talk about things that are true for you? Compare
with a partner. Who can use the most sentences?**

4 | Speaking

**Discuss these questions in groups of three. Try to
use as much of the grammar from this unit as
you can. Spend five minutes planning what you
want to say first.**

1. How do you like the flat/house you're living in now,
   compared to places you lived in before?
2. What's the best place you've ever lived in? Why?
   What made it so good?
3. Is your city better or worse than it used to be ten
   years ago? In what way?
4. Is your country better or worse than it used to be?
   In what way?
5. Can you think of anything that you found a bit
   disappointing the *second* time around – a place, a film,
   a book, a restaurant?

▶ For more information on comparatives, see G3.

Using vocabulary

1 | Phrasal verbs with *up*

Michael's parents split up. There are lots of
phrasal verbs with up. Complete the sentences
below with the correct form of the verbs in the
box.

fill	cheer	mix	get	look	pick

1. If the tickets go on sale at nine, we'd better
   . . . . up early and be there by eight.
2. I'll . . . . you up in the car around seven and
   we can go into town and have a bite to eat.
3. You look really sad! . . . . up! It's not the
   end of the world!
4. I'll just go to their website and . . . . up the
   times of their flights to Zurich.
5. We can . . . . up with petrol before we
   leave.
6. I always . . . . up Pete with his brother Ed.
   They look so similar.

2 | Speaking

Discuss these questions with a partner.

1. Can you think of three reasons why couples split up?
2. Can you think of three things you could do to cheer
   yourself up?
3. What kind of things can you look up?

3 | Talking about disasters

What do you think has happened in these pictures?

With a partner, discuss in which picture each of the following is most likely to be said.

1. Everyone's been evacuated. ☐
2. It all just happened so suddenly. ☐
3. My car's been totally turned upside down. ☐
4. Everything's been smashed to pieces. ☐
5. Luckily, no one's been hurt. ☐
6. It's balanced right on the edge. ☐
7. Everything's gone up in flames. ☐
8. It's spread very quickly. ☐
9. It could go at any minute. ☐
10. It destroyed everything in its path. ☐
11. It's done millions of pounds' worth of damage. ☐
12. They're still trying to put it out. ☐
13. Our roof was blown off. ☐

A

B

C

4 | Speaking

Have there been any natural disasters in your country? When? What happened?

5 | Giving bad news

Notice how the highlighted expressions warn the other person that bad news is coming.

A: I haven't seen Mary for ages. How is she?
B: Oh, *haven't you heard?* She was made redundant last month.
A: Oh, that's awful. She must've been really upset.

A: How's your mother?
B: *Well, actually,* she passed away last month.
A: Oh, I *am* sorry to hear that. Is your father all right?
B: Oh yes, he seems to be coping very well.

A: Can John make it to the party?
B: *I'm afraid not.* We're no longer together.
A: Oh, I'm sorry about that. Is everything OK?

Make short dialogues by matching the questions 1–8 to the answers a–h.

1. Can you give me a lift home?

2. Do you think I could get that camera back off you sometime soon?

3. Have you heard from Jan recently?

4. Is your grandfather any better?

5. So, has Peter had his results yet?

6. Are you feeling all right, Steve?

7. Hello, how are you?

8. I thought you had a dog.

a. I'm afraid not. We're very worried about him. But then, he *is* ninety.

b. Oh, fine thanks. Well, actually, I think I'm getting the flu, so I'd stay away if I were you.

c. I don't know how to put this, but I think I lost it last night while I was out. I'm really sorry, but I've searched everywhere and I can't find it. I'll get you another one. I'm extremely sorry.

d. We did. But unfortunately, it ran out into the street and was run over. I'm afraid we had to have it put down.

e. I'm sorry, I'm afraid I can't. I lost my licence last week – had a bit too much to drink and got stopped by the police!

f. Well, actually, I haven't – not for about six months – we had a bit of an argument last year.

g. Well, actually, no. I've just had some very bad news.

h. Well, yes, I'm afraid he has. He didn't pass – so he's got to re-sit part of his exams in July.

🎧 **Go back and underline the expressions used to introduce the bad news. Now listen and check your answers. Then work in pairs reading the dialogues.**

> **Real English: have it put down**
>
> If an animal is seriously ill or badly injured, you take it to the vet and he *puts it down*. Another way of saying this is he *puts it to sleep*.

6 | Role play

Imagine you live in one of the places shown in the pictures on page 18. A friend has rung you, not knowing what has happened. Give them the bad news. For example:

A: Hello, is that you, Jack? This is Ron in Sydney.
B: Hi, Ron, how are things down under?
A: Well, actually, it's like an inferno. Everything's on fire. The bush … trees … houses …
B: And are you all right?
A: For the time being, I think we are.

Now change partners. Think of five questions your friend might ask you about the terrible situation you are in.

1. .... ?
2. .... ?
3. .... ?
4. .... ?
5. .... ?

Now role play a similar conversation to the one you've just had. This time, use a different picture and the questions above.

I really get a kick out of it. • What kind of things do you do in your free time? • I read a lot of novels. • I'm really into board games. • What kind of programmes do you usually watch? • I don't really buy that many magazines. • I wait till they come out on DVD. • What sort of music are you into? • I only usually go to classical concerts. • You can't beat a live gig. • Gardening! I'm a total shopaholic. • Are there any good clubs you'd recommend? • I wish I could play the xylophone! • I've never been to an art gallery in my life! • It should be right up your street. • I was wondering if you were doing anything this Friday? • I don't know very much about art, but I do know what I like. • I'm completely hopelessly hooked on computer games.

3 Your interests

Using vocabulary

1 Free time

Which of the following do you like doing in your free time? Mark each one in this way:

O	**if you do it often**
S	**if you do it sometimes**
N	**if you never do it**

- listening to classical music
- going to see bands
- going clubbing
- playing an instrument
- reading
- working out at a gym
- watching videos
- going to art exhibitions
- going to an evening class
- playing a sport
- eating out
- going round junk shops
- playing computer games
- t'ai chi or something like that

> **Real English: junk**
>
> Junk is stuff of little value which you consider useless, for example, old furniture, books, CDs, or other things you have no use for.

Use your dictionary to translate any vocabulary you are unsure of. Find out what you have in common with your partner.

2 | Not as often as I used to

Listen to June, a bus driver, talking about how she spends her free time. As you listen, complete the time expressions she uses below.

1. Not all that . . . .
2. All the . . . .
3. Not as . . . . as I'd like to.
4. About . . . . fortnight.
5. . . . . I can.
6. A . . . . of times a year.
7. Hardly . . . .
8. Not as often as I . . . . to.

Practise saying the eight expressions above.

3 | How often do you ...?

Ask and answer with a partner. When you answer, try to use some of the expressions in Exercise 2.

How often do you ...

1. have your hair cut?
2. get up early on Saturdays?
3. see your parents/grandparents?
4. cook in the evenings?
5. work in the evenings?
6. see your best friend?
7. have friends round for dinner?
8. read in English?
9. watch films in English?
10. buy presents for friends?
11. go away for the weekend?
12. go to the cinema?

4 | *How-* questions

How- questions are useful for asking for more information.

> How much did it cost?
> How long did it take you?
> How difficult was it?

Make how- questions by adding an adverb, an adjective, or a quantity word like much to these questions.

1. A: How . . . . did it take you to learn to play the guitar as well as that?
    B: About ten years. I started when I was really young, though.

2. A: How . . . . is your work from your home?
    B: About an hour's drive, I think.

3. A: How . . . . did you move here?
    B: Oh, ages ago. In fact, I've forgotten how long!

4. A: How . . . . does dinner usually cost you?
    B: It varies, but I suppose about £8 or £9.

5. A: So how . . . . have you been learning English?
    B: Ever since I can remember. I started when I was really really young.

6. A: How . . . . can you speak Chinese?
    B: I guess I'm OK, but I could be better.

7. A: How . . . . is it to learn Chinese?
    B: Some people say it's the most difficult language to learn as a foreigner.

8. A: How . . . . do you go away, then?
    B: Every couple of months, I suppose, providing I've got the money.

9. A: How . . . . people do you need in a team?
    B: Usually it's eleven, but you can also play with five.

10. A: How . . . . are you about your exams?
    B: Very! But I'm trying not to think about them too much!

Now write questions you would like to ask a partner. Then work in pairs to find the answers.

1. How much . . . . ?
2. How often . . . . ?
3. How long ago . . . . ?
4. How far away . . . . ?
5. How difficult . . . . ?
6. How easy . . . . ?
7. How many . . . . ?

Listening

1 | Speaking

Discuss these questions with a partner.

1. Do you have much in common with the rest of your family? What interests do you share?

2. Do you think men and women tend to be interested in different kinds of things?

3. Is it best to marry someone who ...
   - shares all your interests?
   - shares none of your interests?
   - shares a few of your interests, but has some of their own?

4. Is there something you would really like to be able to do, but have not yet had the opportunity to do?

2 | Before you listen

Dan and Helena have only just started going out together. They are not finding it easy to decide what to do with their evening. Cover the conversation. As you listen, try to decide which of these statements is the most accurate.

1. They have nothing in common.
2. They have lots in common.
3. They have less in common than they think!

Listen again and complete the gaps in the conversation.

So what shall we do tonight?

Dan: So what do you feel like doing tonight? Any ideas?

Helena: Well, I'd quite like to see a film, or, I don't know, see if there's any good bands around, if you're into bands.

Dan: Yes, that's an idea. (1) . . . . music do you like, then?

Helena: Oh, all sorts, really, you know, a lot of pop and I quite like blues and jazz and (2) . . . .

Dan: Oh, really? I'm more into dance music myself, so maybe ...

Helena: Well, (3) . . . . , we could always go and see a film. I like really scary things.

Dan: What? You mean like *Halloween*?

Helena: Yes, that kind of thing, and I also (4) . . . . action movies, you know, car chases, guns, bombs, anything that's fast and exciting.

Dan: Oh, right. To be honest with you, I'm not really (5) . . . . violent films.

Helena: You're kidding! And I thought this was going to be the perfect relationship!

Dan: (6) . . . . ! But it doesn't sound like we've got all that much in common, really, does it?

Helena: Oh come on, there must be something we can do!

Dan: Let me think. Well, I suppose we (7) . . . . go clubbing.

Helena: What? Somewhere like Paradox?

Dan: Is that the new place that's just opened?

Helena: Yes, just last week. Right, so (8) . . . . going clubbing, then?

Dan: OK. Why not? Do you go much yourself?

Helena: No, (9) . . . . , actually. A couple of times a year, I guess.

Dan: Oh, me too now, but I (10) . . . . a lot more when I was younger – almost every weekend. The thing was, though, it just got to me after a while, staying out dancing all night and then having to go to work (11) . . . . in the morning. I'm getting a bit too old for it now.

Helena: Oh, well, that's that off the menu, then! So, what shall we do then?

Dan: I don't know. (12) . . . . get a video and a curry, and have a nice quiet evening in in front of the telly?

Helena: Oh, you've got to be joking! We're not in our graves yet. I mean, that's the kind of thing my parents are probably doing (13) . . . . ! Look, it's not what I'd normally do on a Monday night, but let's give clubbing a go! It might be a laugh.

> **Real English: The thing was ...**
>
> This is a natural way to add extra details or an explanation.
> The thing is ... introduces a problem, an excuse, or a difficulty of some kind.

3 | Speaking

Do you and your friends ever have problems trying to decide what to do in the evenings?

At what age are you too old to go clubbing? Twenty-five? Thirty? Forty? Never?

Using grammar

1 | Agreeing

If we share someone's interests, we can say:

A: I really love classical music.
B: Really? What's your favourite piece? *or*
So do I. Who's your favourite composer? *or*
Me too! Especially Mozart.

When we agree with a negative idea, we say:

A: I don't really like classical music.
B: Neither do I. *or* Me neither.

2 | Grammar in context

For each of these statements only two responses are correct. Cross out the incorrect one in each group.

1. A: I really love Mexican food.
   B: So do I. / Me too. / So have I. It's great, isn't it?

2. A: I don't really like much modern fashion.
   B: Neither do I. / Me neither. / Me too. It's dreadful.

3. A: I'm not really keen on big Hollywood movies.
   B: Neither do I. / Neither am I. / Me neither. They're so predictable.

4. A: I've seen all the Bond films.
   B: So have I. / Neither have I. / Me too. Some are better than others.

5. A: I'd love to go to Africa sometime.
   B: So do I. / So would I. / Me too. It sounds amazing.

6. A: I hate most classical music.
   B: Me too. / Me neither. / So do I. It doesn't do anything for me, I'm afraid.

3 | Auxiliary verb practice

Use *So* + auxiliary + *I* or *Neither* + auxiliary + *I* to agree with the following.

1. I prefer coffee without milk.
2. I don't like things that are too sweet.
3. I'm going to stay in tonight and do nothing.
4. I've just booked my summer holiday.
5. I never go abroad.
6. I'd love to meet someone really famous.
7. I was born in Australia.
8. I can't stand sea water.

▶ For more information on using auxiliaries, see G4.

Real English: What kind of films are you into?

If you are into something, you are very interested in it.
She's really into health food.
He's into alternative medicine.
Tell your partner about something you're really into.

Using vocabulary

1 | Not really keen

If we do not share someone's interests, we often soften the way we express this. Notice how really is used in these examples:

A: I really love classical music and opera.
B: Oh, do you? I'm not really very keen on it myself. *or*
It's not really my kind of thing, I'm afraid. *or*
I don't really like things like that.

Without really, these statements would sound quite strong and even rude. Make short dialogues by matching the statements 1–6 to the responses a–f.

1. I love nearly all winter sports. ☐
2. Going out with a crowd of friends and having fun, that's what I really like doing. ☐
3. I'm really interested in politics. ☐
4. I'm really into older music, you know, before 1967. ☐
5. My favourite kind of things are comics and cartoons. ☐
6. I'm really into roller-blading. It's a bit like roller-skating. ☐

a. Oh, it's not really my kind of thing, I'm afraid. I don't really understand what makes all the parties different. They all seem the same to me!

b. Really? I'm not really very keen on them myself. I once broke my leg skiing and it put me off – for life!

c. Are you? It's not really my kind of thing. I'm always worried I might get hurt.

d. I don't really like things like that myself. I don't see the point of them. I prefer a good novel – the longer the better!

e. Are you? I'm not really that keen on anything before 1980.

f. Do you? It's not really my kind of thing, I'm afraid. I prefer to go out with just one or maybe two people. I hate crowds.

🎧 **Now listen and notice how all the responses give extra information. Go back and underline all uses of really. All the language in this course is carefully chosen to help you to learn useful natural English. Complete these collocations from the exercise above.**

1. winter . . . . .
2. have . . . . .
3. interested . . . . . politics
4. It's not my . . . . . of thing.
5. get . . . . .
6. classical . . . . .
7. I don't see the . . . . . of it.
8. It . . . . . me off . . . . . life.

2 | I really love it

Do you like doing these activities or not? Discuss with a partner using expressions from this page. Explain why.

| golf | snorkelling | cycling | tennis |
| surfing | football | skiing | singing |

Reading

1 | Interests

Look at the examples below of two people talking about hobbies and interests they had in the past, but don't have any more.

> **Speaker 1:** I used to collect cans when I was younger, like coke cans. I lived near the sea and I'd find them on the beach. I grew out of it after a while and I can't remember what happened to all the cans.
>
> **Speaker 2:** I used to have a train set when I was younger, but I just lost interest in it once I got into music.

Think of two hobbies you used to have when you were younger. Tell your partner as much as you can about them. Try to use the following:

1. I used to collect ....
   when I was younger. I kept them in a .... I grew out of it when I was ....
   years old.

2. I used to play .... when I was younger.

When we ask about people's interests and hobbies, we often ask the question:

What do you do when you're not working/studying?   *or*
What do you do in your free time/spare time?

It sounds a bit strange if you ask:
What are your hobbies?

2 | While you read

Now read the text about collecting.

Are you a bag person?

Come on, admit it! You can't resist classy carrier bags. You have some cheap and nasty bags from the local supermarket which you put your rubbish in. But somewhere at home you've got a collection of bags that you wouldn't part with for the world. An Armani bag? A Gucci one? Or maybe it's that one from the Duty-Free Shop at Kuala Lumpur Airport? They prove that you're the sort of person you'd like to be.

Recently, a London gallery held an exhibition to celebrate the carrier bag. They asked thirty top artists and designers to design a carrier bag for thirty shops which took part in the exhibition. The show was a tremendous success because it seems we are all secret carrier bag collectors. Some people go into expensive designer shops and buy the cheapest thing – just to get one of their bags. Others don't even bother buying anything. They just ask straight out for a free bag for their collection. It seems that it's not the bag we want. It's what it represents. That's why we throw away our boring Tesco and Marks and Spencer bags, but make sure our Harrods or Louis Vuitton ones remain in perfect condition.

3 | Speaking

Discuss these questions with a partner.

1. Which is your most treasured carrier bag? Where did it come from?
2. What makes a classy carrier bag?
3. Do you collect anything else which might seem strange to other people?
4. Do you ever wear any designer clothes? Why/why not?

Using vocabulary

1 | Idioms focus

Complete the idioms in the sentences below with the words in the box.

| accounting | own | street | taste | cup |

1. I must admit, I don't really like this kind of music. It's not really my . . . . of tea.
2. If you're into action movies, you really should go and see *Explosive Device*. It should be right up your . . . .
3. You like Disney movies! I can't believe it! Oh well, each to their . . . .
4. My favourite kind of food is cheese – blue cheese. I know it's an acquired . . . .
5. You're into techno music? Well, there's no . . . . for taste, I suppose.

Match the idioms 1–5 above to their meanings a–d.

a. Different people like different things. (two idioms)
b. I don't really like that kind of thing.
c. I'm sure you'd like it.
d. It's something you learn to like gradually.

2 | Speaking

Ask and answer these questions with a partner. Try to use some of the idioms in Exercise 1 above when responding.

1. What kind of food do you like?
2. What kind of things do you usually do at the weekend?
3. What kind of music are you into?
4. What kind of things do you like watching on TV?
5. What kind of films are you into?
6. What kind of things do you like doing in class?
7. What kind of restaurants do you like going to?
8. What kind of things do you like reading?

3 | Expressions with *thing*

Complete the sentences below with the expressions in the box.

• it's just not the done thing	• the thing is
• it's just one of those things	• one thing after another
• for one thing	• I don't know the first thing about

1. I've had such a dreadful day. It's just been . . . . since I got up.
2. I don't know why you're asking me. . . . . cars. Ask Mark.
3. A: I'm sorry to hear you've lost your job.
   B: Yes, well, ... , I guess. We could all see it coming.
4. Whatever you do when you're in Indonesia, don't use your left hand to offer or take things. . . . .
5. I'd love to come with you, but, ... , I've already agreed to go out with Samantha.
6. A: So why don't you like him, then?
   B: Well, ... , you can't trust anything he says, and for another, he's a bit of a show-off.

Thing/things is a useful word in English. Find three more thing expressions you like in a dictionary. Tell your partner what you have chosen and why.

4 | Speaking

Are any of the following just not the done thing in your country? Discuss with a partner.

1. using your left hand to pass things
2. burping after dinner
3. starting to eat before everybody else
4. blowing your nose in public
5. asking how much someone earns
6. women smoking
7. living together before you're married

Think of three things you don't know the first thing about. See if anybody in the class can teach you a bit about them!

25

That's not what you'd expect. • It's not the sort of thing my parents would approve of. • He's a bit off the wall. • It's something different, I suppose. • Not just what everybody else does. • Something really individual. • But isn't it a bit dangerous? • Won't you end up getting hurt? • Hunting makes me sick! • Does it give you a buzz? • It's not everybody's cup of tea, I know. • You wouldn't catch me in one of those things. • But people get killed doing that! • It should be banned if you ask me. • I wouldn't be seen dead doing that kind of thing! • If you don't start when you're young, it's hard to get the hang of it. • People think I'm crazy, but I don't care! • It's an expensive hobby. • Sometimes I ask myself why I do it!

4 Unusual interests

Using grammar

1 | The *-ing* form as a verb

Tell a partner which of these things you enjoy doing.

- planning your summer holidays
- playing the piano/violin/guitar
- helping homeless people
- raising money for sick animals
- collecting things (e.g. stamps, phonecards, etc.)
- going folk dancing
- going to the theatre
- studying a foreign language
- going camping or youth hostelling
- going abroad
- surfing the net
- gardening or visiting gardens
- mountaineering or hill-walking
- reading
- painting or drawing
- singing or acting

Complete these sentences with the ideas above.

1. No wonder John's eyes are so sore. He spends his whole life . . . .

2. This French friend of mine's just got back from New York where he spent most of the winter . . . . at a school in Brooklyn.

3. Kevin feels very strongly about animal rights. He spends a lot of time . . . .

4. Pedro wants to be the next Pavarotti. He spends all his free time . . . .

5. His mother really loves her plants and flowers. She spends all her time . . . .

6. I've spent ages . . . . , and I'm finally off in three days. Two weeks in the sun!

7. Bill has just splashed out £100 on these new boots. You know he goes . . . . nearly every weekend, don't you?

8. Marie works with poor people in the inner city. She spends every Saturday night . . . . at a hostel in the city centre.

Did you notice the two different kinds of -ing patterns in the sentences 1–8 above?

a. *I go ...-ing* + time expression
b. *I spend* + time expression + *...-ing*

Go back and underline the time expressions in the sentences 1–8. Then decide if these time expressions fit best into pattern a or b.

whenever I can	all my life
most of my evenings	half my life
all my Saturday mornings	quite often
as often as I can	on Tuesdays

Now complete these sentences about your own interests.

9. I go . . . . almost every week.
10. I go . . . . quite a lot in the summer.
11. I spend most Sundays . . . .
12. I sometimes feel like I spend half my life . . . .

Tell a partner what you have written.

2 | The *-ing* form as a noun

We can use the -ing form to talk about an activity which is the subject of a sentence.

Mountaineering can be pretty dangerous.

Use your own ideas and the ideas in Exercise 1 to complete these sentences in pairs. For example, the answer to number one might be ballroom dancing. What do you think?

1. . . . . is all right for old people, but not for people in their twenties.
2. I know . . . . can be very dangerous, but there's no need to ban it, just because some people get killed every winter.
3. . . . . around the Greek islands in the summer is great fun.
4. . . . . is all right if you've got the time and the money.
5. . . . . is more useful than learning Chinese – unless, of course, you happen to be Chinese!
6. . . . . is a very worthwhile thing to do.
7. . . . . is something I've always wanted to do, but I've just never had the time.
8. . . . . is all right for women, but not for men.

Now compare your ideas with your classmates.

Real English: alright / all right

In British English some people write alright as one word. Others write it as two. Writing it as one word tends to be more informal. In this course it is always written as two words.

3 | All right

Make short dialogues by matching the questions or comments 1–7 to the responses a–g. Each dialogue contains a different use of all right.

1. Are you feeling all right now?
2. I'm really nervous about making the speech.
3. Is everything all right, sir?
4. Is your coffee all right?
5. Shall we take the car?
6. Just listen to that wind. I hate flying in weather like this!
7. Is it all right if I borrow your video for the weekend?

a. Well, actually, it's a bit cold.
b. Yes, thanks. The room's perfect.
c. Yes, thanks. I'm much better.
d. Yes, all right. It'll be quicker than the train.
e. Yes, sure – so long as you're careful with it.
f. Don't worry, it'll be all right on the night.
g. Now, calm down. Everything's going to be all right.

Practise reading out the dialogues with a partner. Then cover the responses a–g. Your partner will read out the questions and comments 1–7. See if you can remember the exact responses.

4 | More *-ing* forms in use

Good listeners check they understand what is being said to them. This encourages the speaker to give more information. You might have to interrupt to do this. Look at the following very useful 'checking' technique.

A: I love music.
B: What? Do you mean just listening to it or actually playing an instrument?
A: Both, really. I play the drums in a band at weekends and I've got piles of CDs at home.

Make short dialogues using the words in brackets and the pattern you have just seen. Then practise the dialogues with a partner.

1. A: I'm really interested in boxing.
   B: (watch it / box yourself)
   ....?
   A: No way! You'd never catch me in the ring! No, I just love watching it.

2. A: I really love American football.
   B: (watch / play)
   ....?
   A: Oh, I'm in a team. We play every Sunday.

3. A: I really love Chinese food.
   B: (go to Chinese restaurants / make it yourself)
   ....?
   A: No, I make it myself – all the time. You must come round sometime.

4. A: I'm really into art.
   B: (go to galleries / paint yourself)
   ....?
   A: No, I wish I could paint. I just like going round galleries.

5. A: I'm very interested in culture.
   B: (youth culture / Beethoven and things like that)
   ....?
   A: Well, all sorts. Fashion, music, dance, clothes, anything, really.

Reading

1 | Speaking

Discuss these questions with a partner.

1. Do you think men and women are treated equally in your society? Why/why not?

2. Should women be allowed to do exactly the same sports and jobs as men?

2 | Before you read

You are going to read an article about the way in which women's position in British society has – and hasn't! – changed. To help you understand the text better, here are a few definitions:

- A licence gives you permission to do something.
- If something is a spectacle, it is strange or interesting to watch.
- If you counter an argument, you give the opposite view.
- If you are unstable, you are not mentally fit.
- If you commit suicide, you kill yourself.

3 | While you read

Now read the article and underline any examples of discrimination mentioned.

It's a man's world?

For the last thirty years, we've been told that the war of the sexes is over and that women now have equal rights with men. To try to prove this, some have pointed to the way in which women have reached the highest offices. Mrs Thatcher, for example, led Britain for thirteen years, whilst many other countries have also recently elected their first female leaders.

In the traditionally male-dominated world of sport, women have also made great progress. In kick-boxing, for instance, two young Scottish women have forced their way into the British team. Whilst many conservative commentators may disapprove, Kate Kearney and Teresa Dewan are proud of the fact that they can not only take on men, but can even beat them. 'We usually give them a good fight,' said Teresa, 'but a man never likes to be beaten by a woman. They usually go off in a huff afterwards. You should see their faces!'

However, several recent news stories have highlighted the fact that women are still being discriminated against in all areas of life. A survey last year showed that on average women earn 30% less than men and that in many companies, there is still a glass ceiling, preventing women from getting the top jobs. As if this wasn't bad enough, evidence also suggests that women do more than their fair share of the work in the home. Women today have the burden of having to go out and fight for their rights in the workplace – and are then still expected to come home and cook and clean.

Sadly, despite the success of women like the Scottish kick-boxers, sexism is also still alive and well in sport. The unofficial world women's lightweight boxing champion, Jane Crouch, is today waiting to hear whether the British Boxing Board of Control (BBBC) will allow her to continue her career. The BBBC is deciding whether women boxers will be allowed to box officially or whether they will have to remain in the shadowy world of unofficial boxing.

Miss Crouch could expect to earn around £100,000 a year if she is given a licence. However, there has been much opposition to the spectacle of women in the boxing ring. There was laughter at the BBBC inquiry this week when it was suggested that women should not be licensed to box because they were biologically and emotionally unstable.

To counter these arguments, Miss Crouch's lawyer, Dinah Rose, said sarcastically: 'We are all taking a hell of a risk allowing women to pilot aeroplanes, aren't we? Perhaps all women airline pilots should be tested to see if they suffer from emotional instability.'

'I would certainly want research on that, if I were responsible for them,' replied Adrian Blackson, the BBBC's chief medical officer. 'And perhaps we should also say that only men are stable enough to look after children,' Miss Rose asked, to which Mr Blackson could only respond by saying, 'That's an interesting question.'

Miss Rose went on to suggest that it was men who were more likely to be unstable, to commit violent crimes or commit suicide. Mr Blackson told the inquiry that until further research had been done, the BBBC should not allow Miss Crouch to box.

4 | Speaking

Discuss these questions with a partner.

1. Do you think any of the things mentioned in the article happen in your country?

2. Do you think there is discrimination against any groups of people (other than women) in your society?

5 | Comprehension check

Now answer these questions about the text.

1. How do male kick-boxers react when they are beaten by women?

2. What's stopping women from getting top jobs in companies?

3. What does BBBC stand for?

4. Does Dinah Rose believe that women make bad pilots?

6 | Vocabulary check

Complete these sentences with words from the text.

1. A sports person who wins a very important competition is the . . . .

2. The place where boxing matches take place is called a boxing . . . .

3. If you say something which is the opposite of what you believe, because you want to mock or insult someone, you say it . . . .

4. If you study something in detail to gain new knowledge about it, you do . . . . on it.

Now complete these sentences with words from the text.

5. You can expect to . . . . £30,000 a year.

6. There's a lot of . . . . to the proposed landfill site.

7. I think we're . . . . a big risk if we don't go to the doctor immediately.

8. If you commit a violent . . . . , you should go to prison for a long time.

Using vocabulary

1 | Boxing joke

Practise telling this joke in pairs. Think about which words to stress and where to pause. Who tells the joke better, you or your partner?

When I was a kid, we couldn't afford a TV, so one day, my dad drilled a hole through the wall, which meant we could look into the house next door. After that, we used to watch the boxing and the wrestling every night ... until we finally realised that the neighbours didn't have a TV either.

2 | Violent or dangerous?

Make sure you understand what these sports are. Are they violent, dangerous, or both?

boxing	bungee jumping	climbing
snowboarding	water-skiing	skiing
wrestling	horse-racing	canyoning
canoeing	kick-boxing	football
sky-diving	hang-gliding	scuba-diving

Now talk about the activities above using these structures:

I'd quite like to ...
I wouldn't ... even if you paid me! I'd be scared of ...

Why do you think so many people like sports like boxing or bullfighting?

Have you got any dangerous interests?

Using grammar

1 | *Would* and *'d*

The responses a–e use would, wouldn't or the contracted form 'd. Make short dialogues by matching the sentences 1–5 to the responses a–e.

1. I'm not really very keen on going out tonight.
2. If you want a ticket, I'll get you one.
3. Could you possibly give me a lift home?
4. I've no idea where to go on holiday.
5. I think I'll have the Madras curry.

a. I would if I could, but I can't, I'm afraid. I've got to leave early today.
b. Well, I'd quite like to go somewhere exotic.
c. If you'd rather, we could always stay in instead. I don't mind either way.
d. I wouldn't if I were you! It's really hot!
e. That'd be great, if you could.

2 | Grammar in context

Complete the sentences below with the expressions in the box.

that'd be great	if you'd rather
I'd quite like to	I would if I could

1. A: So what do you feel like doing tonight?
   B: . . . . go out for a meal, if that's all right with you.
2. A: Do you want a lift?
   B: Oh, thanks. I'm in a real hurry to get home.
3. Look, it's not that I don't want to see you. . . . . , but I just can't. I'm out of the country all that week.
4. . . . . go to the party on your own, that's fine by me.
5. Well, if you could persuade Jim to come to the lecture this evening, then . . . . , but don't worry if you can't.
6. A: I'm really sorry you can't come with us tonight.
   B: Well, you know, ... , but I've really got to finish this work.
7. I'm really very tired. . . . . go to bed, if that's all right.
8. . . . . come a different weekend, that's fine. It's all the same to me.

Here are three common expressions with 'd and wouldn't:

> You'd never catch me in a boxing ring!
> I wouldn't be seen dead wearing leather trousers!
> I wouldn't go parachuting even if you paid me!

Use them to say something amusing about yourself.

▶ For more information on how to use *would*, see G5.

Real English: Do you want a lift?

You ask this question when you offer to take someone in your car. Look at these examples:
Could you give me a lift to the station?
You couldn't give me a lift, could you?
I'll give you a lift if you want.

This is different from the expression thumb a lift, which means that you are hitch-hiking.

3 | Reaching decisions

With a partner, try to agree what to do in each of these situations. Use the expressions with *would* from Exercise 1.

1. An important guest is visiting your home town. You have been asked to take them out and show them the best it has to offer. What would you suggest to them?
2. You and a friend have just won £1,000 in a lottery. How would you most like to celebrate?
3. You and some friends are totally broke, but want to have a nice day out tomorrow. You have absolutely no money to spend. Where would you go?

Once you have reached your decisions, join up with another pair and reach a group decision.

1 | Tenses

Choose the correct form.

1. I'm looking / I look for a new job at the moment.
2. My dad is liking / likes playing golf a lot.
3. I'm doing / I do odd jobs now and then.
4. She's running / She runs her own business from home and always has.
5. I'm working / I work this weekend, I'm afraid.
6. How often are you having / do you have your hair cut?

2 | Multiple choice

Choose the correct alternative.

1. He's ... .
   a. a bit of a show-off   b. a bit too show-off

2. He's ... .
   a. quite fun to be with   b. a bit of fun to be with

3. a. To learn English is not easy.
   b. Learning English is not easy.

4. A: I don't really like this kind of food much.
   B: a. Me neither.   b. Me too.

5. A: I don't really like places with lots of people.
   B: a. So do I.   b. Neither do I.

6. Pete spends a lot of time out in the country ... .
   a. hill-walking   b. to hill-walk

7. I spend ... .
   a. as often as I can studying
   b. most of my evenings studying

8. How ... people are coming tonight?
   a. many   b. much

9. A: Do you want to go out somewhere later on tonight?
   B: To be honest, ...
   a. I'd rather just stay in   b. I rather just stay in

10. ... swimming in the lake when I was younger.
    a. I had gone   b. I used to go

Compare your answers with a partner and discuss your choices.

3 | Comparing

In sentences 1–5, cross out the option which doesn't match the statement in the box. The first one is done for you.

> The country is much worse than it used to be.

1. It used to be much ~~more~~ / less violent than it is now.
2. People aren't as rude / polite as they used to be.
3. Unemployment is higher / lower than it used to be.
4. There used to be a lot more / less crime than there is now.
5. The cities aren't as clean / dirty as they used to be.

Now do the same in sentences 6–10.

> The country is much better than it used to be.

6. It isn't as safe / dangerous as it used to be.
7. Inflation used to be much lower / higher than it is now.
8. It's easier / more difficult to find a job than it used to be.
9. They're finally spending less / more on health and education than they used to.
10. There didn't use to be nearly as many policemen / drug addicts on the street as there are now.

4 | Speaking

Do you think your town/country has changed for the better or for the worse? Tell your partner what you think and why.

5 | Conversation

Put the jumbled conversation below into the correct order.

a. So, do you feel like doing anything tonight? `1`
b. Oh, really. I didn't know you had a brother. How old is he? ☐
c. Well, actually, I'm already going to see a film with my brother. ☐
d. You mean action movies and that kind of thing? ☐
e. Yeah, that kind of thing. So, what were you thinking of doing tonight, anyway? ☐
f. And do you get on with him all right? ☐
g. Yeah, he's great. We get on really well. He's into the same kind of films as me. ☐
h. About thirty-two or thirty-three, I think. I can never really remember. He's a good bit older than me. ☐

6 | Look back and check: Describing people

Look back at the language for describing people on pages 8, 9 and 11. Tick all the words you can remember. Then ask your partner about anything you have forgotten.

Use as much of this language as possible to describe another student in the class. Can your partner guess who you are talking about?

7 | Expressions

Complete the sentences below with the expressions in the box. All the expressions are from units 1–4.

I'm afraid I can't	not really keen
haven't you heard	one of those things
I would if I could	cheer up

1. A: Where's Jim? Hasn't he turned up yet?
   B: Oh, ... ? He's been taken ill and rushed to hospital.

2. Look, it's not that I don't want to see you. I mean, ... , but I just can't get away from work until after seven.

3. A: Could you look after my kids on Friday for a few hours?
   B: No, sorry, ... I'm already doing something else.

4. A: I'm sorry I broke your vase.
   B: Don't worry about it. It's just . . . .

5. A: So, what do you think? Do you like my new tie?
   B: No, I can't say I do really. I'm . . . . on that colour.

6. A: . . . . ! It's not the end of the world.
   B: I suppose not, but I still feel bad about it.

How many different endings can you think of to follow: 'Oh, haven't you heard?' as in number one above?

How many different endings can you think of to follow: 'I would if I could, but...' , as in number two above?

8 | Collocations

Match the verbs 1–8 to the best collocations a–h.

1.	do	a.	for myself
2.	run	b.	the net
3.	go	c.	self-employed
4.	surf	d.	for the weekend
5.	work	e.	a lot of work
6.	go away	f.	well with my family
7.	get on	g.	clubbing
8.	be	h.	my own business

Now match 9–16 to the best collocations i–p.

9.	hand down	i.	a report
10.	finish off	j.	someone a big hug
11.	break into	k.	religion and politics
12.	give	l.	the building
13.	be stuck	m.	a lot of damage
14.	steer clear of	n.	clothes
15.	evacuate	o.	in a traffic jam
16.	do	p.	the bank

Who would do each of the things in numbers 9–16 above and why?

9 | Real English

Match the statements and the questions 1–8 to the responses a–h.

1. What's all that noise?
2. Boxing is all right for men, but not for women.
3. Do you want a lift?
4. So, how long have you been collecting phonecards, then?
5. Can you get there by seven?
6. What's your little brother like then? Is he OK?
7. How do you get on with your in-laws?
8. He's great, isn't he, that new teacher?

a. That's a pretty conservative view, isn't it?
b. Do you think so? I'm not that keen on him.
c. It's the neighbour from hell again.
d. Only if you're going my way.
e. Pretty well, I suppose, all things considered.
f. No, not really. The thing is, I'm supposed to be meeting Jim at 6.30.
g. I suppose I've always been into it, really.
h. You're joking, aren't you? He's a pain in the neck!

You have one minute to memorise the responses a–h. Now cover Exercise 9 above. Your partner will read out the statements and questions 1–8. How many responses can you remember?

10 | Idioms

Make sentences with idioms by matching the beginnings 1–7 to the endings a–g.

1. It never rains,
2. You're making a mountain
3. We don't always see eye
4. My car is on its last
5. I'm up to my eyes
6. It's not really my
7. It's just not

a. in work at the moment.
b. legs.
c. out of a molehill.
d. the done thing.
e. cup of tea.
f. but it pours.
g. to eye.

11 | What can you remember?

With a partner, note down as much as you can remember about the two texts you read in units 2 and 4.

Surprise for Jailbird Dad

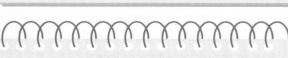

It's a man's world?

Now compare what you remember with another pair. Who remembers more?

Which text did you enjoy more? Why?

12 | Vocabulary quiz

Answer these questions with a partner. Then compare your answers with another pair. Who got most answers right?

1. How do you get your driving licence?
2. If you want to do well in your career, are you ambitious or greedy?
3. Do vegetarians drink milk and eat cheese?
4. If you hardly ever do something, does it mean that you do it very often or very rarely?
5. Where does a retired teacher teach?
6. If you are messy, are you tidy or untidy?
7. If someone kills themselves, do they commit suicide or suffer from suicide?
8. If you are keen on another person, do you want to start a relationship with them or not?
9. If someone with red hair is called a redhead, what is someone with blonde hair called?
10. Where are you likely to be if you are having a pint?
11. If you were a laid-back sort of person, how often would you be in a huff with someone – often or hardly ever?
12. Is a biography a book someone writes about their own or another person's life?
13. Do criminals make crimes or commit them?
14. How do you get on with someone if you're not on the same wavelength?
15. A friend of yours is described as narrow-minded. Does it mean they are open to new ideas or are their ideas fixed in a negative way?
16. If you have no brothers or sisters, are you a single child or an only child?
17. When do you need to get things off your chest?
18. Can you think of three things a hurricane could do to a house?
19. Does a boxing match take place in a ring or a square?
20. How well do you know an acquaintance?

Learner advice: The authors speak!

Discuss these statements with a partner. What do _you_ think?

1. I need to learn more grammar and do more grammar exercises in class.
2. You can say more with vocabulary than you can with grammar.
3. English grammar is very complicated.
4. It's important to know all the grammar terminology.
5. What's more useful when you go abroad – a grammar book, a coursebook, a dictionary or a phrasebook? Why?

Now read this text and see how the authors of this book answer the questions above.

Last month, a student, Carlos, showed me his copy of a famous English grammar book and said: 'I bought this. It's very useful. I'm working my way through it. I'm doing two units a day. I'll finish in two months' time. I'll be fluent by then.' I actually groaned at this and Carlos noticed. 'You don't think it's a good idea, then? But I really need more grammar. I still don't know how to do reported speech.'

Carlos wasn't the first student to ask me a question like this – or to buy that grammar book. In fact, I've had conversations like this with hundreds of students, and I understand how they feel. Of course it's good to use grammar correctly and grammar does help us speak more accurately. Also, a book which promises to cover all aspects of English in a hundred units looks attractive to students. However, learning a language doesn't really work like that!

To begin with, grammatical accuracy comes slowly. Even people who've lived in Britain for twenty years still make grammatical mistakes, but that doesn't stop them getting good jobs or making friends. Grammar mistakes rarely stop you being understood. Also, there's no proof that doing grammar exercises and studying rules makes you more accurate. Some of the best foreign speakers I've ever met don't even know what the present perfect is – but have no trouble using it! Similarly, if you're always thinking about grammar rules, it can stop you being fluent. Native speakers speak fast because they remember and re-use chunks of language repeatedly. Unfortunately, most grammar books don't give you much access to this kind of language, but instead give unnatural examples.

Believe it or not, over 80% of all verbs used in English are in the present simple or the past simple – and you've already studied both of those a lot. You probably still make mistakes because you haven't learned the easiest ways of saying things in English yet – usually this means you haven't learned enough collocations, idioms and fixed expressions.

A lot of grammar is used in a limited way and you learn it best by looking at typical examples. There are plenty throughout this book. There is a lot of grammar in this book and we show you how it's used in everyday speech. If you want to think more about grammar, how it works and how to use it, read the Grammar introduction on pages 157–158.

Discuss these questions with a partner.

1. Do you use any books to help you study English at home?
2. Has this text made you change your mind about anything?
3. Is there anything you strongly disagree with here? Why?

I've decided it's time to leave home. • I can't make up my mind. • Good for you! • I'm sure you've made the right decision. • I don't want to get stuck in a dead-end job. • You don't get a second bite at the cherry. • It's a once-in-a-lifetime opportunity. • I've got something important to tell you. • I don't know if you want to hear this. • I wouldn't mind becoming a doctor or something. • It was the biggest decision of my life. • You'll meet lots of interesting people and see lots of interesting places. • It just feels like the right thing to do. • How come you're marrying her and not me? • What on earth made you decide to do that? • I hate to admit it, but I'm starting to get cold feet. • It's time to get off the fence! • Change is the only constant in life.

5 Big decisions

Using vocabulary

1 Tough decisions

What is the most important decision you have ever made in your life? Did it turn out well or badly?

On your own, put the following decisions in order, from the most difficult to make (1) to the easiest to make (8).

- [ ] deciding to change your job
- [ ] deciding to get married
- [ ] deciding to start a family
- [ ] deciding to work abroad
- [ ] deciding to stop smoking
- [ ] deciding to get divorced
- [ ] deciding to move house
- [ ] deciding on a name for your child

Compare your answers with a partner. Can you think of any other tough decisions not listed above?

2 Who did what?

Now listen to these three people talking about their experiences of some tough decisions. Listen carefully and write down their decisions.

3 What a nightmare!

Check you understand the expressions in the box below. Use a dictionary to help you translate any vocabulary you're unsure of.

> I felt really pleased with myself.
> It was total chaos.
> It was a real weight off my shoulders.
> I couldn't stand it any more.
> What a nightmare!
> After that, it was plain sailing.

Listen to the three people again and tick the expressions when you hear them.

Use the expressions to talk about experiences you have had.

1. ....

2. ....

3. ....

Using grammar

1 | Giving explanations

When we explain why we did something, we often talk about what **had been happening** (the past perfect continuous) before we did what we did. Look at these examples:

A: So why did you decide to move out of your old flat?
B: It was mainly because I hadn't been getting on with my flatmates for ages, so I just decided I needed a place of my own.

A: So how come you started smoking?
B: Well, all my friends had been smoking for ages and they'd been trying to get me to start, so eventually I just gave in.

Complete these short dialogues by putting the verbs in brackets in the past perfect continuous.

1. A: So why did you decide to go to India, then?
   B: Well, I .... a lot about it since Sally told me about her trip, so I just took a month off work and went on my own. (read)

2. A: So what made you decide to stop eating meat?
   B: Well, I .... about it for a while. A few of my friends were vegetarians and they .... to convince me for ages, so I just decided to give it a go. (think, try)

3. A: So how come you finally bought a computer?
   B: It was really because for years I .... all my writing on this ancient typewriter, so I decided to splash out. (do)

4. A: So how come you two split up, if you don't mind me asking?
   B: Well, basically, we .... constantly for months, and, to be honest, we weren't really enjoying each other's company. (argue)

5. A: I hear you've moved into a flat, Jim?
   B: Yes, I .... in the university hostel since I left home. I thought it was time to get a place of my own. (live)

6. A: So, you and Karen didn't move back to Sweden after all?
   B: No, we .... second thoughts for a while, so we decided to stay here in Cardiff, at least for the time being. (have)

Go back and underline the time expressions. Then read the dialogues with a partner.

2 | Grammar pair work

Ask each other these questions. Use your imagination and the past perfect continuous when you answer.

1. So how come you decided to get engaged?
2. So what made you decide to buy your own flat?
3. So why did you finally decide to get a job?
4. So why did you decide to get rid of your cats?
5. So how come you gave up salsa dancing, then?
6. So why on earth did you get rid of your TV?

Tell your partner about a big decision you've made, and then explain the background to that decision, using these structures:

I'd been -ing.
I hadn't been -ing.

> For more information on how to use the past perfect continuous, see G6.

Real English: Basically, ...

This is a common way to introduce an explanation.

A: *So why do you need to learn English, then?*
B: *Well, basically, my boss told me I had to.*

A: *How come you sold your car?*
B: *Well, basically, I just couldn't afford to keep it running.*

What other reasons can you give for selling an old car?

Using vocabulary

1 | Idioms focus

Complete the idiomatic expressions in the short dialogues below with the words in the box.

sailing	cake	stone	nothing	done	depth

1. A: It must've been really hard learning Spanish.
   B: No, not really, I already speak Italian, so it was a piece of ....!

2. A: Did Lee give you your money back?
   B: Eventually, yes, but it was like getting blood out of a .... He's so mean!

3. A: Did you go and give blood in the end?
   B: Yes, and I'm glad I did. There was .... to it! I didn't feel a thing.

4. A: So how come you decided to quit the class?
   B: Oh, everyone else was so much better than me. I felt totally out of my ....!

5. A: Did it take you long to get used to living in Greece?
   B: Well, the first six months were quite hard, but after that it was all plain ....

6. A: Why not try and get a work permit and stay?
   B: That's easier said than .... It's fine if you've an EU passport, but I'm Chilean.

2 | Talking about jobs

Which jobs can you see in these pictures?

surgeon	mechanic	builder
chemist	social worker	soldier
bouncer	policewoman	pilot
fireman	postman	model

Now complete these sentences in ways that are true for you by adding the relevant jobs.

I wouldn't mind being a . . . .
I'd quite like to be a . . . .
I could never be a . . . .

Compare your answers with your partner and explain your choices. These expressions might help you explain why a job does or doesn't really appeal to you.

On the positive side:
I imagine it'd be really rewarding.
I think it'd be a really creative job.
I imagine it'd give you a lot of freedom.
I'm sure the money would be good.
It wouldn't be all that demanding.
You'd meet a lot of people.

On the down side:
You'd have to work really long hours.
I imagine it'd be really stressful.
I think it'd get really boring after a while.
It'd be dangerous.
It'd be dirty.
I've got a feeling it'd drive me mad.
The money wouldn't be very good.
You'd end up doing the same thing every day.

Using grammar

1 | Second conditionals

The first conditional uses the present simple:
If I get that job, it'll be really well-paid.

The second conditional uses the past simple:
If I had a job like that, I'd go crazy.

Complete the paragraph below with the past simple of the verbs in the box.

be	earn	exist	have	meet	want

Some people spend half their life wishing their lives were better – it really annoys me. 'If I (1) . . . . a bit more more money – if I (2) . . . . a better job – if I (3) . . . . the right man or woman for me.' It drives me mad. There is no perfect job or perfect partner! And people say things like 'If I (4) . . . . so busy, I'd do this or that', but that's just an excuse. If they really (5) . . . . to do it, I'm sure they could find the time. If the word 'if' (6) . . . . , the world would be a much happier place.

Make second conditional sentences using the words in brackets. For example:

(you / look better / if / wear / suit)
I think you'd look better if you wore a suit.

1. (Rachel / understand / if / you explain it / her)
   I'm sure . . . .
2. (if / we have more time / look round / museums)
   It's a shame. . . . .
3. (I / buy one / if / not be / so expensive)
   The fact is, ...
4. (if / I / not have any children / I / travel round the world)
   I often think that . . . .
5. (life / be easier / if / everybody / tell / the truth)
   I often think that . . . .

2 | Likely or unlikely?

Choose the most suitable verb form – past for an unlikely situation:

If I won a lot of money, …

and present for a likely or more likely situation:
If I pass my exam, …

1. If I meet / met the Prime Minister, …
2. If everybody thinks / thought like me, …
3. If I live / lived to be seventy, …
4. If I live / lived to be 120, …

Now finish the sentences 1–4 with your own ideas or choose from a–d below.

a. I'd probably have great-great-grandchildren.
b. I don't know what I'd say to him.
c. the world would be a better place!
d. I'll be quite happy.

> ➤ For more information on how to use second conditionals, see G7.

Using vocabulary

1 | Decisions, decisions

Deciding on your career is one of the biggest decisions you'll ever make in your life. Complete the sentences below with the words in the box.

wise	wrong	unpopular
immediate	joint	right

1. We definitely made the . . . . decision coming by train. It's so much easier than driving.
2. Look, we've got three days to make up our minds about it. It's not as if we need to make a(n) . . . . decision or anything, is it?
3. A: I've decided to stay and finish my course. It would be mad to leave it now.
   B: I think that's a(n) . . . . decision.
4. Oh no, look at the traffic. We made the . . . . decision coming this way.
5. The government's decision to raise income tax to 35% has been very . . . .
6. Some of our friends think it was my idea to give up our jobs and move to the country, but it wasn't. We'd both talked about it for years. It really was a(n) . . . . decision.

2 | Speaking

Discuss these questions with a partner.

1. Has your government made any unpopular decisions recently?
2. Have you made any joint decisions recently? Who with? What about?
3. Have you ever made a wrong decision?

Listening

1 | Before you listen

You are going to hear a man talking about some big decisions he's made. The expressions in the box are all connected to these decisions. Discuss with a partner what you think he decided to do.

> pass a physical
> stuck in front of a computer all day
> It's dead!

2 | While you listen

Phil and Jason are both in the same evening class and are chatting during the coffee break. Listen to them talking about some big decisions.

Cover the conversation. As you listen, try and answer these questions.

1. What big decisions has Jason made?
2. Why?

Listen again and try to fill in the gaps in the conversation.

3 | Speaking

Crawley is a nice quiet town in the country about half an hour by train from London. It's near Gatwick Airport, so there are a lot of jobs. It's got good schools and few social problems. Where would you rather live – London or Crawley?

Would you like to move to another town – or even another country – or are you happy where you are?

Forty a day!

Phil: Just time for a quick smoke. Oh sorry, do you want one?

Jason: No, thanks. I gave up years ago.

Phil: (1) ....! I've given up even trying to give up!

Jason: Yeah, it's a nightmare, isn't it?

Phil: (2) ....! I don't know how you managed it.

Jason: Well, it's funny, but it was my job that did it. I mean, (3) ...., and you know it's destroying your lungs, don't you, and I knew I wouldn't be able to become a fireman if I didn't give up.

Phil: So, what's becoming a fireman got to do with it? Is it the fire risk or something?

Jason: No, it's just that (4) .... pass a physical to get in, and I wouldn't be able to do that if I was smoking forty a day.

Phil: Forty a day! Just as well you gave up! So, (5) .... you decided to become a fireman anyway?

Jason: Mm, I'd have to think about that. I suppose it all goes back to when I got out of college. I wanted to do something exciting and different, you know, and a friend of my dad's was in the local fire brigade.

Phil: Oh, right. So, (6) ....?

Jason: Yes, he helped me get the job. I mean, I knew I didn't want to (7) .... sitting in an office pushing bits of paper round a desk or stuck in front of a computer screen!

Phil: Yeah, I know exactly what you mean. I'm half blind already! So, (8) .... move to London, then? Was it for work or because of a relationship or what?

Jason: Well, it was mainly work, but also because I was just (9) .... where I was living at the time.

Phil: It was down in Crawley, wasn't it? It's pretty quiet down there, isn't it?

Jason: Quiet? Yeah, it's dead. There's absolutely nothing to do there.

Phil: (10) ....?

Jason: What? Becoming a fireman?

Phil: No, no, moving to London, I mean.

Jason: Oh yeah, (11) .... I love it. I don't think I could live anywhere else now.

Phil: No, it's the same for me. It gets you after a while, doesn't it? It's like a drug.

Real English: Good for you!

This is a common way of congratulating someone.
A: *I've just passed my driving test.*
B: *Good for you!*

Using vocabulary

1 | How come?

**How come is an alternative way of saying why.
Look at these examples:**

Why did you decide to move to London?
How come you decided to move to London?

Why did you decide to do that, then?
How come you decided to do that, then?

Why are you leaving early?
How come you're leaving early?

Practise saying the expressions above.

Re-write these sentences starting with why.

1. How come you paid so much for your car?
....

2. How come you got here so early?
....

3. How come you refused the invitation?
....

4. How come you didn't accept the job in LA?
....

5. How come you're so interested in Tibet?
....

6. How come there's no beer left in the fridge?
....

**Now complete these sentences with how come
or why.**

7. So, ... you're studying English?
8. So, ... did you choose this school?
9. So, ... did you decide to do that, then?
10. So, ... you chose to study that?
11. So, ... do you want to go to Iceland?
12. So, ... you decided to move there, then?

**Now ask your partner two interesting questions
starting with how come.**

2 | Jokes!

**Complete these 'How come?' jokes with
the correct response in the box below.**

- I wanted to be near my mum!
- Because I left the plane tickets on it!
- They didn't look!
- I want to be ready in case there's an accident!

1. A: How come you drive with your brakes on?
   B: ....

2. A: How come you were born in New Zealand?
   B: ....

3. A: I wish I'd brought the piano with me.
   B: How come?
   A: ....

4. A: When I was a kid, I ran away from home.
      It took them six months to find me.
   B: Six months! How come it took them so long?
   A: ....

3 | Explaining your decisions

**Here are six expressions for explaining why you
made certain decisions. Put the words in the
correct order.**

a. got / with / we / just / each / other / bored
....

b. always / I've / been / in / it / interested
....

c. always / to / wanted / I'd
....

d. just / with / up / I / fed / it / got
....

e. just / I / felt / it / like
....

f. him / of / friend / recommended / mine / a
....

**Now complete these short dialogues with the
expressions a–f above.**

1. A: Why did you decide to write a book?
   B: .... ever since
      I was at school.

2. A: So, how come you went to Dr Martin?
   B: .... and I'm
      glad I did. He's wonderful.

3. A: So, why did you decide to stop dancing lessons?
   B: .... I mean,
      it was fun to begin with, but it started eating up
      all my free time.

4. A: So, what on earth made you decide to dye your
      hair grey?
   B: .... I thought
      it might make me look more mature.

5. A: So, what made you study Greek philosophy?
   B: ...., believe it
      or not!

6. A: So, why did you and Jane split up?
   B: ....
      It's sad, I know, but that's life, I suppose.

Tell a partner about:
- **something you got fed up with.**
- **something silly you just felt like doing.**
- **something you've always been interested in.**

I'm really scared of flying. • Landing and take-off is the worst. • I've got no head for heights. • This is a no-smoking airline, I'afraid. • Smoking is permitted only in the areas designated. • I'd never fly with them! • Can I see your boarding card, pleas • It's like kissing an ashtray! • It's a free country. • Passive smoking. • I just don't have the will power to give up. • You're mo likely to get killed crossing the road. • Mind your own business! • I get really nervous just before take-off. • It's the safest for of transport. • I always fly economy class. • This is a security announcement. • Toilets engaged. • Please have your passpo ready for inspection. • Did you have a pleasant flight? • I got a really cheap ticket online. • I had the prepare a special vegetarian meal for me. • The recycled air irritates my sinuses.

6 Flying

Reading

1 | Your captain speaking

With a partner, discuss whether you think these statements about air travel are true or false. Why?

1. Only you or members of your family may pack your luggage.
2. No aerosols are allowed in any luggage.
3. Only two items of hand luggage may be carried on board.
4. No cigarettes or alcohol are allowed on board.
5. The use of mobile phones is strictly prohibited.
6. No toy weapons are allowed on board.

Can you think of other rules which apply to these things when flying?

7. smoking during take-off and landing
8. using a CD player
9. wearing high-heeled shoes in an emergency
10. where to put your hand luggage
11. using the toilet
12. seats in the upright position
13. wearing seat belts during the flight
14. special seat belts for babies

2 | Before you read

You're going to read an article that features air travel, the law and smoking. Check that you understand the words in the box below, using a dictionary to help you if necessary. Then put them into the correct categories.

handcuffed	fined	
nervous	on board	puff
cabin crew	light up	prosecuted
touched down	arrested	refuelling

air travel: . . . .

the law: . . . .

smoking: . . . .

With a partner, discuss what you think the article is going to be about.

3 | While you read

🎧 **Read this article about a woman whose craving for a smoke landed her in big trouble – at 30,000 feet! When you've read it, answer these questions.**

1. Why did Joan Norrish light up on the plane?
2. When was she arrested?
3. What happened to her after that?

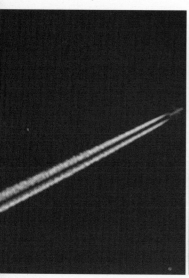

The cost of a cigarette

A businesswoman's desperate need for a cigarette on an eight-hour flight from America resulted in her being arrested and handcuffed, after she was found lighting up in the toilet of a Boeing 747, not once but twice.

Joan Norrish, aged 33, yesterday became the first person to be prosecuted under new laws for smoking on board a plane, when she was fined £440 at Uxbridge magistrates' court. Ms Norrish, from Radwinter, Essex, said: 'I'm such a nervous passenger, and I couldn't have handled the flight without a cigarette. If they'd told me I couldn't smoke on board, I would've avoided going by plane altogether.'

Ms Norrish first attracted the attention of the in-flight staff when she had her first puff in the toilet after the plane touched down for refuelling at New York's JFK airport. One and a half hours later, she went into the lavatory again, causing passengers to complain to the cabin crew. However, on inspection, they could find no sign of cigarettes in the toilet, and were concerned that Ms Norrish may have hidden the cigarettes, thus adding to their fears for the safety of the plane.

Relations between Ms Norrish and the crew soon got worse, as Ms Norrish turned violent when the plane landed at Heathrow, where the police were alerted. She was subsequently arrested and handcuffed.

Outside the court, Ms Norrish commented on her fine. 'It was quite high, much higher than I was expecting. It all seems like an awful lot of fuss over just a couple of cigarettes.' Ms Norrish is being encouraged to appeal against the fine by a pro-smoking organisation who have offered her legal aid. A spokesman for the group said: 'This is yet another example of the way in which smokers are being discriminated against and marginalised in society. We generate millions of pounds for the government every year through the taxes we pay – and yet we are treated like second-class citizens. We're banned from smoking in all kinds of public places and people expect us to stand outside in all weathers if we want to smoke. It's got to stop!'

However, anti-smoking lobbies have welcomed the judge's decision and have claimed that there is no excuse for endangering the lives of others by lighting up in public. 'This is a step in the right direction,' a spokeswoman said, 'and we look forward to the day when all smoking is banned.'

4 | Speaking

Discuss these questions with a partner.

1. Do you have any sympathy for Ms Norrish? Why/why not?

2. Is smoking banned in your country? Can you think of anything else that is?

3. Are you more pro- or anti-smoking? Why?

5 | Vocabulary check

Complete these sentences with words from the article.

1. I quit after two years working there. I just couldn't have . . . . the pressure any longer.

2. If I'd known we'd get delayed for six hours, I would've . . . . flying altogether.

3. When we . . . . down, there was a great big crash. It was really scary.

4. I've looked everywhere for her. She's just totally vanished. There's no . . . . of her anywhere.

5. Since the war ended a few years ago, ... between our two countries have improved a lot.

6. It was lovely this morning, but it's suddenly . . . . really cold, hasn't it?

7. Has the postman been yet? I'm . . . . some important mail today.

8. I was going to complain, but I didn't want to make a . . . . I hate it when I feel like everybody's looking at me.

9. I'm going to apply for . . . . aid so I can take them to court.

10. I'm a fireman and we're going on strike next month. We're sick of being treated like second-class . . . .

Using vocabulary

1 | Flying vocabulary

Match the words 1–10 to the words a–j to make collocations which are commonly used to talk about things to do with flying.

1.	your boarding	a.	entertainment
2.	the drinks	b.	flight
3.	an eight-hour	c.	locker
4.	the overhead	d.	crew
5.	your oxygen	e.	stopover
6.	the in-flight	f.	trolley
7.	the smoking	g.	card
8.	the emergency	h.	section
9.	the cabin	i.	exit
10.	an unscheduled	j.	mask

Discuss these questions with a partner.

11. Have you ever had to use your oxygen mask?

12. Can you remember things falling out of the overhead locker?

13. When was the last time you went on a really long flight?

14. What is the longest flight you have ever been on?

2 | Role play

Now imagine you have just touched down after the worst flight ever. You had problems with all of the things in Exercise 1 above. You're going to phone a friend back home and tell them about your journey. Spend five minutes planning what you are going to say. Ask your teacher for help if necessary.

3 | Watch, see, look

On a long flight, do you watch the in-flight movies? Complete these sentences with the correct form of watch, see, or look.

1. Could you have a look on the TV page to .... what's on after the news?

2. A: Can you .... anything wrong, doctor?
   B: No, your throat .... fine.

3. I think I'll .... the match on TV tonight.

4. The amount of food at the wedding was incredible. I've never .... anything like it!

5. I want you to .... him closely. I think he's up to something.

6. Here, ... out of the window. Have you ever seen a car like that before!

7. Can you .... my bag while I go to the loo, please?

8. When the sky is this clear, you can .... for miles from up here. It's fantastic!

9. Have you .... that new film yet? It's great.

10. I've .... everywhere for my wallet. I can't .... it anywhere.

Do you have three different words for look, see and watch in your language? Do you use them in the same way as the examples above?

4 | Flying joke

🎧 Try to guess the ending of this joke. Listen and check. Then tell it to each other in pairs and decide who tells it better. These people then tell it to the class, who vote on who tells it best.

Alfred had never flown before and was extremely nervous. He was flying across the Atlantic to visit his sister, who had emigrated to Canada. When he got on the plane he found he was sitting in a window seat. After a few minutes, the person next to him arrived – an enormously fat American. Not long after the plane took off, the American fell asleep and began to snore loudly. It was obvious to Alfred there was no way he could get out, even to get to the toilet, without waking the man up.

After the in-flight meal had been served, the plane entered an area of severe turbulence. The American continued to snore. Alfred, however, started to feel sick. He was desperate to get to the toilet. Finally, he was sick – all over the man's trousers. The American didn't wake up, but he just continued to snore. Alfred didn't know what to do.

As the plane touched down, the American finally woke up and saw his trousers. Alfred turned to him and said, '.................?'

What is your worst flying story?

Using vocabulary

1 Adjectives: strong comparatives

Here are expressions which show that the end result of something was different from our expectations.

A: How was your flight?
B: It was terrible – much worse than I thought it would be.

A: What was the food on the plane like?
B: It was good – much nicer than I'd expected.

Using these two examples, think of answers to the following questions. Here are some words and phrases to help you.

fine	much hotter
great	much nicer
went well	much better
interesting	much easier
nice	
sweltering	

1. How was your exam?
2. What was the weather in Tunisia like? Is it hot at this time of year?
3. So, you've moved into your new house. How did it go?
4. How did you feel about your presentation the other day? Were you happy with it?
5. What did you think of the restaurant? Was it nice?
6. So, how was the exhibition? As good as all the advertising said it would be?

Now ask your partner questions about some things you know they have done or seen recently. They should answer as above. Continue the conversations for as long as possible.

2 Strong adjectives

Look at ways of responding in the examples below.

A: Having someone throw up all over you is quite unpleasant, isn't it?
B: Unpleasant? It's disgusting!

A: That guy on the plane was quite fat, wasn't he?
B: Fat? He was enormous!

We often respond by repeating an adjective as a question and then adding another stronger adjective. Respond to these questions or comments in a similar way using the strong adjectives in the box below.

tiny	freezing	boiling	shocked
terrifying	dead	enormous	gorgeous

1. A: It must've been really hot in Greece.
   B: ....
2. A: Oh, you're from São Paulo originally, are you? It's a pretty big city, right?
   B: ....
3. A: How's your flat? It must be a bit cold with all this snow we're having.
   B: ....
4. A: It's pretty quiet down in Devon, isn't it?
   B: ....
5. A: You must've been pretty surprised when you read the report in the papers.
   B: ....
6. A: It's a bit small in here, isn't it?
   B: ....
7. A: So, is he good-looking, then, your new boyfriend?
   B: ....
8. A: It must've been a bit scary, going so high up like that.
   B: ....

It is important that you can keep conversations going. Here are A's next comments a–h from the conversations above. First match them up. Then listen to the conversations. Finally, practise reading them with a partner.

a. There's no way you'll catch me doing that again!
b. That's why I've decided to have central heating put in.
c. That's why I moved to a small town out in the country.
d. You can hardly swing a cat in here!
e. That's why we made sure the hotel had air-conditioning.
f. That's why I decided to move to the city!
g. You'll die when you see him!
h. That's why I contacted my solicitor straightaway.

Using grammar

1 Gerunds and infinitives

Look at these two patterns:

Verb + gerund
There's no way you'll catch me doing that again.

Verb + infinitive
That's why I've decided to move to the city.

Some verbs can take either pattern, but the meanings may be different:

I clearly remember posting your letter.
I must remember to post your letter.

Mark each verb in this way:

G	**if it only takes the gerund**
I	**if it only takes the infinitive**
G/I	**if it can take either**

1. try to do / doing
2. ask him to do / doing
3. promise to do / doing
4. suggest to do / doing
5. forget to do / doing
6. expect to do / doing
7. love to do / doing
8. remember to do / doing
9. enjoy to do / doing
10. avoid to do / doing
11. begin to do / doing
12. prefer to do / doing
13. carry on to do / doing
14. manage to do / doing
15. start to do / doing
16. plan to do / doing

Now cross out the impossible verb forms.

2 Practice

Complete these sentences in ways that are true for you. Use the gerund or the infinitive.

1. I'll never forget . . . .
2. I must remember . . . .
   this week.
3. I promised . . . . ,
   but I didn't.
4. I'm always forgetting . . . .
5. I've never quite managed . . . .
6. I usually avoid . . . .
   if I can.
7. There's no way you'll catch me . . . .
8. I'm planning . . . .
   sometime in the next couple of years.

Tell your partner as much as you can about what you have written.

3 Grammar check

Verbs often work together in specific patterns. Circle the correct form in these sentences.

1. Why did you decide to learn / learning English?
2. Well, because I wanted going / to go to America.
3. Well, because I was interested in travelling / to travel.
4. Well, because I was fed up with working / to work in the evenings.
5. Well, I was really bored with doing / to do the same thing every day at work.
6. Because I was trying getting / to get into university and I needed it for my exams.
7. Because I was hoping to go / going to Australia for six months.

4 Grammar in context

With a partner, think of two possible answers for each of these questions, starting with the words given.

1. A: So, why did you leave your job?
   B: I wanted . . . .
   I was fed up . . . .
2. A: So, how come you decided to move to Milan?
   B: I was bored . . . .
   I was interested in . . . .
3. A: So, why did you break up with your fiancé(e)?
   B: I wanted . . . .
   I didn't want . . . .
4. A: So, how come you suddenly decided to stop smoking?
   B: I was trying to . . . .
   I was just fed up with . . . .

> For more information on how to use gerunds and infinitives, see G8.

Using vocabulary

1 | Smoking

Complete these collocations by adding the missing words.

a. a heavy / a chain / an occasional
. . . .

b. smoke a / light a / put out a
. . . .

c. king-size / low-tar / mild / menthol / strong . . . .

d. . . . . lighter / packet / ends / advertising

e. give up / start / stop / be anti- . . . .

Now complete these sentences with collocations from a–e above.

1. I used to be a really . . . . smoker, you know, fifty a day, but now I'm just a(n) . . . . smoker.

2. I've been trying to . . . . smoking for years now. I wish I'd never . . . . in the first place!

3. Where can I . . . . this cigarette? Is there an ashtray or something around?

4. I saw this old homeless guy in the streets yesterday picking up all the old cigarette . . . .

5. Cigarette . . . . is banned on television in some countries.

6. The link between . . . . and lung cancer has now been proved.

2 | Speaking

Discuss these questions with a partner.

1. Do you know anyone who smokes? What kind of smoker are they?

2. Do you know anyone who's given up? How did they manage to do it?

3. How do you feel about cigarette advertising?

3 | Playing for time

We often need to pause when we are asked difficult questions, to give us time to think. We do this by using 'delayers'. Listen and practise saying these 'delayers'.

> **So how come you decided to start smoking?**
>
> Why did I start smoking?
> That's a good question.
> That's a difficult question.
> Well, I'd have to think about that.
> I'm not really sure.
> Um, I don't really know.
> Why? I haven't really thought about that.

With a partner, take turns asking and answering the questions below. Before answering, use delayers to give you thinking time.

1. How come you decided to wear those clothes this morning?

2. Why did your parents call you (your name)?

3. What made you decide to sit next to me today?

4. Why do you think everyone ends up learning English and not French, German or Spanish?

5. What makes English so hard to learn?

4 | Role play

Pick someone in the class to pretend to be a famous person. For a couple of minutes, the rest of the class should prepare to ask them difficult questions about their life and experiences. The famous person should answer the questions, remembering to use 'delayers' if they need time to think.

I've got a really hectic weekend coming up. • I think I'll just laze about. • I just live for the weekend. • Doing anything interesting this weekend? • We're popping over to Paris for the weekend. • Can I crash out on your floor tonight? • I always go to the car boot sale. • I just love Sunday morning breakfasts. • Have a good weekend. • I'm going on a picnic in the country with some friends. • I usually spend Saturday morning doing the week's washing. • I've got to clean the flat up. • I think I'll just go and wander around the shops. • We're having some people round for dinner tonight. • It's not my idea of an exciting weekend. • What're you up to tonight? • Would you mind watering the plants while I'm gone? • Thank God it's Friday!

7 Your weekend

Using vocabulary

1 A typical weekend

Here is a list of things people do at weekends. Tick the ones you do. Think of some others.

- do the weekly shopping
- have a lie-in
- have people round
- tidy up your house/flat/room
- wander around town
- go out with friends for a meal
- go to church
- stay in and relax
- do some studying
- catch up with your e-mails
- go out for a walk
- go to the cinema/the theatre/ a concert
- clean the car
- catch up with work
- visit your parents/grandparents
- play football/tennis

Compare your answers with a partner.

> **Real English: What are you up to this weekend?**
>
> This is a common way of asking what your plans are.
>
> *What are you up to tonight?*
> *What are you up to on Saturday?*

2 Planning expressions

🎧 **Listen to Gavin talking about his plans for the weekend. Tick the expressions you hear.**

1. I guess I'll probably . . .
2. I imagine I'll . . .
3. I wouldn't mind . . . if I get time.
4. If I get the chance, I'll . . .
5. I hope to . . .
6. Unfortunately, I've got to . . .
7. I'm going to try to . . .
8. I'm planning to . . .

Now practise saying the expressions above.

3 Speaking

Discuss these questions with a partner.

1. When was the last time you just had a night in front of the telly? What did you watch?
2. Do you know anybody whose house is a tip?
3. When did you last have a big night out? Did it take you long to recover?

Using grammar

1 | Four different future forms

Here are four common ways to talk about the future.

1. 'll

That's the phone. I'll get it.
Wait for me. I'll only be a minute.
I think I'll have the chicken.

2. going to

Look at those black clouds. It's going to rain.
We're going to catch the early train.
We're going to go to New Zealand this winter.

3. present continuous

We're meeting in town tomorrow.
I'm leaving at the end of the month.
I'm going out to the cinema tonight.

4. present simple

We leave for Calcutta tomorrow morning.
The last bus leaves at 11.15.
India play Australia in the final next month.

With a partner, discuss which of the following best describes each group of sentences.

a. We use this form because there is some kind of evidence *now* for the future event. This might be a decision, a plan, or something you can see.

b. We use this form for things which are as certain as a timetable.

c. We use this form for things we've already arranged.

d. We use this form to give a reaction, an opinion or a decision at the moment of speaking.

2 | Grammar discussion

Read these sentences. Then discuss the question in brackets after each sentence.

1. I'm going to tidy up the house tomorrow morning. (When did you decide?)

2. We land at eight in the morning US time. (How do you know?)

3. I'll call in on the way home from work. (When did you decide?)

4. We're having my grandparents for Christmas dinner. (Is this a plan?)

You will learn best from good, natural examples.

3 | Grammar check

Complete the sentences below with the correct form of the verbs in the box.

get in do (x2) go give sneeze

1. A: What're you up to this afternoon? Any plans?
   B: I think I .... some gardening if it's nice.

2. According to the timetable, the earliest bus .... at seven.

3. A: Did you manage to post that letter?
   B: Oh, I'm sorry. I completely forgot. I .... it on my way home tonight. I promise!

4. Sorry I can't make it to class tonight. I .... out to dinner with some friends.

5. As soon as I pass my driving test, my father .... me his old car.

6. Pass me the paper hankies. Uh, uh, uh, I ....

4 | Grammar in context

Make sentences by matching the beginnings 1–4 to the endings a–d.

1. I'm just going to have a quiet night in tonight,

2. I've got to work really late tonight,

3. I'm so pleased that my exams are over

4. My mother's arriving tomorrow,

a. so I'm planning on having a lie-in tomorrow.

b. so I've got to get up really early and meet her.

c. and watch a bit of TV.

d. that I'm going to go out and celebrate tonight.

Now make sentences by matching the beginnings 5–8 to the endings e–h.

5. I've been going out such a lot lately

6. I'm just going to take it easy tonight

7. I've got a big night on Friday

8. I'm just going to stay in tonight because

e. because my brother's wedding's on Saturday.

f. I've got some things to do around the house.

g. because I was out until three last night at a party.

h. that I'm just going to stay in tonight for a change.

Ask some other students: 'So, what're you up to this week?'

> For more information on how to use these structures, see G9.

Listening

1 | While you listen

It's Friday evening. Ken and Steve have both just finished work for the day, and are about to go home. Listen to them talking about their plans for the weekend.

Cover the conversation. As you listen, try to answer this question.

What are Ken and Steve doing this weekend?

Listen again and fill in the gaps in the conversation.

Thank goodness it's Friday!

Steve: Thank goodness it's Friday! This week's been dragging on forever.

Ken: Tell me about it! So, what are you up to this weekend?

Steve: Oh, nothing special, really. This evening, I'm (1) .... for dinner with my parents.

Ken: Oh, that should be nice.

Steve: Yes, we're going to this little French place near where I live. The food's great there, and then tomorrow I've got to get up really early – at least for me! – and do some cooking, because I've (2) .... some people (3) .... in the afternoon. And I'll have to give the place a really good clean as well. And, I'm not sure, but I think (4) .... be going out after that – to see a film or something. We haven't really planned anything. What about yourself?

Ken: Well, tonight I'm (5) .... going out with some people from my old job, but I don't really feel like it any more. I'm feeling really tired.

Steve: So you're just going to (6) ...., then?

Ken: Yes, because tomorrow night I've got a big

night. I'm going to my friends Pete and Rachel's party. It's on a boat.

Steve: Oh, that sounds great. (7) ....?

Ken: Down by the river. You know, in the docks.

Steve: Oh yes, I know where you mean. I went to a party there myself (8) ....

Ken: Right. Is it OK down there?

Steve: Yes, it's great, but it's (9) .... big. There's not that much room on the boat.

Ken: Mm, sounds cosy!

Steve: Oh, yes, you can get really close to people! Lots of sweaty bodies!

Ken: I don't think it's (10) .... that sort of party!

Steve: Well, you never know. If you're lucky it might become one! No, I'm only joking, it's actually a great place for a party.

Ken: Good. I'm really (11) .... to it. But then on Sunday, unfortunately, I've got to do some things for work.

Steve: No rest for the wicked! Well, listen, I (12) .... give you a ring on Sunday, then, just to hear all about your quiet night out down on the river!

Real English: Tell me about it!

You say this to people when they tell you something negative and you want to sympathise because you have had a similar experience.

A: *I've had so many bills to pay this week. I can't believe how much it costs to have my own flat!*

B: *Tell me about it! My place is costing me a fortune!*

Are there any more expressions in the conversation which you have not met before or find surprising?

2 | Speaking

Discuss these questions with a partner.

1. Who do you think is going to have a better weekend – Steve or Ken?

2. Do you ever get that Friday afternoon feeling or that Monday morning feeling?

3. Have you ever been to a party on a boat? What was it like?

4. How often do you go out for dinner with your parents? What kind of places do you go to?

5. Are you usually too tired on a Friday to want to go out in the evening?

Using grammar

1 | More ways of talking about the future

Here are some more ways to talk about things in the future. All are common in spoken English.

1. I've got somebody coming round.
   I've got some friends arriving from Spain tomorrow.

2. I've got to do something.
   I've got to get up really early tomorrow to take my father to the airport.

3. I'm supposed to be doing something, but ...
   I'm supposed to be playing football on Saturday, but I've got a bit of a cold.

4. I might be doing something.
   I might be going to the coast for the weekend, but I haven't decided for sure yet.

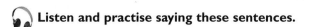 **Listen and practise saying these sentences.**

With a partner, use one of the patterns 1–4 to tell someone that …

1. a friend has arranged to come to your flat to help you with some homework on Sunday.

2. you've arranged to go shopping with a friend on Saturday, but you'll probably stay at home.

3. you've thought about going to the cinema, but you're not sure yet.

4. you have to do a lot of work this weekend because the deadline for your essay is Monday, and you haven't even started it yet.

5. your flat is really untidy. You know you must clean it this weekend.

6. there's a possibility your friend, Steve, is having a party tomorrow night.

7. you've arranged to meet some friends on Sunday for lunch, but you don't know if you'll feel like it because you're going to a party on Saturday!

8. your mother has arranged to visit your new flat on Saturday afternoon.

> ▶ For more information on how to use these structures to talk about the future, see G10.

2 | Role play

Imagine you want to invite your partner to a special event (e.g. the wedding of a relative, a day at the races, a masked ball). However, your partner can't come and will make an excuse. Practise using the example below.

A: Debbie and I are getting married next Saturday and we'd really like you to come to the reception in the evening.

B: Oh, I'd love to, but I'm afraid I can't. I've already arranged to go away for the weekend.

A: That's a shame. Is there no way you could put it off?

B: Well, I would if I could, but we've already booked the tickets.

A: Oh well, too bad. We'll save you a piece of the cake!

Do you find it easy to turn down invitations?

Would you turn down an invitation to any of the things shown in the pictures on these pages?

3 | Famous futures

What's your favourite song?

Can you complete these lines from famous songs? Each uses a future form. In one of the examples, you will need the spoken form of going to – gonna.

shall	'll	gonna

1. We . . . . overcome.
2. I . . . . tell you what I want; what I really, really want.
3. She . . . . be coming round the mountain when she comes.
4. Everything's . . . . be all right.

Find some more song lyrics which include future forms.

Here are three famous quotations, each using a future form. Which is your favourite?

'When I was young, I was told, 'You'll see when you're fifty.' I am fifty and I haven't seen a thing!'
Erik Satie

'Old men are dangerous. It doesn't matter to them what is going to happen to the world.'
George Bernard Shaw

'I disapprove of what you say, but I will defend to the death your right to say it.'
Voltaire

Can you say this short poem?

Tomato Ketchup
If you do not shake the bottle,
None'll come, and then a lot'll.

4 | Pronunciation

In the conversation Steve said: 'I'll have to give the place a really good clean'. Practise saying these common sentences with 'll.

1. Right, I'll see you later.
2. It'll be all right on the night.
3. She'll be with us in five minutes or so.
4. What'll you say to your boss?
5. How'll we recognise each other?
6. You'll regret it.
7. I'll see what I can do.
8. There'll be a lot of people you know there.
9. So, where'll we meet, then?
10. I'm sure we'll meet again.

In what kind of situation would you say number 6?

Using vocabulary

1 | Collocations with *go*

Below are six sentences with go for talking about your plans for the weekend. Cross out the wrong collocation in each group.

1. I'm going on a date / a day-trip to Cambridge / shopping tonight / a guided walk.
2. I'm going out to see a film / my friend up in Yorkshire / a bar tonight / see a musical.
3. I'm going out for shopping / a walk / the day on Saturday / a drink with some friends.
4. I'm going away to the mountains / Brighton this weekend / France for three days / the pub.
5. I'm going out to get something to eat / some things for the house / some shopping / driving.
6. I'm going fishing with my dad / shopping / some shopping / clubbing tonight.

Compare your answers with a partner, then make six statements about what you plan to do next weekend, using the vocabulary above.

Answer these questions.

7. Do you like going to bars?
8. How often do you go away for the weekend?
9. When was the last time you went away somewhere?
10. Have you ever been fishing? What did you catch?
11. What was the last day-trip you went on?

2 | Vocabulary check

What is the difference between a meeting, an appointment and a date?

Make sentences by matching the beginnings 1–4 to the endings a–d.

1. I've got an appointment ☐
2. I've got a blind date with ☐
3. I've got a meeting with ☐
4. I'm meeting up with ☐

a. my boss at four, which should last until six or so.
b. some friends of mine later for a drink.
c. at the dentist's at five. I'm dreading it.
d. this friend of a friend.

Now make sentences by matching the beginnings 5–8 to the endings e–h.

5. I'm going to go and visit ☐
6. I'm going round to ☐
7. I've got a date with ☐
8. I'm meeting ☐

e. a friend's tonight.
f. some friends later on this evening.
g. a friend of mine in hospital this afternoon.
h. this gorgeous guy/girl I met yesterday.

Real English: a friend's

This is how you talk about a friend's house or flat.
We're meeting at Steve's before going round to Stewart and Jane's.
We often also say *Steve's place* or *Jane's place*.
Whose place do you go to most often?

3 | Speaking

Discuss these questions with a partner.

1. What is the difference between a date and a blind date? Have you ever been on a blind date?
2. How often do you have a dentist's appointment?
3. Do you ever have to go to meetings? Who with?
4. Do you remember your last date, meeting or appointment? What about your first date?

4 | Plan a weekend

In pairs, plan an ideal weekend. Think about whether you want to …

- stay at home or go away somewhere.
- relax or keep busy.
- stay in the town or go out into the country.
- be on your own or with friends.
- eat out or at home.

Now talk to another partner and tell them about your plans for your ideal weekend.

Next, plan a really cheap weekend with your new partner. When you have done this, talk to a different student and compare your plans.

5 | Festivals

Are you interested in going to festivals such as the one shown in the pictures? It's Samhuinn (pronounced *Savin*) – an old Celtic festival, held in Edinburgh to celebrate Hallowe'en (All Souls) and the end of summer. Do you have anything like this in your country?

6 | Idioms focus

Steve used the expression 'No rest for the wicked!' at the end of his conversation with Ken on page 50. We use this expression to make fun of friends when they have to work – and we don't! Complete the common idioms below with the words in the box.

> choosers   joking   me   see   devil   present

a. Long time no . . . .!
b. Talk of the . . . .!
c. Beggars can't be . . . .!
d. Rather you than . . . .!
e. There's no time like the . . . .!
f. You must be . . . .!

Complete these short dialogues with the idioms a–f above.

1. A: Hello, Jack, ...!
   B: I know. I haven't seen you for ages.
2. A: When are we going to plan the party?
   B: Well, ..., is there?
3. A: We're going to the opera tonight.
   B: Opera? . . . .! I can't think of anything more boring!
4. A: I think Jane's just a bit annoyed because of what happened earlier.
   B: Oh, ...! Here she comes now. Let's ask her about it.
5. A: Look, the cheapest flight leaves at midnight and gets in at four in the morning.
   B: Let's take it! . . . .!
6. A: I was wondering if you could lend me £50 till next Friday.
   B: . . . .! I'm still waiting for the £5 I lent you last week!

Which of these idioms do you think you'll use most often? Why?

Hi, come on in. • You're the first one here, actually. • The music's awful. • Turn it down a bit, will you! • This is Paul. • Pleased to meet you. • Do you know anyone else here? • Who else is supposed to be coming? • Do you want to dance? • The food's over there. • I feel like a fish out of water. • This is brilliant! • Can I get you a drink? • Who's that over there? • What a lovely surprise! • I didn't know you were coming. • I'm ready to go in a minute. • Come on. The night is still young! • Change the music, will you! • Try this, It's delicious. • I feel a bit sick. • Shall I call you a taxi? • I hope you got his phone number. • What'll you have to drink? • Oops, sorry. • I'm sure it won't leave a stain. • Give me the keys! • He's an angry drunk. • I know my limit.

8 Party animals

Using vocabulary

1 | What kind of party?

With a partner, discuss what each of these kinds of parties involves.

- a birthday party
- a dinner party
- a family get-together
- a fancy dress party
- a farewell party
- a house-warming party
- a rave
- a stag night/a hen night
- a surprise party

Which of these kinds of parties do you enjoy going to the most? And the least? Why? Are there any you've never been to?

> **Real English: a rave**
>
> A rave is a party with hundreds of young people and very loud dance or techno music, often held in a warehouse or other large empty building. Sometimes the venue is kept secret till a few hours before it starts so that the police will not know about it. People discover where the rave is taking place by ringing a special number or finding out via the Internet.

> **Real English: a stag night/ a hen night**
>
> These refer to the parties usually held before two people get married. A stag night is when the bridegroom gets together with his male friends. A hen night is when the bride has a night out with her girlfriends.

2 | Party collocations

Complete the sentences below with the correct form of the verbs in the box.

break up	gatecrash	invite	sort out
finish	go on	ruin	throw

1. It was a great party. It . . . . until the small hours.
2. My girlfriend dumped me in front of everybody. It really . . . . the party!
3. The neighbours complained about the noise and, in the end, the police turned up and . . . . the party.
4. We had a lot of trouble with these guys who tried to . . . . the party. We told them they weren't invited, but they just wouldn't listen!
5. What time did the party . . . . ?
6. Hey, remind me later. I must remember to . . . . Louise and Arthur to the house-warming.
7. You know Russell's leaving soon, don't you? I think we should . . . . some kind of farewell party for him.
8. Have you . . . . everything for the office Christmas party yet? Do you need a hand with anything?

3 | Speaking

Discuss these questions with a partner.

1. Have you ever gatecrashed any parties? Have any of your parties ever been gatecrashed?
2. What kind of things would ruin a surprise party? A dinner party? A family get-together? A fancy-dress party? Have you ever been to a party which was ruined by something?
3. What's the longest party you've been to?

4 Planning a party

You are going to have a party. Put the following in order of importance.

- lots of food
- loud fast music
- really slow music
- lots of your friends
- some new people
- lots of different kinds of things to drink
- somewhere with atmosphere

Now compare your order with a partner and try to agree.

5 Planning expressions

Re-order the jumbled conversation below about organising a party.

a. Right, I'll bring some music if you sort out the food. How does that sound? `1`

b. Brilliant. I'm looking forward to it already. ☐

c. Yeah, OK, no problem. I'll try and bring crisps and things like that. What about the invites? ☐

d. Well, to be honest, I'd rather organise the music, if it's OK with you. Couldn't you do the food? ☐

e. Oh, I'll do those. I'll be seeing most people at school this week, so that'll be easy. ☐

Now underline the expressions above that you could use when planning a party.

> **Real English: the invites**
> The normal word is invitations. Invites is common in informal speech.

6 Role play

You and your partner have got £100 to organise a party for some friends. Plan it together. Here are some of the questions you will need to discuss.

- What kind of party do you want to have?
- When are you going to have it and where?
- What do you think you'll need to buy?
- How many people are you going to invite?
- Will your party have a theme?

Now walk around the class and invite as many people to your party as possible. Use the following:

We're having a party on … night. Would you like to come along?

When you are asked to someone else's party, make sure you ask these questions.

- Whereabouts is it?
- When's a good time to turn up?
- Should I bring anything?

If you have already accepted an invitation to another party on the same night, make sure you turn down the new invitation using an expression from the role play on page 51.

7 Speaking

When you are invited to a party at a friend's, what do you normally take as a present? What present would you give in these situations?

1. A friend is getting married.
2. It's your best friend's eighteenth birthday.
3. A friend is moving into a new flat.

Look at the picture below. What do you think each object is for? Would you like to get any as presents? What would you say if you were given any of the others?

Reading

1 | Collocations

Before you read the article, complete the sentences below with the phrases in the box.

> led to calls for tighter laws
> lose control
> suffering from shock
> ended in tragedy
> organised crime
> got out of hand

1. Our holiday in Canada was supposed to be the trip of a lifetime, but the whole thing nearly .... when our hired car went off the road in the middle of the mountains.

2. One of the problems with mind-altering drugs is that people who take them can sometimes .... and end up doing really stupid or dangerous things.

3. The demonstration was meant to be peaceful, but the whole thing .... and ended up as a full-scale riot.

4. Most murders in London are connected to ...., rather than individual criminals working alone.

5. The massacre of fifteen students in America has .... on the possession of guns.

6. After the crash, three passengers were taken to hospital ....

2 | Before you read

The article on the right is called 'Rave to the grave' and contains the six collocations in the box in Exercise 1 above. Discuss with a partner what you think the connection between them might be.

3 | While you read

Now read the article and see if you were right.

Rave to the grave

A rave party nearly ended in tragedy last night, when over a hundred people fell through the floor of the fourth-floor flat they were dancing in and into the flat below. Amazingly, no one was killed, although seven people were taken to hospital suffering from shock. The party was organised by a group called Tribal Spiral, and was held in a deserted flat on a housing estate in East London. It is believed that the extremely high volume of the techno music being played weakened the structure of the floor.

Bert Jones, aged 64, who lives in the third-floor flat below, said: 'I must admit, I hadn't really noticed the party going on. I'm a bit hard of hearing and I didn't have my hearing aid in, but I could feel the vibrations from somewhere. I just thought it must be kids messing around upstairs somewhere. Then, the next thing I knew, there was an almighty crash in the living room, so I ran in and the place was full of dust and plaster and people screaming. I just couldn't believe my eyes. I got the shock of my life, I can tell you. Now I'm waiting for the council to send someone round to fix things.'

The incident follows a number of complaints about techno parties all over the capital and public outcry about raves. A recent tabloid headline screamed, 'SPACED OUT! 11,000 YOUNGSTERS GO DRUG CRAZY AT BRITAIN'S BIGGEST EVER DANCE PARTY', while the number of drug-related deaths at raves has risen dramatically over the last year. All of this will undoubtedly lead to calls for tighter anti-rave laws. The government is already considering introducing a new law which will help police crack down on unofficial gatherings of this kind. They are proposing a bill which will allow police to break up any groups of more than twenty people listening to 'music with repetitive beats' and also intend to make club owners responsible for any drugs being sold on their premises. A spokesman for the Metropolitan Police said, 'Things are getting out of hand, and obviously what worries us the most is that where you have rave parties and where you have drugs, you're bound to come up against organised crime. We'd obviously appreciate any new law which gave us more powers to tackle this problem.'

David Goodyear, a Stepney ambulanceman, claimed that many of the partygoers at the Tribal Spiral event had failed to notice the floor had collapsed. Most of the young people just carried on dancing – a fact he put down to the mind-altering affects of Ecstasy and other so-called 'dance drugs'.

However, there are signs that young people themselves are already looking for alternatives to the rave scene. One of the most successful new clubs to have opened this year is the Domino Club. Here, young people sit around drinking cocktails whilst a DJ plays laid-back jazz. There isn't much dancing – instead, the club-goers play board games such as Scrabble and Monopoly. Another club which has become very popular is The Big Chill, which is held in a church called the Union Chapel. Ironically, maybe young people today are closer to God than the government and the police realise!

4 | Comprehension check

Without looking back at the article, try to correct these false statements using the exact words from 'Rave to the grave'.

1. The party was held in Tribal Spiral's flat.
2. Dancing weakened the structure of the floor.
3. Bert Jones is fixing his flat himself.
4. This is the first complaint there's been about techno parties in London.
5. There's been a small increase in the number of drug-related deaths over the last year.
6. The dancing stopped when the floor collapsed.

Now go back and see if you remembered the exact words correctly.

5 | Speaking

1. What's the noisiest party you've ever been to?
2. Why do you think young people take drugs?
3. Is your country 'hard' or 'soft' on drug-taking?
4. Is organised crime a problem in your country?

6 | I just couldn't wait

In the article, Bert Jones said: 'I just couldn't believe my eyes.' Can you remember why?

What do you think just means in these expressions?

a. I just couldn't make up my mind.
b. I just couldn't bear it any longer.
c. I just couldn't wait.
d. I just couldn't resist them.
e. I just couldn't believe my eyes.

Now complete these sentences with the expressions a–e above.

1. Sorry I've started without you, but I was expecting you at five. I got so hungry that . . . . There's still a little bit of chicken left if you want it.

2. When I saw what he'd done to his hair, ... ! It was bright pink and green!

3. A: Did you manage to get some shoes?
   B: Oh, it was awful, it really was. I went into dozens of shoe shops and tried on I don't know how many, but . . . . So, in the end, I didn't buy anything!

4. The meeting was supposed to run from nine till six, but after a couple of hours it got so boring . . . . So I made my excuses and left.

5. I know I'm supposed to be on a diet, but the cakes all looked so delicious that . . . . Oh well, I just won't eat all day tomorrow now!

7 | Speaking

Discuss these questions with a partner.

1. Have you ever been in a situation where you just couldn't believe your eyes?
2. When was the last time you had to admit to someone that you just couldn't resist something?
3. When was the last time you just couldn't make up your mind? What about?
4. When was the last time you got so bored by something that you just couldn't bear it any longer?
5. Have you ever been so annoyed by somebody that you just couldn't bear it any longer and had to say something? What did you say? How did they feel? Did it make you feel better?

abulary

:s

**and the meaning of the
...below. Then ask some
other students ...your class the questions.**

1. Do you know anyone who is a member of a political party?
2. What kind of things do left-wing political parties believe in?
3. What kind of things do right-wing political parties believe in?
4. What are the main political parties in your country?
5. Which party came to power in the last election?
6. Which party leaders in your country do you think are strong/weak at the moment?
7. Are any political parties banned in your country? Why?
8. What was the last political party to be set up in your country?
9. Have any parties in your country split over the last few years?

2 | Do, make

Complete these sentences with the correct form of do or make.

1. I think he'd .... a very good leader.
2. The People's Party didn't .... very well in the last election.
3. I don't know why they .... him party leader. He's completely incompetent.
4. They've .... a big difference since they came to power. Things are much better now.
5. I can't .... up my mind who to vote for.
6. We've got to try and .... a decision by tomorrow.
7. I wouldn't take those pills if I were you. They won't .... you any good!
8. At some time in our life, we all .... something wrong and we all .... mistakes!
9. Do you think you can .... the shopping later, if you get time?
10. I'm only here for a few days, so I want to .... the most of my time.
11. I've got an important client coming over later, so please .... an effort to look your best.
12. I don't know why you like this kind of music! It doesn't .... anything for me.

3 | Talking about the law

In the 'Rave to the grave' article, you read that the government is considering introducing a new law. Can you remember why? Look back at page 56 if you need to.

Now make four sentences about laws by matching the beginnings 1–4 to the endings a–d.

1. They're going to introduce a new law to ban
2. They're going to introduce a new law to protect
3. They're going to introduce a new law to crack down
4. They're going to introduce new tax breaks to encourage

a. on illegal street trading.
b. smoking in all public places.
c. people to have more children.
d. the environment.

Now make four more sentences by matching the beginnings 5–8 to the endings e–h.

5. They're going to relax the drinking laws
6. They're going to tighten the immigration laws
7. They're going to change the old adoption laws
8. They're going to legalise

e. because they're out of date.
f. to allow pubs to stay open longer.
g. genetic cloning.
h. to make it more difficult for people to get into the country.

4 | Role play

In groups of three, you are going to set up your own political party. You will need to decide the following:

- what you want to ban
- what you will crack down on
- what tax breaks you will give and who to
- what laws you're going to tighten
- what laws you're going to relax
- if you're going to legalise anything

Decide on a name for your party and then go round your class campaigning. Your teacher will then organise a class election. You're not allowed to vote for your own party!

5 | Political quotes

Do you agree with the three quotations below? Why/why not?

The natural relationship between a journalist and a politician should be that of a dog towards a lamppost.
Henry Mencken

Power tends to corrupt and absolute power corrupts absolutely.
Lord Acton

I must study politics and war so that my sons may be free to study Mathematics and Philosophy.
John Adams

Review: Units 5–8

1 | Tenses

Choose the correct form.

1. Before I left home, I haven't / I hadn't been getting on very well with my parents.
2. I'd / I'll die if that happened to me.
3. A: What are you up to tonight?
   B: I'm meeting / I'll meet some friends.
4. A: So, how come you decided to go to the doctor?
   B: Well, I didn't feel / I hadn't been feeling well for ages, so it seemed like the right thing to do.
5. If he does that one more time, I'll / I'd scream!
6. We weren't / We hadn't been getting on very well for ages, so we decided to end the relationship.
7. We'll go / We're going to the cinema tonight. Do you want to come with us?
8. If I'm / I were you, I'd be really upset about it!
9. Will you / Are you going to tell me when it's five o'clock, please?
10. I'll / I've got to go and pick the kids up from school in a minute, so I'll phone you back later, OK?

2 | Multiple choice

Choose the correct alternative.

1. How come … ?
   a. you bought such an old car
   b. did you buy such an old car
2. Did you manage … ?
   a. finding those shoes   b. to find those shoes
3. It was really … .
   a. much more better than mine
   b. much better than mine
4. I really enjoy … .
   a. living here   b. to live here
5. I was really fed up … .
   a. with sitting around all day b. to sit around all day
6. I'm going … .
   a. on a day-trip to Bath
   b. out for a day-trip to Bath
7. I'm supposed … .
   a. playing tennis   b. to be playing tennis
8. Don't worry. … .
   a. It's just a simple mistake
   b. It just is a simple mistake
9. I always try to avoid … .
   a. talking to him if I can   b. to talk to him if I can
10. I can still remember … .
    a. watching her leave   b. to watch her leave

Compare your answers with a partner and discuss how you made your choices.

3 | Conditionals

Make sentences by matching the beginnings 1–6 to the endings a–f.

1. If he does that one more time,   ☐
2. If he did that to me,   ☐
3. I'd give that a miss   ☐
4. I won't be able to do that   ☐
5. I'd be able to do that   ☐
6. I'll buy that for you   ☐

a. I'd leave him.
b. if you don't find the instructions.
c. if I had the money.
d. if I get a Christmas bonus.
e. I think I'll scream.
f. if I were you.

With a partner, discuss what you think 'that' could mean in 1–6 above.

Now use these five sentence starters to tell a partner some things about yourself.

7. If I was a man/woman, …
8. If I spoke better English, …
9. If I was older, …
10. If I wasn't sitting here, …
11. If I could take a year off, …

4 | Conversation

Put the jumbled conversation below into the correct order.

a. So, what are you up to this weekend?   1
b. I don't know. I haven't got a clue. I suppose it depends how good my Greek gets.   ☐
c. Don't you think it'd get boring after a while?   ☐
d. Studying? Oh right, your Greek course. How come you decided to start that?   ☐
e. I'm going away to Wales. Would you like to come?   ☐
f. It couldn't be more tedious than being stuck in front of a computer all day!   ☐
g. Oh, I'd love to, but I'm afraid I can't. I've got to do some studying.   ☐
h. Well, I suppose it was because I've always wanted to live and work on a Greek island.   ☐
i. I know what you mean. I'm half-blind already. So, you think you'll get a job out there, then?   ☐

5 | Look back and check: Adjectives

Look back at the strong adjectives and follow-up comments on page 45. Tick all the words you can remember. Ask a partner about anything you have forgotten.

Can you think of some instances from your own life where you could use some of the words and phrases? Tell a partner as much as you can about them.

6 | Expressions

Complete the short dialogues below with the expressions in the box. All the expressions are from units 5–8.

make up my mind	you'll regret it
I just felt like it	that's a good question
what a nightmare	I would if I could

1. A: Why did you go and have all your hair cut off?
    B: I don't know. . . . .

2. A: They lost all my luggage and then we got delayed for three hours.
    B: Oh, no! . . . . !

3. A: Can you give me a hand to move this table?
    B: No, sorry. . . . . , but I've got to rush. I'm late for work.

4. A: I'm just going to have one more cream cake.
    B: I wouldn't if I were you. !

5. A: So, how long have you been doing t'ai chi for, then?
    B: . . . . I'd have to think about it really.

6. A: Did you buy anything in the end?
    B: No, nothing. I just couldn't . . . . what I wanted.

Can you think of three other sentences you might respond to by saying: 'Oh no! What a nightmare!'?

Can you think of three other sentences you might respond to by saying: 'I wouldn't if I were you. You'll regret it'?

7 | Collocations

Match the verbs 1–10 with the b[est collocations] a–j.

1.	watch	a.	smoking
2.	make	b.	your cigarett[e]
3.	go out	c.	really early
4.	stop	d.	a photograph
5.	go	e.	too much TV
6.	take	f.	for a meal
7.	get up	g.	at home
8.	put	h.	a big decision
9.	stay	i.	everywhere for something
10.	look	j.	on a date

Now match the verbs 11–18 to the best collocations k–r.

11.	gatecrash	k.	a fuss
12.	eat up	l.	a new law
13.	feel	m.	a job
14.	introduce	n.	them like second-class citizens
15.	accept	o.	pleased with myself
16.	treat	p.	income tax
17.	make	q.	all my free time
18.	raise	r.	a party

Discuss these questions with a partner.

19. What eats up most of your free time?
20. When was the last time you had to look everywhere for something? Did you find it in the end?
21. Have you ever made a big fuss? Why? What happened?
22. Have they introduced any new laws in your country recently?

8 | Real English

Match the statements 1–6 to the responses a–f.

1. I'm going to Guinea Bissau next year.
2. I'm going to study in Edinburgh for a year.
3. It's so expensive here in London, isn't it?
4. What are you up to this weekend?
5. Doing anything tonight?
6. Did you get an invite to Ann's party?

a. Tell me about it! I've already spent most of the money I came with!
b. Good for you! You'll have a great time.
c. No, I didn't even know she was having one!
d. Yes, I am, actually. I'm going round to Jane's.
e. Where on earth is that?
f. I'm going to my country cottage on Friday night.

You have one minute to memorise the responses a–f. Now cover Exercise 8 above. Your partner will read out the statements 1–6. How many responses can you remember?

Idioms

Make sentences with idioms by matching the beginnings 1–8 to the endings a–h.

1. It's a real weight
2. No rest
3. After that it was
4. It'd drive
5. Long time
6. Talk of
7. Beggars can't
8. Rather you

a. plain sailing.
b. me mad.
c. be choosers.
d. the devil.
e. off my shoulders.
f. for the wicked.
g. than me.
h. no see.

10 What can you remember?

With a partner, note down as much as you can remember about the two texts you read in units 6 and 8.

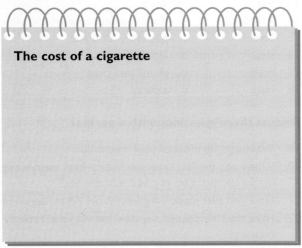

The cost of a cigarette

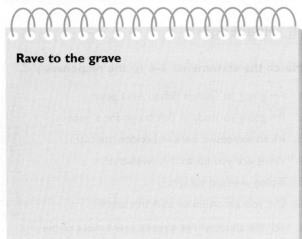

Rave to the grave

Now compare what you remember with another pair. Who remembers more?

Which text did you enjoy more? Why?

11 Vocabulary quiz

Answer these questions with a partner. Then compare your answers with another pair. Who got most answers right?

1. If there's no sign of someone, does that mean that you can't find them anywhere or that they haven't sent you a letter?
2. How many different kinds of parties can you think of?
3. Could you be arrested for lighting up on a plane?
4. If you spent the weekend just messing around, what did you do?
5. What's the difference between left-wing and right-wing?
6. Who would break up a party and why?
7. When you go to the dentist's, do you make an appointment or a date with him?
8. If you don't like, for example, eating frogs, would you say: 'I wouldn't eat a frog if you paid me' or 'I wouldn't eat a frog if you asked me'?
9. If you and some friends go to a nice little French place, what are you going to do?
10. If you're a heavy smoker, does it mean you're fat or that you smoke too much?
11. What is the difference between going shopping and doing the shopping?
12. Does a plane touch down at the beginning, in the middle, or at the end of a flight?
13. If something drags on, does it happen really quickly or does it take forever?
14. If you can be on board a plane, can you be on board a boat?
15. How could a government tighten laws on drinking? On immigration?
16. Are your relations the same as your relatives?
17. Do you go on a day-trip or have a day-trip?
18. You play tennis on one and you might end up in one if you're arrested. What is it?
19. Is a cosy room large or small?
20. Where do you work if you are one of the cabin crew?

Learner advice: The authors speak!

Discuss these questions with a partner.

1. How do you learn vocabulary? Do you think you do it well or badly?
2. Do you read texts to learn vocabulary? What kind of texts?
3. What do you do if you don't understand a word?
4. What kind of dictionary do you use?
5. Do you translate words into your language? Why/why not?

Now read this text and see if you are like any of the students mentioned.

I was teaching my class this morning and the phrase "I got ripped off by the taxi driver coming from the airport" appeared in a reading text. Several students asked: 'What does "rip" mean?' I have to admit, I find this question a bit depressing, because it means some of my students are still thinking in terms of single words rather than phrases or expressions. I am patient and reply: 'It's not "rip". The expression is "I got ripped off". It means "I paid more money than I should have paid". Normally the taxi ride to the city centre costs ten euros, but this guy charged me … how much?' Several students shout out, 'Thirty, forty euros.' I then asked if anyone has ever been ripped off and several students answered. Someone even gave a translation in Spanish, which I speak. Great. Unfortunately, while all this was happening, two other students were using their bilingual dictionaries. One of them had one of those computer ones which make a really annoying beeping noise. 'Ah, it means "tear, break"?' he asked. 'No!' I re-explained and we did another exercise which again included the phrase "ripped off". The second student then asked, 'What does "rip" mean?' I felt like screaming.

What can I tell you about all this, apart from the fact that students not listening drives teachers mad? I think there are several important things to say. Firstly, *don't* underline single words: ask your teacher about the whole phrase. If you want to compare how a word from your language is used, ask your teacher, for example, 'Can you say there was *big* traffic?' Also try to notice any new combinations of words you already know. For example, the phrase "I need to go out and let my hair down" was in a text the other day. I asked people if they knew it and a couple of students pointed to their hair. They were wrong! The expression means "to relax and party" – maybe dancing and laughing a lot. If you get a dictionary, make sure it has examples of these kinds of expressions – and maybe whole phrase translations.

There is lots of work on idioms and collocations in this Coursebook, and on page 167, there are lists of them for you to translate and remember.

Has the text made you change your mind in any way about the way you study?

So what did you get up to last night? • You went out where? • It's not really my sort of place. • What a bore! • Who did you say you bumped into? • I bet you've never even been there! • We didn't get in till two in the morning. • What was it like? • Oh, did you? • I went round to a friend's place. • You'd have enjoyed yourself. • You should've come. • It was one of the best nights of my life. • You must be exhausted. • Believe it or not, I'm too old for that sort of thing! • I was bored out of my mind • That's the last time you'll catch me there! • It was a total rip-off. • The food was awful. • It's *the* place to be. • The music was out of this world. • It wasn't the same without you. • You look terrible. What time did you get in last night? • We were up until the wee small hours. • It was an older crowd

9 Last night

Using vocabulary

1 Lifestyle

What sort of lifestyle do you lead? Do you go out every evening or are you the stay-at-home type?

Read these descriptions of what some people did last night.

1. I went out for a walk around town.
2. I rang my sister.
3. I watched the semi-final on TV.
4. I just had a quiet night at home.
5. I went to my evening class.
6. I finished painting the kitchen.
7. I had an early night.
8. I visited my neighbour in hospital.
9. I tried to find a cheap flight on the Internet.
10. I went to the laundrette.

Which of these things do you do? Which do you never do?

Listen to four people talking about what they did last night. When you have decided what they did, tick the correct number in the list above.

A

B

C

D

2 So how was your night?

Complete the sentences below with the words in the box.

absolutely	house
catch up	loads
depth	seat
halfway	single
horrendous	taking it up

1. I had a terrible time. I didn't know a .... person there.
2. I had a terrible time. The service was ....
3. I had a terrible time. We had .... nothing in common.
4. I had a terrible time. I was completely out of my ....
5. I had a terrible time. I fell asleep .... through.
6. I had a great time. We got on like a .... on fire.
7. I had a great time. I met .... of interesting people there.
8. I had a great time. It was really nice to .... after all this time.
9. I had a great time. I'm thinking of .... more seriously.
10. I had a great time. I was on the edge of my .... the whole way through.

With a partner, practise asking and answering these questions using the answers above. Try and keep each conversation going for as long as you can.

a. So how was the play?
b. So how was your date?
c. So how was your Italian class?
d. So how was the party?
e. So how was the meal with your friends?

3 Speaking

When was the last time you had a great time? A terrible time? Why?

4 | Collocations with *get*

In Exercise 1 on page 64, one speaker said they were quite tired when they got in from work. There are many collocations with get. Complete the sentences below with the words and expressions in the box.

surprise	bus
upset	wet
a job	a call
something to eat	money
my hair cut	lost

1. I got . . . . last night. Do you like it? I think it's a bit too short at the back myself.

2. I tried to get some . . . . from the cash machine last night, but it wasn't working.

3. I got . . . . from an old friend of mine last night. I hadn't spoken to her for ages, so that was nice.

4. I was really hungry, so I popped out to get . . . .

5. I got really . . . . last night watching TV. I watched that documentary about Hiroshima.

6. I've never seen rain like it – I got really . . . . on the way home last night.

7. I got a real . . . . last night. An old school friend of mine turned up out of the blue!

8. Hey, you won't believe it. I've finally got . . . . I start next Monday.

9. My car broke down, so I had to get the last . . . . home.

10. I walked around town a bit, but ended up getting . . . . I had to ask someone where I was!

Go back and underline the get expressions.

You can use get with all of the following words. Use them to say something true about yourself or people you know.

annoyed	angry	upset
better	soaked	worried
tired	married	sleepy
well paid	lazy	pregnant

When was the last time you ...

- had to get a taxi home?
- got in really late?
- got stuck in traffic?
- got stopped by the police?

5 | Problem words

With a partner, discuss the [ ] between the highlighted wo[ ] sentences.

a. I had a chat with her.
   I had a talk with her.

b. We gossiped about the boss.
   We talked about work.

c. I did the washing-up.
   I did the washing.

d. I went to a disco.
   We ended up going to a disco.

e. I missed the last bus home.
   I really missed her when she was in Spain.

f. I went out last night after work.
   I left work last night about five.

Now complete these sentences with the sentences a–f above.

1. Yes, Mr Fairhurst, ... about it. I'm sure Eve won't be late again.

2. I bumped into Marie yesterday, which was nice. . . . . about, you know, nothing much, but it was nice to see her.

3. I had a drink with Bill last week. . . . . and nothing else all evening!

4. Some of us went for a drink after work the other day. It was awful. . . . . for ages. I'm glad he wasn't there!

5. I haven't got anything to wear tomorrow. It really is time . . . .

6. Just look at all those dirty dishes. It's time . . . .

7. I had a crazy evening. I met some old friends and we went out for dinner and then eventually . . . .

8. My legs are killing me this morning! . . . . and didn't stop dancing all night!

9. I'm really annoyed. I didn't get home until two last night. . . . .

10. Jane came back last week. . . . .

11. . . . . and just went straight home.

12. I should have known better. . . . . with a few people from my department and I didn't get in till 3 am. I feel terrible.

Before you listen

Are there any places you would never go out to in your town? Why not?

2 | While you listen

🎧 **Rose and Lucy are having breakfast in the kitchen of the flat they share. Listen to them talking about what they did last night. Cover the conversation. As you listen, try to answer these questions.**

1. What did Rose and Lucy do after work?
2. What time did they go to bed?

Listen again and try to fill in the gaps in the conversation below.

> **Real English: get a cab**
>
> Cab is correct spoken English for a taxi.
> *You get a cab. I'll walk.*

3 | Speaking

Discuss these questions with a partner.

1. Have you ever been chatted up by someone much younger than you? What happened?
2. What's the worst club, disco or party you've ever been to? What made it so bad?
3. How often do you eat foreign food? What's your favourite?
4. Do you ever feel you watch a bit too much TV and that you should go out a bit more instead?

> **Real English: I bet he hadn't even started shaving.**
>
> It is very common for friends to make comments to each other starting I bet ... .
> *I bet John's going to ask Angie to the party!*
> *I bet you're wishing you'd gone!*
> *I bet their car will break down!*
>
> We say I bet ... when we are fairly sure that what we are saying is true.

The Worst Disco in Town!

Lucy: Hey, Rose, there's a letter for you.

Rose: Thanks. You must've got in late last night. I didn't even hear you come in – and (1) .... after one.

Lucy: I did, actually, yes. I went and met some old friends from college that I hadn't seen for ages.

Rose: Oh, (2) ....? That must've been nice.

Lucy: Yes, we had a drink and a chat and caught up with all the gossip. You know what it's like.

Rose: Uh-huh.

Lucy: Then we had (3) .... and then another drink and then we (4) .... going on to this awful disco in town.

Rose: Oh, did you? Which one? Not Stardust! No, surely not Stardust?

Lucy: I'm afraid it was, actually – and it was really terrible, just full of kids and the music was so loud (5) .... It was like being back at school all over again. Kids of fourteen acting as if they were eighteen!

Rose: I could've told you that!

Lucy: This boy came up to me – you know, bottle of beer in his hand, acting all macho, and asked me to dance! I bet he hadn't even started shaving!

Rose: And did you?

Lucy: What? Dance with him? (6) .... ! Then I told him I was thirty-five!

Rose: You're so cruel.

Lucy: Well, I just figured it was better he found out (7) .... that I was old enough to be his mum!

Rose: I thought you were supposed to be there talking to old friends.

Lucy: I was, but there was so much noise, you couldn't really have a proper conversation. And then to top it all, I missed the last train home and had to get a cab and (8) .... three!

Rose: Didn't you? You must be feeling exhausted this morning, then.

Lucy: Yeah, I could do with another hour or two in bed, that's for sure. (9) .... , what about you? How was your night?

Rose: Oh, it was OK. I just did a bit of shopping on my way home, cooked myself some ramen noodles.

Lucy: Cooked yourself (10) ....?

Rose: Ramen noodles, you know, just Japanese noodles.

Lucy: Oh, OK.

Rose: They're really quick and easy, and then I just did a bit of tidying-up, you know, nothing amazing or anything, read for a bit, watched (11) .... – some film – you know the kind of thing that's on late on Channel 4. Actually, I was so tired, I fell asleep in the middle of it!

Lucy: Oh, don't! You're making me feel even more exhausted!

Using grammar

1 Responding with auxiliary verbs

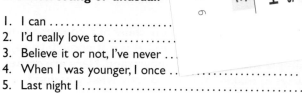

🎧 **Look at these common ways of responding to what someone says. Then listen and practise saying the expressions in colour.**

Auxiliary question + follow-up question

A: I met our old English teacher on the train last night.
B: Oh, did you? How is she?
A: She's fine, she's working at another school now, teaching younger kids.

Auxiliary question + follow-up comment

A: Hey – great news! I've just passed my driving test!
B: Oh, have you? Congratulations. You must be really pleased.
A: Yes, it's excellent. Now all I need is the money for a car.

First respond to the statements 1–8 with an auxiliary question. For example: *Can you? Have you?* **Then add one of the follow-up comments a–h.**

1. A: I'm a pretty good cook, believe it or not.
    B: .... ? ....

2. A: I've just come back from Paris.
    B: .... ? ....

3. A: I had a fight with my boy/girlfriend yesterday.
    B: .... ? ....

4. A: I was thinking of going to the circus this weekend.
    B: .... ? ....

5. A: I think I'm getting the flu.
    B: .... ? ....

6. A: I usually play football on Saturdays.
    B: .... ? ....

7. A: Eventually, I'd like to end up living overseas.
    B: .... ? ....

8. A: I'm going to see Marco tonight.
    B: .... ? ....

a. Who do you play for?
b. How was it?
c. Say 'Hello' from me.
d. Have you sorted everything out yet?
e. Keep away from me, then.
f. Where's it on?
g. So, when are you going to invite me round for dinner, then?
h. Anywhere particular in mind?

With a partner, practise reading out the dialogues above, but add a third comment – as in the two examples at the top of the page.

2 Talking about you

**Complete these sentence s ...
are true for you. If you can,
are interesting or unusual.**

1. I can ....
2. I'd really love to ....
3. Believe it or not, I've never ..
4. When I was younger, I once .. ..
5. Last night I ....

Now tell a partner what you've written. Your partner should respond first by using an auxiliary question and then by adding a follow-up question or comment. Try to continue these conversations for as long as you can.

▶ For more information on how to use auxiliary verbs when responding, see G11.

...g sure you understand

...do you feel when you don't understand ...mething someone has just said to you? How do you deal with this problem?

When someone says something in a conversation that you don't understand, it is not enough to say simply that you don't understand. Here are some ways of making it clear exactly what you don't understand.

A: I surfed the net last night.
B: You did what last night?
A: Surfed the net – played around on the Internet.

A: I went on holiday to Phuket last year.
B: You went where?
A: Phuket. It's a beach resort in Thailand.

🎧 **Listen and practise the dialogues above with a partner.**

Now complete these dialogues by writing questions to make it clear exactly what you don't understand.

1. A: My car cost over two grand.
   B: ....?
   A: Over two grand, two thousand pounds.

2. A: I had dinner in Bellini's last night.
   B: ....?
   A: In Bellini's, that new Italian place.

3. A: I downloaded this great article last night.
   B: ....?
   A: I downloaded an article, you know, copied it off the Internet.

4. A: I arrived here on Boxing Day.
   B: ....?
   A: On Boxing Day, you know, the day after Christmas, 26th December.

5. A: I went bungee jumping last year in Canada.
   B: ....?
   A: Bungee jumping, you know, when you jump from a bridge with elastic round your legs.

6. A: This shirt cost me eighty quid.
   B: ....?
   A: Eighty quid, you know, eighty pounds.

7. A: I found a baby wren in my garden today.
   B: ....?
   A: A baby wren. It must've fallen out of its nest.

8. A: We went to Alton Towers at the weekend.
   B: ....?
   A: To Alton Towers. It's a kind of theme park, like Disneyland, but much smaller.

Compare your answers with your partner, then practise the dialogues above in pairs.

Real English: My car cost over two grand.

In informal spoken English a grand is one thousand pounds. In number six in Exercise 3 eighty quid is informal British English for eighty pounds.

4 | Not until

In the conversation on page 66, Lucy says: 'I didn't get in until three.'

Why didn't she say: 'I got in at three?'

Complete these sentences by choosing the more appropriate of the two choices.

1. I had to work late, so ... .
   a. I got home at seven
   b. I didn't get home until seven

2. The traffic on the way was really heavy, so ... .
   a. I didn't get there until nine
   b. I got there at nine

3. We managed to get the bus OK, so ... .
   a. we were there by nine
   b. we weren't there until nine

4. I was a late starter. ... .
   a. I didn't have a girlfriend until I was twenty-one
   b. I had a girlfriend when I was twenty-one

5. I just had a fairly quiet night. ... .
   a. I didn't get to bed until eleven
   b. I went to bed at eleven

6. There were three standing ovations. The concert ... .
   a. finished at 11:30
   b. didn't finish until 11:30

7. I'm not too bad at English, considering ... .
   a. I didn't start studying until I was eighteen
   b. I started studying when I was eighteen

8. I was so busy that ... .
   a. I had breakfast at midday
   b. I didn't have breakfast until midday

Can you explain your choice in each example?

5 | Discuss

With a partner, answer these questions. Try to use not until ... . Give reasons for your answers. You don't have to tell the truth.

1. What time did you get in last night?
2. When did you have your first boy/girlfriend?
3. What time did you go to bed last night?
4. When did you start studying English?

▶ For more information on how to use not ... until, see G12.

6 | Linking ideas

On page 66, Lucy talked about the disco:
'It was so loud, I could hardly hear myself think.'

This is a common way of linking two ideas:
I was very tired.
I fell asleep in the middle of the film.
→ I was so tired, I fell asleep in the middle of the film.

Make sentences by matching the beginnings 1–8 to the endings a–h.

1. It was so cold,
2. I was so exhausted,
3. I was so hungry,
4. It was so hot,
5. His conversation was so dull,
6. I was so angry,
7. I was so worried,
8. The film was so bad,

a. I could've killed him!
b. I rang the police.
c. I could hardly breathe.
d. I walked out halfway through.
e. I just went straight to bed as soon as I got in.
f. I could hardly stop myself from yawning.
g. my hands felt like they were going to fall off.
h. I could've carried on eating all night!

Listen, then say all these sentences, making sure you stress so.

7 | More conversations

With a partner, complete these dialogues using ideas of your own. For example:

A: So, how was that club you went to?
B: Terrible! The music was so loud, I just had to leave.

1. A: So, what was that film like you saw last night?
   B: Well, to be honest, it was so bad, ...
2. A: What was the food like in that French place you went to?
   B: Really good. It was so delicious, ...
3. A: So, did you do anything special last night?
   B: No, I was so exhausted, I ... .
4. A: So, how did your meeting go last night?
   B: Terrible, it was so ... , I ... .
5. A: So, did you sort everything out with your boss yesterday?
   B: No, I got so ... , I ... .
6. A: So, did you pass your driving test?
   B: No, I'm afraid not. I was so ... , I ... .

For more information on how to use this linking structure, see G13.

8 | Role play

There's a thief in the class!
At 8 pm last night, a terrible crim
committed – your teacher's car w
from the school car park. The pol
two students from this class.

1. **The class decides which two students are most likely to have committed the crime. The pair of suspects leave the room to prepare their story. They should try to use as much language from this unit as possible.**
   (Where were you when the crime happened? Who were you with? What were you doing? All the details are important!)

2. **The rest of the class prepare to interview the two students.** (What will you ask them?)

3. **Student 1 comes back into the room alone and is interviewed by the class. When the interview is finished, student 2 comes in to be interviewed.**

4. **When both students have been interviewed, the class vote. Are they both guilty? Is only one guilty? What should happen to them? Decide on a suitable punishment!**

...e you been all my life? • He's old enough to be your father! • I only like men with money. • Looks don't matter to... He's a bit of a lad, if you ask me. • You'd never catch me going out with someone who wears red socks! • I think I'm i... ...ve. • Excuse me, would you like to come home and see my stamp collection? • I usually go for Scandinavians. • Are you trying to chat me up, because if you are, you can get lost! • We've decided to go our separate ways. • Go jump In the river! • He'... a bit of a nerd. • I prefer older men. • I'm not prejudiced, of course. • I don't find him attractive at all. • I don't know what she sees in him. • It's a match made in heaven. • It just wasn't meant to be. Our marriage is on the rocks. • The honeymoon is over.

Relationships

Using grammar

1 | Judging by appearances

Which of the people in the picture below do you find most/least attractive? Why?

Complete these sentences by adding looks, looks like or looks as if.

1. He/she . . . . he's/she's got some kind of disease.
2. He/she . . . . a model or something.
3. He/she . . . . a bit of a nerd.
4. He/she . . . . a bit dull.
5. He/she . . . . he/she wouldn't say boo to a goose.
6. He/she . . . . quite sexy.
7. He/she . . . . a real creep.
8. He/she . . . . he's/she's about to collapse.
9. He/she . . . . a bit down.

2 | Speaking

Do you think any of the sentences 1–9 in Exercise 1 describe the people in the picture below? Compare what you think with a partner.

> For more information on how to use these structures, see G14.

Real English: a real creep/a bit of a nerd

Creep is a very negative word used to describe someone very weird – usually male – who makes women feel uncomfortable. Nerd is a negative word used to describe someone – usually male – who is so obsessed with a hobby, such as computers, that they haven't really developed any social skills.

Have you ever met anyone like this?

Using vocabulary

1 | Descriptive adjectives

First decide if these adjectives describe character or appearance or both. Then mark them **P** or **N**, depending on whether you think they are positive or negative.

☐ muscular	☐ flirty
☐ pushy	☐ sexy
☐ plain	☐ macho
☐ forward	☐ unpredictable
☐ warm	☐ dishy
☐ quiet	☐ mature
☐ skinny	☐ cuddly
☐ down-to-earth	☐ hairy

Now describe someone else in your class to your partner using some of the adjectives above. See if they can guess who you're talking about.

> **Real English: dishy**
> If you find someone dishy, you find them physically attractive. Some dictionaries say that this is a rather old-fashioned word, but many young British people in their twenties use it, particularly women.

2 | I bet

When we make guesses about people based on their appearance, we often use *I bet* + a statement. **For example:**

A: He looks like a bit of a nerd.
B: I know. I bet he's studying computing or something like that.

A: He looks a bit mad.
B: I know. I bet he likes playing practical jokes on people.

With a partner, have conversations like this about the people in the pictures at the bottom of the page.

3 | Chat-up lines

If you chat somebody up, you talk to them in a friendly way to show that you're attracted to them. 'Chat-up lines' are openings that people use when they want to chat you up.

Decide which of the following you think are the best and worst chat-up lines. Compare your answers with a partner.

1. Do you come here often?
2. Someone call heaven – I think they're missing an angel.
3. What's a nice girl/guy like you doing in a place like this?
4. Are you here by yourself?
5. Excuse me, but have you got a light?
6. Can I get you a drink?
7. Has anyone ever told you you've got really lovely eyes?
8. What are you doing afterwards?

Has anyone ever tried to use these chat-up lines – or similar versions in your own language – on you? Have you ever used any yourself? Can you think of any other chat-up lines you've ever heard? Did they work?

Reading

1 | What turns you on?

Which of the following are most important for you in a partner or friend? Give each of the following ideas a score (1–5): 1 means you think it is not important; 5 is very important.

money

sense of humour

age

looks

nationality

dress sense

intelligence

cooking ability

honesty

religion

2 | Prepositions

Before you read the article, complete these sentences with a suitable preposition. Check your answers after you've read the text.

1. It was awful when I had to break the news of our grandmother's death . . . . my brother.

2. My girlfriend's a belly-dancer. I was worried that my parents wouldn't approve . . . . her.

3. I've been going out . . . . my boyfriend for almost six years.

4. Personally, I don't really go . . . . blondes. I much prefer brunettes.

5. He kept on asking me all these really personal questions, so I just told him it was none . . . . his business!

6. It took the children a long time to come to terms . . . . the death of their rabbit.

3 | Before you read

What do you think a mixed marriage is? What advantages and disadvantages do you think there are to mixed marriages?

4 | While you read

Now read the article and see if any of your ideas are mentioned.

Is she really going out with him?

The latest census in the UK has confirmed that inter-racial marriages are increasingly common, leading many journalists to claim that we are a totally tolerant society. However, despite what the census might suggest, the truth is that the vast majority of us tend to eventually marry a partner not only of the same race, but also of the same religion, class, age and background. While mixed marriages of various descriptions may be on the increase, prejudice and social and family pressures are still very much alive, and love cannot always overcome them. We talked to two couples about their experiences.

A religious divide

Rachel McCarthy and David Brown decided to leave Belfast, the city in Northern Ireland that they both grew up in and where their parents still live, when they got married last year. Rachel is a Catholic and David is Protestant. The two halves of the Christian religion are still deeply divided in Northern Ireland, and although the bombing and killing which occurred between the two communities has largely stopped, as Rachel and David know, people in mixed marriages are often ostracised and verbally abused. 'We actually found it difficult to find a place to live in Belfast because areas tend to be either Catholic or Protestant. That's really why we left. Over here, we just look the same as everyone else and no one really knows – or cares – that we have different backgrounds. It has been very difficult, though, because we haven't had any support from our families. Neither sets of parents have really come to terms with our relationship and that's obviously been very painful.'

The age gap

Jamie Brodlin is twenty now and has been going out with his partner, Jane Fisher, for three years. Believe it or not, Jane has just turned sixty! They met when Jamie was out clubbing with three friends. Jane was working in the cloakroom and when Jamie came up to her and started chatting her up, she thought he was pulling her leg. 'I thought he was just some lad with too many beers inside him who was doing it all for a bet. It was only later when he phoned me up to ask me out on a date, I realised just how mature and sensible he really is.'

Jamie says: 'To be honest, I never have gone for girls my own age. I tend to find them a bit immature. They usually just want to talk about music and shopping, whereas you can have a proper conversation with someone who's older. I guess Jane was quite a bit older than my previous girlfriend, but there was just something about her and about the way she moved and hung up the coats that caught my eye. She's a very warm and appealing sort of woman. My mates did think it was a bit weird, but I just told them it's none of their business, and now they don't really ask about Jane. Jane often stays in with my parents when I go out clubbing. She says she's too old for that kind of thing these days, which is fine. I was worried that my parents wouldn't approve of her when I first broke the news to them, but they've been fantastic. They found it a bit difficult to accept I was in love with someone old enough to be my gran, but when they met her, they just got on really well. I don't know if we'll ever get married. We'll see. We haven't really talked about it.'

5 | After reading

Did the article mention any advantages or disadvantages to mixed marriages that you didn't think of?

Do you think the two relationships described in the article are likely to last? Why/why not?

Which of the two couples …

1. get on well with their parents?
2. have been insulted in the street?
3. faced a lot of discrimination?
4. don't socialise very much together?
5. have been ignored by most people in their society?

Now go back and underline the parts of the article which confirm your answers.

6 | Word check

Complete these sentences with words from the article.

1. Marriages between people of different religions is . . . . common now.
2. There was a lot of family . . . . on me to become a doctor.
3. My mum didn't approve of my girlfriend, but I got a lot of . . . . from my sister.
4. A: Excuse me, but is there somewhere I can leave my coat?
   B: Yes, there's a . . . . just at the top of the stairs.
5. He's a typical macho . . . . , you know, always out for a good time with his mates.
6. I don't know about you, but personally I don't find that kind of man very . . . . He's a bit too tall for me.

> **Real English: I thought he was pulling my leg**
>
> If someone pulls your leg, they are joking with you.

Using vocabulary

1 | Speaking

Discuss these questions with a partner.

1. Have you ever gone out with anyone much older or younger than yourself?
2. How do you feel about relationships where there's a large age difference?
3. How would your parents and friends react if you started going out with someone much older or younger than you?
4. How would you feel about marrying a divorcee? Why?
5. How do you know when you're in love?
6. Would you consider marrying someone if there was a big age difference? What do you think of relationships between these pairs of people?

   a. a man of fifty and a girl of eighteen
      a woman of fifty and a boy of eighteen

   b. a man of twenty-five and a girl of eighteen
      a woman of twenty-five and a boy of eighteen

   c. a man of eighty and a woman of thirty
      a woman of eighty and a man of thirty

How would you complete these statements?
I wouldn't get involved with anyone who …
I'd never marry someone who …

Can you think of any famous people who have had relationships with people much older or younger than themselves?

2 | Stages of a relationship

Decide in which order you think the following would probably occur. Use a dictionary or ask your teacher to help you with any vocabulary you are not sure of.

a. My wife/husband and I are separated. ☐
b. I'm getting married next week. ☐
c. We've just got engaged. ☐
d. I'm going out with him/her. ☐
e. My marriage is on the rocks. ☐
f. We're having marriage guidance counselling. ☐
g. I proposed to her/him last night. ☐
h. We're in the process of getting divorced. ☐

Now compare your order with your partner and explain your choices.

Do any of the sentences a–h above describe any people you know?

Using grammar

1 | Expressions with modals

Complete the fixed expressions in the short dialogues below with the modal verbs in the box.

```
can   might   must   could   couldn't   should
```

1. A: I used my best chat-up line on her, and then she went and told me she was married!
   B: I .... 've told you that. I thought it was common knowledge.

2. A: Paddy's must be one of the best clubs in town.
   B: You .... say that again! What a night!

3. A: The food there was terrible – again!
   B: Well, you .... 've known better after what happened last time.

4. A: Does Rob ever invite you round to his place?
   B: You .... be joking! Rob never invites anyone round to his place.

5. A: I went for a walk with my parents yesterday afternoon, down by the river.
   B: Oh, that .... 've been nice. You had some lovely weather for it.

6. A: So, did you have a good chat with Steve last night?
   B: Not really, no. It was so loud in the pub, I .... hardly hear myself think!

7. A: Did you see Jamie trying to chat up the cloakroom attendant last night?
   B: Yes, I know. I just .... believe it. She's old enough to be his grandmother.

8. A: We climbed over the fence and went for a swim in their pool last night.
   B: You .... be mad doing that! They've got an alsatian and a rottweiler!

9. A: My husband forgot my birthday – again!
   B: You never know. He might be planning to surprise you later.
   A: Yes, right! And pigs .... fly!

Complete the nine expressions used above.

1. .... been nice.
2. .... say that again!
3. .... be joking!
4. .... be mad!
5. .... believe it!
6. .... told you that.
7. .... hardly hear myself think!
8. .... known better!
9. Pigs .... !

2 | Grammar in context

With a partner, choose which of the nine expressions in Exercise 1 is the best response to the following.

1. We spent the whole day on the beach yesterday.
2. Can you believe they wouldn't let me in because I was wearing jeans?
3. There were so many kids there yesterday, weren't there?
4. That guy Mike we met last night is a bit of a nerd, don't you think?
5. So, what was that exhibition you went to last week like? Any good?

3 | I could do with ...

Look at another useful modal verb expression from the conversation that you heard in Unit 9 between Rose and Lucy.

Rose: You must be feeling exhausted this morning, then.
Lucy: Yeah, I could do with another hour or two in bed, that's for sure.

Complete the sentences below using I could do with and one of the expressions in the box.

```
a bit more time        a break
more money             a good night's sleep
something to eat       a lie-in
some help              a holiday
```

1. Is anyone free? .... This thing's really heavy.

2. Hey, can we pop in here for a snack? I didn't get a chance to have anything earlier. ....

3. I'm so tired staring at this computer screen. ....

4. I haven't quite finished it yet. .... , to be honest.

5. I've been up to my ears in work this month. .... , I can tell you!

6. I've been out every night this week. .... tomorrow, that's for sure.

7. I'm pretty tired. .... tonight, if possible.

8. I'm pretty happy at work, but .... I mean, I always end up broke by the end of the month.

> ▶ For more information on how to use modals, see G15.

Using vocabulary

1 | Tend to

In the article on page 72, Jamie said that he **tends to** find girls his own age a bit immature.

We often use **tend to** after the subject of a sentence and before another verb. It means 'generally, but not always'. We also use it a lot to talk about our habits.

Complete these sentences in ways that are true for you and then compare your answers with your partner.

1. I tend to watch about . . . . hours of TV a day.
2. I tend to spend about . . . . hours a week studying English.
3. I tend to go to bed at about . . . . most nights, and I tend to get up at around . . . .
4. I tend to spend about . . . . most days.
5. I tend to try and . . . . at least twice a week, if I can.
6. I tend to eat chocolate maybe . . . .
7. I tend to do some sport or some exercise maybe . . . .
8. I tend to . . . . every weekend, if I have the time, of course.

Who's harder-working, you or your partner? Who's healthier? Who's lazier?

2 | Discuss

Do you agree with these statements? Tick those you agree with and compare your answers with a partner. Try and explain your choices.

1. Men tend to eat more junk food than women.
2. Women tend to be much more careful drivers.
3. Women tend to take longer to get ready to go out.
4. Men tend to be much more selfish.
5. Men tend to be more into sports.

The class will now split into male/female groups and your teacher will give you a few minutes to come up with some more ideas about the differences between men and women. Make sure each sentence uses **tend to** – you don't want to start World War Three, do you!

Once you have come up with a list you all agree with, find a partner of the opposite sex and explain what you have written. Do you agree on the differences between the sexes or does one sex tend to have more ridiculous ideas than the other?!

Have I ever told you about the time I got locked in the loo of a jumbo jet? • You're pulling my leg, aren't you? • You'll neve
believe what happened to me this morning. • It's all very well for you to laugh, but you wouldn't have liked it if it'd happene
to you. • Do you think I was born yesterday?! • Did you hear what happened to Max? • Now I've heard everything! • So, t
cut a long story short. • I don't believe a word of what you're saying. • A spider in her ear? • It's one of the strangest thing
that's ever happened to me. • And if you believe that, you'll believe anything. • No, honestly. It's the truth. • Really? Really!
Can you keep a secret? • That's a likely story. • Let's keep this just betwee
you and me. • Sally just loves it when I tell her a bedtime story.

11 Telling stories

Listening

1 Before you listen

Have you ever not recognised somebody you knew? When? What happened? How many different reasons for not recognising someone can you think of?

2 While you listen

🎧 **Diane and Cathy are taking the underground across London, chatting as they go. Listen to Diane talking about a strange thing that happened to her.**

Cover the conversation. As you listen, try to answer these questions.
1. Where and when did this happen to Diane?
2. What was the problem? What happened in the end?

Listen again and try to fill in the gaps in the conversation.

> **Real English: pinch his wallet**
> If you pinch something, you steal it. Pinch is a very informal word.

3 Speaking

Do you ever ignore people you know? In what situations?

What's the strangest/most interesting thing that's ever happened to you while you were travelling?

Hair today, gone tomorrow!

Cathy: So, we've got to take this one and then change at Cannon Street, right?

Diane: Yes, that's it. Hey, (1) .... what happened with me and my dad on the underground last year?

Cathy: No, go on, what?

Diane: Well, (2) .... , I decided to get all my hair cut off, right? I always used to have really, really long hair – ever since I was about fourteen or fifteen, you know – way down past my shoulders – parted in the middle like curtains. So, (3) .... , about a week after I had it all cut off, you know – really short – and I looked quite different.

Cathy: Yeah, I bet.

Diane: So, anyway, (4) .... home on the tube, and I was half asleep because it was five or six o'clock and I was just standing there, (5) .... – and little did I know that my dad was actually coming back from a business trip abroad, passing through London on the underground to get his train back to Durham. And (6) .... ? He got into the same carriage as me! The doors closed behind him. So there I am, standing there face to face with my own father! I don't recognise him at first, but then I think, 'Ah, that's my dad,' and, of course, he's obviously only seen me with really long hair for the last ten years, and so (7) .... there, staring at him and he (8) .... on glancing at me nervously, thinking, 'Who's this lunatic staring at me?' and I'm thinking – you know, it's the strangest feeling not being recognised by your own dad – so I just stood there thinking, 'Well, (9) .... just get off at the next stop without telling him, or (10) .... risk giving him a nervous breakdown and a heart attack by saying, 'Hello, dad?' But, anyway, (11) .... I went, 'Hello, dad' and he went, 'Diane!' and then said how he was getting really worried because he thought I was a pick-pocket or a drug addict (12) .... who'd been getting ready to pinch his wallet or something – and, um, yeah, that was a pretty strange and funny thing.

Cathy: Yeah, *really* strange.

Using vocabulary

1 | Hairstyles

Match the descriptions 1–8 to the pictures A–H.

1. He's got spiky hair.
2. She's got curly hair.
3. She's got a fringe.
4. He's got dreadlocks.
5. She's got dyed red hair.
6. She's got pigtails.
7. She's got hair extensions.
8. He's got short back and sides.

Have you ever thought of changing your hairstyle, dyeing your hair or bleaching it blond?

Have you ever had a really bad, unusual or different haircut? How did people react to it?

2 | Slang

In the conversation you heard pinch his wallet. Match the slang words 1–8 to the neutral equivalents a–h.

1. Chuck it to me.	a. lost his temper
2. Have you got a fag?	b. stolen
3. They went out boozing.	c. throw
4. My bicycle's been nicked.	d. sell
5. I've decided to flog the car.	e. drinking
6. It only cost ten quid.	f. cigarette
7. He's a really nice bloke.	g. pounds
8. He flipped his lid.	h. man

Always be careful with slang. You may think you know what a slang word means, but sometimes it has an extra meaning. In the examples in this exercise, boozing means drinking in order to get drunk. Slang is a dangerous area in all languages and you should always check with a teacher before using it.

3 | Speaking

Discuss these questions with a partner.

1. Have you ever flipped your lid? Why?
2. Has anything of yours ever been nicked? What happened?

4 | Different kinds of stories

Complete the sentences below with the words in the box. Then underline the expressions formed with the words.

bedtime	old	hard-luck
inside	tall	love

1. The story of Romeo and Juliet must be one of the world's greatest . . . . stories.

2. I ended up sitting beside this guy who'd just got divorced and lost his job. I spent the whole six-hour flight listening to his . . . . story.

3. A: The lift's broken down again!
   B: The same . . . . story, then!

4. The kids say they won't go to sleep unless you go up and read them their . . . . story.

5. You're a friend of Jane's. Nobody understands why she's leaving. Come on, you must know the . . . . story!

6. A: Jason told everyone at work that he'd won £10,000, but then managed to leave it in a taxi!
   B: I wouldn't believe a word he says. It sounds like another one of his . . . . stories.

5 | Speaking

Discuss these questions with a partner.

1. What are the most famous love stories in your country?

2. Do you know anyone who tells tall stories?

3. What bedtime stories can you remember from when you were a kid?

6 | Storytelling expressions

🎧 **First complete the dialogue below with the words in the box. Then listen and check your answers.**

well	really	go on
you're joking	so	anyway

A: Did I tell you about what happened to me in France last year?

B: No, I don't think you did. (1) . . . .

A: (2) . . . ., I was on holiday with my parents in this little village near the sea, and we ran out of money.

B: (3) . . . .? That's awful.

A: Yes, (4) . . . . we went into town to find a cash machine – which we did, no trouble. (5) . . . ., when we put the card in the machine, it just started spitting out loads and loads of money.

B: (6) . . . .! So did you keep it?

A: Of course we did! Wouldn't you?

Practise reading out the dialogue with a partner.

7 | Telling a story

Look at the pictures below and try to imagine the stories. The expressions below will help you tell the stories. Work with a partner. Use one expression from each group and plan how to tell each story.

A. Introducing your story

Did I ever tell you about the time I . . .
I must've told you about the time I . . .
Did I ever tell you about this friend of mine who . . .

B. Giving background details

A few years ago, when this friend of mine was . . .
Last August when my family was on holiday in . . .

C. Introducing the problem

All of a sudden, . . .
Then suddenly, . . .

D. How the problem was solved

Well, what happened in the end was . . .
Eventually, . . .
Luckily, . . .

E. Finishing off the story

It was one of the funniest/silliest/strangest/worst things that's ever happened to me!
Looking back on it, it was all very exciting/ interesting/ strange/upsetting.
It seems funny now, but it didn't seem like that at the time!

▶ For more information on tense usage in storytelling, see G16.

Using grammar

1 | -ing clauses

In the conversation on page 76, Diane says: 'I was just standing there – minding my own business.'

Notice that she did *not* say: 'I was standing there. I was minding my own business.'

Cross out the words which are not needed in these sentences.

1. I saw a man. He was breaking into a car.
2. Two firemen died. They were trying to get a child out of the blazing flat.
3. The car broke down. It was going up the hill.
4. He had a heart attack. He was playing golf.
5. I was standing outside the bank. I was waiting for a bus.
6. The police caught them. They were trying to break into the shop.
7. We caught sight of the Queen. She was driving past on the way to the funeral.
8. We had to wait ten minutes. We were standing outside in the pouring rain.
9. Some children were in the shop. They were stealing sweets.

Look back at the conversation on page 76 and complete these sentences.

10. It was five or six o'clock and I was just standing there,. . . . .
11. My dad was actually coming back from a business trip abroad,. . . . .
12. He keeps on glancing at me,. . . . .

2 | Practice

With a partner, complete these sentences by adding as many -ing clauses as you can.

1. There was this really strange-looking guy,. . . . .
   . . . .
2. I was rushing around madly,. . . . .
   . . . .
3. On Thursday I was driving along,. . . . .
   . . . .
4. So there we were, in this fancy restaurant,. . . . .
   . . . .
5. My uncle was sitting there in the bar,. . . . .
   . . . .
6. There was this huge crowd outside the parliament building,. . . . . and . . . .

Now report some of your sentences to the whole class and see who has made the funniest examples.

3 | Pronunciation

 Listen and notice where the speaker pauses:

There was this great big dog, sitting there, barking at me.

Listen to these short sections of speech and mark the pauses.

1. It was five or six o'clock and I was just standing there, minding my own business.
2. My dad was actually coming back from a business trip abroad, passing through London.
3. He keeps on glancing at me, thinking, 'Who's this lunatic staring at me?'
4. I was dancing about in the street, acting like a fool.
5. I was lying there on the ground, screaming in pain.

Now listen again and underline the strongest stress like this:

There was this great big <u>dog</u>, <u>si</u>tting there, <u>bar</u>king at me.

Practise saying the sentences above, stressing the correct syllables and pausing in the right places. Then do the same with the sentences 1–12 in Exercise 1.

4 | Speaking

Re-tell your story from page 78 to a different partner. This time, try to use some -ing clauses.

> For more information on how to use *-ing* clauses, see G17.

Reading

1 | Before you read

Have you ever heard of anyone putting an animal into a microwave or finding a mouse in a pie or anything like that?

2 | While you read

🎧 **Read the article below and then discuss with a partner whether or not you think it's true.**

3 | Speaking

Discuss these questions with a partner.

1. Has anything like this ever happened to you or anyone you know?

2. What would you do if you found the following?
   - a spider in your bath
   - a caterpillar in your salad in a restaurant
   - a mouse in your bedroom
   - a cockroach in your hotel bathroom
   - a snake in your kitchen
   - a spider in a friend's hair (she's terrified of them)

Spider woman

Have you heard the story of the woman who dried her cat in the microwave after it had got wet – or the one about the woman who opened a bag of prepared salad and out popped a fully-grown frog? Whether they are true or not, we love telling each other scary stories. Unfortunately, the story that follows is definitely true.

Recently, a woman living in Kent in southern England went to her doctor. For days she hadn't been able to sleep because of noises in her ear. The doctor told her that this was not unusual. Lots of people have noises in their ears. However, when he looked into her ear, he got the shock of his life. He could see legs and something moving. It was a large spider! The woman was absolutely terrified of spiders! The doctor was able to remove it quickly and set it free.

When speaking to a colleague a few days later, the doctor mentioned that that was the first time he had ever found a spider living in someone's ear. His colleague suggested that the spider was probably looking for somewhere warm in order to lay its eggs.

Using vocabulary

1 | Idiomatic language

Colourful expressions are a common feature of storytelling, and help to make stories more interesting. As you study this page, try to think what these expressions would be in your own language.

2 | Idiomatic comparisons

We use strong comparisons to emphasise what we are saying. For example:

It's a great bike. It goes like a bomb!
He's got a great appetite. He eats like a horse!

Complete the sentences below with the expressions in the box.

like clockwork	like dirt
like a chimney	like death warmed up
like a house on fire	like a fish
like a lunatic	like a log

1. I used to have this friend who drank
   . . . .

2. This guy was driving along . . . .

3. He's horrible to his wife. He treats her
   . . . .

4. When I saw myself in the mirror, I looked
   . . . .

5. My granddad used to smoke . . . .

6. The tube system in Tokyo runs . . . .

7. I was so exhausted that I slept . . . .

8. My sister and I get on . . . .

With a partner, check how many of these comparisons you can remember. Cover the list and test each other.

Tell your partner about anybody you know who:

* smokes like a . . .   • drives like a . . .
* eats like a . . .   • looks like . . . in the mornings

Have you ever heard any of the following expressions? Can you guess what they mean?

I've got a memory like a sieve.
I felt like a fish out of water.
She spends money like water.

When was the last time you slept like a log?
Have you ever met anybody who you immediately got on with like a house on fire?

3 | Exaggerating using idioms

In Diane's story about her father not recognising her on the tube, she uses exaggeration in the following way:

. . . so I just stood there thinking, 'Well, shall I just get off at the next stop without telling him, or shall I risk giving him a nervous breakdown and a heart attack by saying, 'Hello, dad'?'

What do you think she really means here? In English, it is very common to exaggerate by talking about illnesses, death, killing, and so on. Complete the sentences below with the words in the box.

died	die	murder (x2)	
death	kill	killing	dying

1. I'm . . . . for a coffee.
2. She gets away with . . . .
3. My feet are . . . . me!
4. It's . . . . trying to get him to do anything.
5. I nearly . . . . when he told me that!
6. I nearly . . . . laughing.
7. I'm sick to . . . . of it.
8. I'd . . . . if anybody else found out.
9. If he does it again, I'll . . . . him.

With a partner, discuss what you think the common exaggerations above actually mean.

Now add one of the sentences 1–9 above to the end of each of the following.

a. I used to be really into dance music, but now
b. I can't wait to get these new shoes off and get into a nice hot bath.
c. I can't wait for the break.
d. That film was so brilliant. It was so funny.
e. And then he said I'd been accepted for the team.
f. Only you know it's a wig.
g. Dad's a bit too easy-going with her.
h. I asked him time and time again to fix it, but
i. That's the second time he's thrown his rubbish over into *our* garden.

Do you have similar expressions in your language? Are there any phrases above you wouldn't feel comfortable using? Why?

But that's absolutely incredible. • I wouldn't have believed it if I hadn't seen it with my own eyes. • I've no idea how he go[t] away with it. • It was kind of weird. • What a funny story. • What was he doing there in the first place? • I've heard a lot o[f] stories, but that beats them all. • That couldn't happen here. • What were the parents thinking of? • Boys will be boys! • [It] was amazing, absolutely amazing! • You should've seen the mess it made. • Is that all it cost? • Not *the* Thierry Henry? • Th[e] car broke down and we were miles from anywhere. • Something similar once happened to a friend of mine • I wasn't bor[n] yesterday, you know! • Do I look stupid? • Truth i[s] stranger than fiction. • I'm not making this up.

12 Difficult to believe

Reading

1 | He used to be so nice!

With a partner, think of three naughty things that children sometimes do. Add them to this list:

1. fight with their brothers or sisters
2. watch videos they shouldn't
3. experiment with cigarettes
4. ....
5. ....
6. ....

On your own, decide which of the above are the most and which the least serious.

Compare your answers with your partner, and explain your choices.

Did you ever do any of the things on your list? Do you know any children who do?

Have you heard the saying 'Boys will be boys'? Does your language have an equivalent?

2 | Collocations

Before you read the text on page 83, make collocations by matching 1–8 to a–h.

1.	cigarette	a.	to the ground
2.	I was grounded	b.	park
3.	it was burnt	c.	their wedding anniversary
4.	to celebrate	d.	the other kids to ice cream
5.	go on	e.	for a week
6.	a theme	f.	was refused
7.	treat	g.	burns
8.	his credit card	h.	a spending spree

3 | Before you read

You are going to read about five different young people being left on their own by their parents. With a partner, try to guess what their stories might be, using the eight collocations above.

4 | While you read

Now read the article and see if you were right. Which story is the most incredible? Why?

Home alone

'Home Alone' is one of the biggest box office successes in movie history. Along with its sequel, 'Home Alone 2', it grossed over half a billion dollars worldwide. If you ask me, they're not particularly funny films. There's too much slapstick humour for my liking – people slipping over or having their faces covered in cream – but there is something about the films which appeals to a deep-held fantasy we all had when we were children: the freedom to escape from our parents and do whatever we wanted.

When I was in my teens, my parents went away for the weekend leaving me and my sixteen-year-old brother to fend for ourselves. We immediately rang up all our friends (and our friends rang their friends) and we had a party. The police came and broke it up at three in the morning because the neighbours were complaining about the noise. When we cleared up the following day, I found hundreds of cigarette burns in the carpet. Luckily, we had an old piece of the same carpet lying around, so I got my younger brother to go round the house and stick little bits in the holes to cover them up. It actually looked quite good and when my parents got back, it seemed they didn't notice a thing and I thought we were in the clear. Unfortunately, when my mum came to do the hoovering later in the week, all the bits we'd put in the holes came unstuck. She was not very pleased and I was grounded for a week, while my brother got away with it because he said I'd forced him into it. Typical! Still, this little story is nothing compared to some of the other horror stories about kids who have been left 'home alone'.

Terry and Jerry Schneider didn't just find a few cigarette burns when they came back, they found their whole house burnt to the ground. The couple had left their two children, aged twelve and fourteen, in the house, while they went on a romantic weekend to Las Vegas to celebrate their wedding anniversary. The children had bought what they thought were indoor fireworks and were playing with them. Unfortunately, the explosive Roman candle they lit was for use *outside* and it soon set fire to the sofa, curtains and carpet in the front room. By the time the children called the fire brigade half an hour later, the fire was already completely out of control.

John Thomas, a ten-year-old from Yorkshire, an area in the north of England, was arrested after he shot a dog and terrorised walkers near his home in Keighley. He had taken the gun from a kitchen cupboard while his parents were out shopping and had decided to do some shooting practice in some fields nearby. 'I didn't realise I could kill anything, I just thought they were pretend bullets,' he explained.

Lamine, a twelve-year-old French boy, went on a ten-day spending spree at the EuroDisney theme park near Paris with the ten thousand pounds he found lying around in his parents' home. As well as treating other children to ice creams, burgers and free rides, he hired a chauffeur-driven car and slept in a three hundred-pound-a-night hotel.

Peter Kerry, a schoolboy of fourteen, went halfway round the world after he stole his father's passport and credit card. He had visited three separate countries in twelve days and spent almost six thousand pounds before he was finally caught: his credit card was refused after his father cancelled it. It wasn't actually the first time it had happened. Two years earlier he spent a week on his own in Germany. 'I like travelling,' he said.

5 | I can't believe it!

We often comment on incredible stories by making questions using the past continuous. These aren't real questions – they are expressions of surprise. We often reply to questions like this using modal verb expressions.

Match each question 1–3 to two of the responses a–f.

1. What were the parents doing, leaving all that money lying around?

2. What were the security guards doing, letting him on the plane?

3. What was the kid thinking of, spending all that money?

a. I know! He could've been a terrorist or something.

b. I know! They should've locked it away more safely.

c. I know! He must hate his parents.

d. I know! He shouldn't have taken it in the first place.

e. I know! They should've checked his passport better.

f. I know! They must have money to burn.

Now write four questions about the article showing what you are surprised about. Use these sentence starters.

What was the writer thinking of,
.................................?

What were Terry and Jerry doing,
.................................?

What was John Thomas thinking of,
.................................?

And what were his parents thinking,
.................................?

Ask a partner your questions. They should try to respond using a modal verb expression.

Using grammar

1 | Past simple and past continuous

Make logical sentences by matching the beginnings 1–8 to the endings a–h.

1. She was just sitting there, reading,
2. Just as I was leaving the house,
3. It was raining really heavily as I was leaving,
4. I was living in Italy
5. I was just going home
6. Just as I went into my daughter's school,
7. While we were trying to decide where to go,
8. I resigned from my job on Friday

a. I remembered the tickets were on my bed.
b. so I grabbed an umbrella.
c. when the big Mafia trials were happening.
d. when this guy suddenly started talking to her.
e. I won this fabulous holiday to Jamaica!
f. and found a better one on Saturday!
g. she came running up to me, crying.
h. when my boss rang and told me I was going to Washington!

Underline the past verb forms in each sentence.

2 | Grammar discussion

One sentence in each of the groups of three below is wrong. Why?

What is the difference in meaning between the other two sentences?

1a. We were cleaning the carpet when we were finding the diamond.
1b. We got the system checked out because we were finding lots of problems with it.
1c. We got the system checked out because we found lots of problems with it.

2a. I was driving through town when I got stopped by this police car.
2b. I was driving through town when I was getting stopped by this police car.
2c. I was driving through town when I realised I was getting really tired.

3a. I was coming home on the tube when I suddenly bumped into an old friend.
3b. I came home on the tube when I suddenly bumped into an old friend.
3c. I came home on the tube when I missed the last bus.

Compare your answers with a partner.

3 | Grammar check

Complete these sentences by putting the verbs in brackets in the past simple or past continuous.

1. As I was on my way back from France, my car . . . . (break down)
2. When I . . . . home last night, I bumped into an old friend of mine. (walk)
3. My mother was tidying my room up when she . . . . the letter. (see)
4. We . . . . along the beach when we suddenly saw a body in the sea. (walk)
5. I . . . . of writing to her when the next thing I knew she turned up on my doorstep. (think)
6. I was talking to a friend on the phone when my dad . . . . rushing into my room. (come)
7. You can imagine how angry he was when he . . . . how much they were charging him. (find out)
8. Oh, it was so stupid! I . . . . some water when I knocked it all over myself. (boil)

When the clock struck twelve on 31ˢᵗ December 1999, where were you and what were you doing?

> ▶ For more information on how to use the past simple and past continuous, see G18.

Using vocabulary

1 | On the way

When we talk about things that happened to us on a journey, we tend to say where we were going. We usually do this by using a verb phrase + *on the way (to)* + place. For example:

As I was on my way back from France, my car broke down.
We stopped off and had something to eat on the way to the match.

Complete the sentences below with the phrases in the box.

a pile-up	almost had an accident
broke down	bumped into
got a puncture	got car sick
got lost	had an accident
stopped off	took a wrong turn

1. We . . . . on the way to Dorset. We had to call someone out from a local garage to fix the engine.

2. We . . . . on the way to Lisa's mum's house. We must've gone up and down the same street about ten times!

3. I . . . . on the way to work the   other day. There's so much glass on the roads nowadays, it makes cycling hell!

4. We . . . . at a beautiful old castle on   our way here and went and had a look around.

5. I . . . . on my way to school the   other day. This guy cut in front of me and I went straight into the back of him!

6. We . . . . on the way to Cologne,   and had to do a U-turn in the middle of the motorway!

7. Rebecca . . . . on the way to   Rushden. She was sick all over the back seat...

8. I . . . . an old friend of mine on the   way to work this morning. I hadn't seen her for ages.

9. We saw . . . . on the motorway on   the way to Malmo. It

2 | Speaking

Have any of the things described in Exercise 1 above ever happened to you? On the way to where? Spend a few minutes thinking about what happened and where. Decide if you'll need to use the past simple or the past continuous and then tell a few other people your stories.

3 | *Trip, tour, travel*, etc.

Complete the sentences below with the words in the box.

trip	tour	travel	journey	flight	travelling

1. A: What time is their . . . . supposed to be getting in now?
   B: About six thirty, I think. It's already been delayed an hour!

2. What a . . . .! Twelve hours on a plane, then six hours on a freezing cold train.

3. I always try and . . . . light, if I can.

4. When I graduated, I worked for a bit and then went . . . . for a year.

5. I was thinking of going on a day-. . . . . to Brighton this Saturday. Do you fancy coming?

6. He's away on a business . . . ., I'm afraid. Try again on Monday.

7. I never . . . . by bus, if I can help it. I much prefer just cycling or walking.

8. I spent a couple of months . . . . round Peru.

9. I can't believe my parents are planning to go on a . . . . to Disneyland when they retire!

10. There's a coach . . . . of the city this afternoon. Do you fancy going?

11. Once you land, have you got a long . . . . ahead of you before you get home?

12. While I was in Granada in Spain, we went on this guided . . . . round the Alhambra, which was really interesting.

4 | Speaking

Discuss these questions with a partner.

1. Have you ever been on a guided tour? When? Where? What was it like?

2. When was the last time you went on a day-trip?

3. What's the longest journey you've ever been on?

4. Would you like to take a year off and go travelling? Where would you most like to go?

5 | Being vague

When talking about things that have happened to us, it is common to use vague or approximate language. Choose the best definition, a or b for the highlighted expressions in these sentences.

1. There must've been about thirty or forty people there.
   a. Either thirty or forty people.
   b. Between twenty-five and forty-five people.

2. He was sort of smiling at me.
   a. It was a particular kind of smile.
   b. It wasn't exactly a smile, but it was more like a smile than anything else.

3. His skin had turned a weird blueish colour and he'd stopped breathing.
   a. It was bright blue.
   b. It wasn't exactly blue, but it was more blue than any other colour.

4. There must have been 500-odd people there.
   a. The 500 people were very strange.
   b. There were approximately 500 people.

5. And the policeman looked at me and said, 'Is this your car?' you know, 'blah, blah, blah.'
   a. And some other things I didn't understand.
   b. I'm sure you can imagine what else he said, and you don't need me to tell you.

6. It must have been built about 1985 or so.
   a. It was built in 1985.
   b. It could have been 1984 or 1986.

7. It cost two hundred and something pounds.
   a. Just a little more than two hundred pounds.
   b. Almost three hundred pounds.

8. And I spoke to that man who works in the office there, you know, what's his name, and he told me . . .
   a. I can't remember his name, but I'm sure you know who I mean.
   b. Please tell me his name.

Real English: sort of / kind of

Sort of and kind of are both very common in spoken English. They are often used when you cannot find the right word to express what you mean. Some people do not like these phrases, but they are extremely common even in educated speech.

It was kind of expensive-looking.
She was sort of annoyed with me.

---

6 | ... or something/... or anything

Look at these two examples:

My dad thought I was a pick-pocket or a drug addict or something.

There was no hot water or showers or anything!

Phrases with or something/or anything are common in spoken English when we want to be vague. Complete these sentences with the language in the box below.

---

or something like that   food or anything
showers or anything   a bit of wire or something
a hammer or something

---

1. He managed to get the lock to work by using . . . .

2. The campsite was horrible. There were no proper toilets or . . . .

3. They must have broken into the car with . . . . They did a lot of damage.

4. I didn't really see the registration number, but I'm sure it started TKP . . . .

5. We flew on one of those budget airlines. There were no drinks or . . . .

> For more information on how to use these structures, see G19.

---

7 | -ish

Adding -ish to an adjective or number is a common way of being less precise.

He's about forty-ish.
Her hair is a sort of reddish brown.

Complete the sentences below with the words in the box.

---

seven-ish	yellow-ish	purple-ish
long-ish	tall-ish	sixty-ish

---

1. He's not retired yet, but I'm sure he's about . . . .

2. When you get malaria, your skin turns a sort of . . . . colour.

3. I think we'll have to get the train about . . . . to get there in time for eight.

4. Although it was red wine, it was a kind of deep . . . . colour.

5. Eva's the one with . . . . dark hair.

6. You'll recognise him. He's a sort of . . . . version of Charlie Chaplin without the moustache.

Reading

1 | While you read

Here are four stories. Three are urban myths and only one is true. Read them and decide which one you think is true.

Urban myths

Safety first!

Did you hear about the plane which crashed somewhere in South America as it was coming in to land?

Apparently, it was fitted with a device which warns the pilot that he's approaching the ground – a Ground Warning Alarm (GWA) system. Some pilots find this warning irritating, so they switch it off.

When the black box was examined, the crash was blamed on pilot error. The decision had been easy to reach. When the plane had been coming in to land, the GWA had gone off, telling the pilot he was too close to the ground. On the tape the pilot can be heard saying, 'Shut up, you stupid machine!' Then you hear the sound of the crash.

True story or myth?

What a rat!

Then there was the story of the couple who were in Thailand on holiday. The morning after they arrived, they found a thin little cat sitting on their balcony.

They immediately fell in love with it. They cleaned it and fed it. By the time they were ready to leave, they couldn't bear to be parted from it. They arranged for the cat to come home with them. Waiting at home was their pet poodle. The poodle and the cat seemed to get on together very well, so the couple decided to go out for dinner. When they got back, they found their sitting room covered in poodle hair and the dog halfway down the cat's throat!

It turned out the cat was not a cat, but an enormous Thai water rat!

True story or myth?

Drowned in a drain

A man from Wakefield in Yorkshire went out one night for a few drinks at his local pub. He left his car in the street near the pub. When he decided to go home, he went out to his car, took out the keys, and then accidentally dropped them down a drain in the road.

He could see the keys down the drain on top of some leaves. So, he managed to lift the drain cover, but the keys were too far down for him to reach. He lay down in order to reach them.

Suddenly, he fell into the drain head first. Just as he did that, it started to rain heavily. Nobody heard his cries for help. The next morning he was found drowned, his head down the drain, his legs sticking up in the air.

True story or myth?

Sunk by flying cow

A few years ago, the crew of a Japanese fishing boat were rescued from the wreckage of their boat in the Sea of Japan. They said that their boat had been sunk by a cow falling out of the sky. Nobody believed them.

A few weeks later the Russian Air Force admitted that the crew of one of their planes had stolen a cow in Siberia and put it into the plane's cargo hold.

At 30,000 feet the cow started to run around the plane out of control. The crew decided there was only one thing they could do. So, they opened the cargo door and the cow jumped out, landing on top of the Japanese fishing boat.

True story or myth?

2 | Speaking

Do you know any other urban myths? If you like this kind of story, they are all on the Web. Find them under 'urban myths'. Bring one in to the next lesson!

9 | Idioms

Make sentences with idioms by matching the beginnings 1–8 to the endings a–h.

1. I nearly	a. a log.
2. I slept like	b. a fish.
3. I could hardly	c. on the rocks!
4. I'm dying for	d. a lunatic.
5. He drinks like	e. might fly!
6. Pigs	f. died laughing.
7. He was driving like	g. a coffee.
8. My marriage is	h. hear myself think!

10 | What can you remember?

With a partner, note down as much as you can remember about the two texts you read in units 10 and 12.

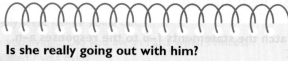

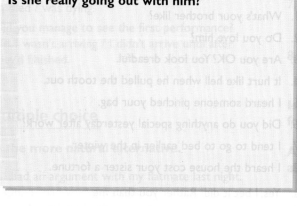

Is she really going out with him?

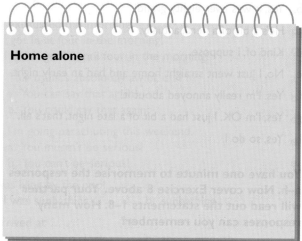

Home alone

Now compare what you remember with another pair. Who remembers more?

Which text did you enjoy more? Why?

11 | Vocabulary quiz

Answer these questions with a partner. Then compare your answers with another pair. Who got most answers right?

1. If you wanted to show someone you were angry with them, would you stare at them, glare at them or glance at them?

2. Can you think of five things you can run out of?

3. Is a sensible person someone who understands their friends' feelings or someone able to make good decisions?

4. If you're 'going out with' someone, what two meanings could this have?

5. If you bump into an old friend, does it hurt?

6. How could my younger brother get away with murder?

7. Is a divorcee someone who is divorced or someone who is getting divorced?

8. If you propose to someone, what is the question you ask?

9. If you get on like a house on fire with someone, do you get on well or badly?

10. Why would you wear a wig?

11. If you're tired, do you go asleep or fall asleep?

12. If you don't have any clean clothes to wear, would you do the washing-up or the washing?

13. If someone tries to chat you up, do they just want to talk to you?

14. If I say: 'That's none of your business', what kind of question have you just asked me?

15. Is someone who kills a lot of people over a period of time a serious killer or a serial killer?

16. Do you surf the net or the beach?

17. Are lads young men or young women?

18. Can you think of three recent blockbusters?

19. If you go to a club, do you leave your coat in the cloakroom or the bathroom?

20. If you find someone appealing, do you like them or not?

Learner advice: The authors speak!

In groups, show each other the notebooks you keep of language you learn in class and/or any vocabulary record books you have. Explain how you record language and what you do with the notes after class. Be honest!

How do you try and learn words and expressions? Who do you think has the best method? Why?

Now read this text and see if you are like the student mentioned.

I was chatting to a student yesterday and she asked me, 'Is "It has typical peacock markings" right?' I looked at her very confused – we had been talking about her visit to Oxford at the weekend.

'Is what right?' I asked.

' "It has typical peacock markings," ' she replied. 'Isn't it right?' She looked at me disappointed.

'It's not that it's not 'right,' I said. 'I mean, the grammar and the words are OK. It's just that . . . well, . . . *why* would you say it? *Who* would you say it to?'

'I don't know. I'll show you later. English has too many words. I'm confused!'

Later on, the student showed me her notebook. It was very full! In the notebook, there was a sentence which had come up in class, followed by an example another student had given.

' "He's a typical Englishman. You know, really polite and well-dressed." '

' "Kasia's a typical Pole. She's very generous and friendly! " '

However, underneath that was the word "typical" with a translation into her language. Then there were about six sentences with the word "typical", including the one about the peacock markings. Then there was a translation of "peacock" and under that the phrase "as proud as a peacock" and "peacock blue" – both with translations. Underneath that was the word "mark" with a translation. Then another ten or fifteen phrases including "Did you mark where it fell?" and "the marks of violence". It must've taken her hours to look everything up and write it down. Then, unsurprisingly, she couldn't remember it.

This book already has a lot of language in it, and your teacher probably gives you more. We've tried to ensure this book includes typical language you'd say. You'd probably be best *just* learning this language first. Even then, there may be language you wouldn't use. Be selective. Think: 'Would I ever say this? When? Who to?' If you don't think it's useful, don't bother trying to learn it. After class, copy the language you learnt into a new book and perhaps put it into new categories. You might want a topic page – e.g. language about cinema – or perhaps grammar categories – phrasal verbs with "up" or phrases with "will". You can then add to each page as you go through the course. Spend five minutes at different times trying to memorise the expressions, but most of all, just try and go out and use them!

Has the text made you change your mind about the way you learn and record vocabulary?

Oh, hello, Liz. • How are you? • Don't you remember me? • What a lovely surprise! • I haven't seen you for ages. • You have
changed a bit. • What're you up to these days? • Not a lot. • I've been travelling. • Oh, that reminds me. • I windsurfed acro
the Atlantic, which was nice. • I keep meaning to do that myself. • How could I forget? • You're looking well. • It must be t
years. • I've completely forgotten your name. • I bumped into Frank the other day. • Well, I'd better be going. • It's been love
seeing you. • Must dash! • Give my regards to Jill. • We've lost touch. • Keep in touch. • We've got two now. • We must ha
lunch sometime. • I haven't seen her since Uni. • Say hello to your mum from m
• We go back a long way. • Have you seen anybody from the old gang?

13 | Old friends

Listening

1 | Eleven questions

Imagine you are attending a reunion of all your
old friends from secondary school. Here are some
of the things you might want to say.

1. Hello, (Carrie,) how are you?
2. I haven't seen you for ages.
3. You haven't changed one bit.
4. You look exactly the same! Not one day older!
5. What've you been doing for the past (ten) years?
6. What're you doing now?
7. Are you married? What does your husband/wife do?
8. Have you got a family?
9. Are you still (afraid of spiders)?
10. Do you still (play tennis)?
11. Where do you live now?

First, work alone and decide how you would
respond to these questions and comments. Then
talk to other students in the class and find out
what you have all been doing.

2 | I haven't seen you for ages

Who is your oldest friend? When did you first
meet?

Can you think of someone you haven't met for a
long time? Why not? Are you still in touch? What
are they up to now?

3 | While you listen

Sharon and Barry are friends who live in the
same area. They've bumped into each other
in the street and are catching up with each
other's news.

Cover the conversation on page 93. As you listen
to them talking about what they've both been up
to, try to answer these questions.

1. What's Barry been up to?
2. What's Sharon been up to?

Listen again and try to fill in the gaps in the
conversation.

Long time, no see!

Sharon: Barry! Hi, how are you? I haven't seen you for ages.

Barry: Hello, Sharon. Long time, no see.

Sharon: I know. So how're you doing?

Barry: I'm all right, thanks. And you?

Sharon: Yeah, not too bad. So, what've you been up to since I last saw you?

Barry: Not a lot – working mostly – (1) . . . . really long hours this week, getting really fed up with it, you know.

Sharon: Really?

Barry: Yeah, but I went down to Kent last weekend, for my grandma's birthday party.

Sharon: Oh, how old was she?

Barry: Eighty-five. It was really great. We (2) . . . . this lovely meal and then we (3) . . . . a walk along the beach. It was good to get out of the city.

Sharon: I bet. I (4) . . . . have a weekend away myself.

Barry: I know. You get to the point where you really need it, don't you? If you don't get out of London from time to time, it starts driving you crazy, you know. (5) . . . . , what about you? (6) . . . . ?

Sharon: Well, on Sunday morning I (7) . . . . that exhibition at the Royal Academy.

Barry: Oh yes, the one there's been (8) . . . . about – dead sheep and pictures of toilet rolls and things.

Sharon: Yeah, my friend Angela – she's at art school – she kept nagging me to go and see it, so I went.

Barry: And what did you think of it? (9) . . . . ?

Sharon: Oh, I (10) . . . . thought it was excellent, really good and challenging. There's only one thing that made you go 'yuk!' – the dead sheep. I think it's meant to shock you, though. Anyway, after that, I (11) . . . . and saw a friend of mine, Richard, for a bit and then we went up to Camden market to do a bit of shopping.

Barry: Oh yeah, it's nice up there on a Sunday, isn't it?

Sharon: Yeah, it's great. And then I (12) . . . . at my mum's, which was nice.

Barry: Oh, that sounds good.

Sharon: Yeah, and apart from that, (13) . . . . things for college, really.

Barry: Uh-huh, still being a good student, then. Oh look, there's my bus into town. (14) . . . . I'll see you soon, then. Bye.

Sharon: Yeah, OK, bye.

4 | Speaking

Has there been an exhibition or concert that caused a big fuss in your country? Why was it so controversial?

What makes you go 'yuk'?

5 | Expressions with *get*

In the conversation, Barry said that if you live in a big city like London, you get to the point where you really need a weekend away. What do you think it means?

Get is a very common verb in English. Here are eight things you can get. Use them to complete the sentences below.

the impression	five years
a terrible shock	to the top
some sleep	a life
a doctor	the message

1. I got . . . . when I saw Mary after all those years. She looked really o

2. That guy got . . . . for knocking down of our neighbours' children. He was driving when was dru

3. Quick, get . . . . ! She's stopped breathing!

4. Sorry, I've been working non-stop for eighteen hours. I really need to get . . . .

5. Do you sometimes get . . . . that Claire is bored with her job?

6. I can't believe you spent the whole weekend studying. You should get out more and get . . . . !

7. I keep dropping hints that I'm not interested, but he never seems to get . . . .

8. He's incredibly ambitious. He'd do anything to get . . . .

Using grammar

1 | Present perfect simple and present perfect continuous

You arrange to meet a friend at seven o'clock. He finally arrives at eight. Which do you say to him – a or b? Explain your choice.

a. Where on earth have you been? I've been waiting here for an hour.
b. Where on earth have you been? I've waited here for an hour.

The next example is very strange. Correct it.
I'm afraid I can't go. I've been breaking my arm.

Which of these sentences sound correct?
1a. You look as if you've been crying. What's the matter?
1b. You look as if you've cried. What's the matter?

2a. Hey! I've been finding your passport.
2b. Hey! I've found your passport.

2 | Adverbs with the present perfect

Look at these common adverbs which are often used with the present perfect:

just almost never completely

Discuss which is the most *likely* in these sentences.

1. I've .... been to Siberia.
2. I've .... bumped into Harry on the tube.
3. I've .... finished. Give me two minutes.
4. I've .... forgotten your name.
5. I've .... got to the end of the book.
6. I've .... had an idea.
7. He's .... had an original idea in his life!
8. I've .... seen something really funny.
9. She's .... got over the death of her son.
10. I've .... seen anything so funny.

3 | Speaking

Use these sentence starters to tell your partner some interesting things about yourself.

1. I've just . . .
2. I've never . . .
3. I've almost finished . . .
4. I've completely . . .

4 | Present perfect collocations

Some verb forms occur very often with the same expressions. Choose the correct expression to complete these present perfect sentences.

1. I've been at college
   a. for the past three years.
   b. since the last three years.

2. I've been travelling
   a. about Africa.
   b. around Africa.

3. I've been studying
   a. for a doctor.
   b. to become a doctor.

4. I've been abroad
   a. studying.
   b. for studying.

5. I've been working
   a. as a volunteer in Africa.
   b. as volunteer in Africa.

6. I've been on a course
   a. to better my English.
   b. to improve my English.

7. I've been away
   a. since two months.
   b. since Christmas.

8. I've been ill
   a. for the past fortnight.
   b. since the past fortnight.

5 | Pronunciation

🎧 **Listen to the intonation pattern of this line from the conversation.**

How are you? I haven't seen you for ages.

Practise the following, which have similar patterns.

1. How are you? We haven't spoken for weeks.
2. How are you? We haven't had a chat for ages.
3. How are they? I haven't seen them for months.
4. How is he? I hear he's just got back.
5. How is she? I haven't seen her for ages.
6. How's your dad? I haven't seen him for years.
7. How is she? I heard she's had a boy.
8. How much was it? I heard it cost a fortune.

6 | Grammar practice

Now ask your partner the questions in Exercise 5 above. Try to keep each conversation going for as long as possible.

▶ For more information on how to use the present perfect simple and present perfect continuous, see G20.

Using vocabulary

1 | Expressions with *point*

You can record expressions in your notebook in different ways. For example, you could put the expression Barry used in the conversation – 'you get to the point where you need a weekend away' – under the heading of get or as an expression with point. Doing both is a good idea.

Here are sentences with some other expressions with point. Complete them with the words in the box.

get	see	make (x2)

1. Do you think you could . . . . to the point, please?
2. Please . . . . a point of being early.
3. I just don't . . . . the point of complaining.
4. If you don't . . . . your point strongly, people will just ignore what you're trying to say.

Now complete the sentences below with the adjectives in the box.

high	turning	strong	sore

5. The real . . . . point in my life was when I was told ten years ago that I only had three months to live.
6. One of Mary's . . . . points is the fact that she never gets annoyed with anyone.
7. Don't talk to Bill about his divorce. It's still a very . . . . point with him.
8. I think the . . . . point of my trip to Africa was standing at Victoria Falls.

Now complete the sentences below with the common expressions in the box.

on the point of	there's no point

9. Jane's working in Greece for a month, so . . . . trying to ring her.
10. I was . . . . leaving when the phone rang.

2 | Speaking

Discuss these questions with a partner.

1. What are the strong and weak points of your English? Grammar? Pronunciation? Vocabulary?
2. Have there been any turning points in your life?
3. What has been the high point of your year so far?

Reading

1 | While you read

🎧 There is a TV programme in Britain called 'Surprise Surprise'. If you want to get in touch with someone you haven't seen for a long time, you contact this programme and they try to put you back in touch – and film the meeting! Some people think this is a very good idea; some think it is a dreadful idea. What do you think?

If you were the programme's producer, which two of these stories would you be interested in? Why?

Long lost friends

Bob's story

When I was in the army, I was very friendly with a chap called Tom Ramsay from Leeds. We lost touch when we left and I wish we hadn't. I would love to meet him again to talk about all the things we went through together.

Jill's story

When I was a young girl of fifteen, I had a baby. My parents forced me to have it adopted. All I know is that she was born on March 14th, 1975 and the people who adopted her lived in York. I would love to meet her. I think about her every day of my life.

Jim's story

I'm now eighty-five. When I was a young lad of fifteen, I spent a summer working on a farm in Kent, picking fruit. I fell in love with a girl called Irene Smithson. She came from Canterbury. At the end of that beautiful summer, we went our separate ways and never met again. My wife died last year. I would love to meet Irene again. I have three children and twelve grandchildren.

Hugh's story

I'm twenty-five and single. I live in Birmingham. Last month, I spent the weekend in London with some friends. On the Saturday night, I met a fabulous girl called Melanie Brown at a disco. We danced together all night and talked for hours. We just hit it off immediately. The trouble was she had a boyfriend who was abroad on business that weekend. She gave me her telephone number, but I've lost it. I'm desperate to see her again. I wish I'd asked her for her address as well. The only thing I know is that she lives in Notting Hill Gate. But that's all I know – except that she had huge brown eyes.

2 | Speaking

Discuss these questions with a partner.

1. Is there anybody you've lost touch with who you'd like to be reunited with?
2. Is there anybody you really wouldn't like to meet again? Why not?

3 | Idioms focus

Decide if these idioms describe a good relationship or a bad one.

1. We got off on the wrong foot, and it was all downhill from there.
2. We decided to go our separate ways.
3. I've got a bit of a soft spot for him.
4. She's good if you need a shoulder to cry on.
5. There's no love lost between them.
6. We just hit it off immediately.
7. They hate each other's guts.

Do you have similar idioms in your language?

Spend two minutes trying to memorise the idioms above. Now cover the sentences 1–7 above and complete the sentences a–g below.

a. Listen, you can always talk to me if you need a shoulder to . . . .

b. A: Have you seen much of Nick and Ling lately?
   B: Oh, haven't you heard? They've gone their . . . .

c. A: Is there something going on between those two?
   B: It's a long story, but basically they just hate . . . .!

d. I met him when I first started work, and we just . . . . immediately.

e. A: He's a bit of an idiot, really, isn't he?
   B: I know what you mean, but I have to admit, I do have a bit of a . . . . for him.

f. A: Those two don't get on, do they?
   B: You can say that again! There's certainly no . . . . between them.

g. A: How come you and Marianne don't get on?
   B: I don't really know. We got off on the . . . . and then it was all . . . . from there!

Think of some people these idioms could describe. Tell some of the other students in your class about them.

Using grammar

1 | I wish

In the text on page 96, Hugh said: 'I wish I'd asked her for her address.'

1. Can you remember why he felt like this?
2. What tense do we use after wish if we want to talk about past regrets?

Complete these sentences by putting the verbs in brackets in the correct form. Some sentences will be negative.

1. I sometimes wish I . . . . my grandfather on my mum's side. (know)
2. I wish I . . . . so much earlier. (eat)
3. I often wish I . . . . more when I was younger. (travel)
4. I really wish I . . . . to see the doctor about it earlier. (go)
5. I sometimes wish I . . . . so much time when I was at university. (waste)
6. I wish I . . . . so much money while I was on holiday. (spend)
7. I wish I . . . . her earlier. (meet)
8. I really wish I . . . . my address book. (lose)

Now match the sentences 1–8 above to the follow-up comments a–h below.

a. I wouldn't be working here if I'd got a better degree.
b. I wouldn't have had to spend so many years of my life on my own!
c. I just don't have the time to do it now.
d. It wouldn't have got so bad if I had.
e. I wouldn't be so badly in debt if I hadn't.
f. I'm going to lose touch with loads of people now.
g. He was supposed to have been a really interesting guy.
h. I feel really sick!

 Now listen and check your answers.

Express regrets that are true for you using these sentences starters.

9. I sometimes wish I'd . . . .
10. I really wish I'd . . . .
11. I really wish I hadn't . . . .
12. I often wish I hadn't . . . .

Tell your partner what you have written and try to explain why you feel like this.

> For more information on how to use wish to talk about things you regret, see G21.

2 | Role play

With a partner, decide which of the four possible stories from the TV programme 'Surprise, Surprise', described on page 96, you would like to act out. Spend five minutes thinking about what you're going to say. Ask your teacher for help if you need to. Then role play the people being reunited.

She paid £500 for it. • You call that art? • It's a masterpiece. • I did it myself. • He pickles dead animals. • I really recommend it. • What's it supposed to be? • It all looks the same to me. • So what exactly is Cubism, then? • Me? Draw? • What do you think of this one? • It's not really my cup of tea. • So you'd recommend it, then? • I'd give it a miss if I were you. • Sound interesting. • It's so detailed, I can't believe it. • I painted this one when I was depressed. • I just love bright colours. • I prefer abstract art. • Dali and people like that. • I like landscapes. • It must be a fake. • I like art, but I'm not really all that arty. • I do a bit of pottery. • I don't know much about art, but I know what I like. • She was ahead of her time. • Oh yes, I agree – very original. • Her work is being exhibited in Soho. • I'm taking an art appreciation class.

14 Art

Using vocabulary

1 | Speaking

Discuss these questions with a partner.

1. Do you ever go to exhibitions? What kind?

2. Has your home town got an art gallery? When was the last time you went to it?

3. What is the best exhibition you have ever been to?

4. The pictures on this page are a portrait of Lunia Czechowska by Amedeo Modigliani and 'Still life with apples' by Paul Cézanne. Do you like them? Can you say why?

5. Have you ever painted, sculpted or drawn? Has any of your work ever been exhibited – perhaps at school?

2 | Recommending

Put the jumbled conversations into the correct order.

Conversation 1

a. I went and saw an exhibition at the Hayward Gallery earlier in the week. `1`

b. So, you'd recommend it, then?

c. Quite good, actually, the photos were really great, quite amazing – some of them.

d. Oh, really? It sounds quite interesting. What was it like?

e. Yes, you should go and see it.

f. It was a collection of photos from the first lunar landing.

g. Oh, did you? What was it?

Conversation 2

a. I went and saw that new exhibition at the National Gallery the other day. `1`

b. Oh, it was this collection of Flemish paintings from the seventeenth century.

c. Oh, did you? Which one's that again?

d. Well, I didn't think much of it myself. It was all a bit dull, you know.

e. No, I'd give it a miss, if I were you – unless you really like that sort of thing, of course.

f. Oh really? What was it like?

g. So, you wouldn't recommend it, then?

Listen and check your answers. Then practise both conversations with a partner, making sure you sound enthusiastic or not, as appropriate.

3 | Recommending expressions

When we talk about an exhibition we've been to, we usually say whether we think it was worth seeing or not. Put the words in order to make recommending expressions.

1. you're / OK / it's / sort / if / into / thing / that / of
....

2. a / must / it's
....

3. recommend / really / I / it
....

4. you / give / if / were / miss / a / I'd / it / I
....

5. visit / well / it's / a / worth
....

6. entrance / not / it's / the / fee / worth
....

7. it's / my / tea / cup / of / really / not
....

Listen and check your answers. Which expressions recommend an exhibition? Which do not?

4 | Practice

Think of an exhibition you've seen. Decide whether you'd recommend it or not. Use Conversations 1 and 2 as models and tell your partner about it. You should begin:

I went and saw an exhibition at … the other day/the other week.

5 | Describing paintings

Here are eight ways of describing paintings. Check that you understand the words, using a dictionary if necessary. Use them to complete the sentences below.

portrait	detailed
landscape	traditional
still life	original
abstract	colourful

1. I think his work is very individual, very .... I've never seen anything else like it.

2. I've just been to a(n) .... exhibition – it's something I've tried to do myself, but my apples always look like peaches!

3. We've got a(n) .... of my great-grandfather at home. He was a general in the army.

4. Renaissance paintings were always very .... You could see all the stitches on the clothes.

5. His most famous .... was a picture of the scenery around his home in Provence.

6. I don't actually like modern art. I much prefer more .... things.

7. I don't like paintings that are all greys and browns. I like really .... things. You know, lots of bright greens and reds and yellows.

8. I don't understand her work at all. It's just too .... for me.

6 | Speaking

Discuss these questions with a partner.

1. You've just learned what a portrait, a landscape and a still life are. What other kinds of art can you think of?

2. What's your favourite piece of art? Why? How would you describe it?

Reading

1 | Before you read

Discuss these questions with a partner.

1. Do you like modern art? Why/why not?
2. What do you think art is for?
3. Do you like any of the works you can see on these pages? Why/why not?

2 | While you read

🎧 **Now read the article and decide how the writer would answer the three questions in Exercise 1.**

Art Attack

It's November, which means it's the time of year when the papers are full of articles by people who are shocked about art. This is because in November the Tate Gallery in London holds the annual Turner Prize exhibition of modern art. Each year four of the best British artists are selected from all those who have exhibited during the year and of these, one is chosen. For the most part, the shock journalists express is not moral outrage, but more of the 'You call that art?!' variety. We are treated to a string of the usual complaints and clichés: 'Anyone could do that!' 'My five-year-old daughter could do better than that.' 'A bed in the middle of a room! Where's the skill in that?' 'Whatever happened to people just painting pictures?' 'Fifty thousand pounds for that! You're pulling my leg.' etc., etc. Well, personally, I'm sick of it – the journalists complaining, that is – not the art. The only thing which is predictable, boring, and money for nothing is their writing. These people just want art to be pretty pictures. For them, it's just an extension of interior design – something which will match the sofa or look good in the bedroom. For me, the worst thing anyone could say about art is that it looks quite nice. Art should make you think. Art should be the result of artists thinking about the world they see and their reactions to it. It shouldn't be about seeing something and saying, 'Oh, that looks nice. I'll paint that and make it look just like a photograph, and I'll take ten years to do it,' which is what these journalists seem to think is required of art.

I have made a selection of some of the previous Turner Prize entrants – I know journalists do not like to spend time doing research for themselves, so I've done it for them. Perhaps they could ask the question Wolfgang Tillmans, a previous winner, poses. 'These scenarios might appear strange to some people, but I try to ask through them, what is so strange here, the scenario in the picture, the world around you, society, your ideas about beauty or my ideas about beauty?'

Richard Long caused outrage with his work, which was a line of bricks laid on the floor of the gallery. He made a similar piece with bits of slate, a kind of grey stone, which he'd found on a walk in the countryside.

Martin Creed won the prize with a piece which involved the audience walking into an empty gallery space and the lights suddenly being turned off and then sometime later turned back on again.

Rachel Whiteread uses common objects as a mould. She fills the inside with concrete and exhibits the sculptures with the objects removed. She has used tables, chairs, bookcases and, most famously, a whole house.

Simon Patterson, in a work called 'The Great Bear', painted a replica of the London Underground map, but replaced the names of the stations with the names of famous people from history.

Chris Ofilli paints religious figures, and as well as paint uses other media such as mud and elephant dung. Mayor Giuliani in New York once tried to ban one of his works of the Virgin Mary because he said it was an insult to the Catholic religion.

Tracy Emin was famous for making an installation of her slept-in bed in the middle of a gallery. She also made a tent and pinned on the inside the names of all the men she'd slept with.

Douglas Gordon won for showing Alfred Hitchcock's thriller, 'Psycho', which he slowed down so much that it took twenty-four hours to play instead of two.

Personally, I don't really care if you don't *like* these pieces; that's not the point. What should be absolutely clear, though, is that these *ideas* are not the work of five-year-olds, but of creative, intelligent adults. It's a shame we can't say the same of some journalists and critics!

3 | Speaking

Look back at the text on page 100 and tick (✓) anything that you agree with, cross (✗) anything that you disagree with or put a question mark (?) if you don't understand something. Compare what you've marked with a partner. Has the article made you change your mind about art in any way? Why/why not?

Ask your teacher about anything you still don't understand.

4 | Collocations

The article said that Richard Long's work made of bricks **caused outrage**. The verb **cause** collocates with several common nouns. Look at these examples and see if you can work out the connection between the nouns that collocate with **cause**.

1. It caused a riot.
2. It caused outrage in the media.
3. It caused an accident.
4. They caused a lot of trouble at the match.
5. It caused a lot of problems at work.
6. It causes a lot of suffering.
7. It caused a lot of damage to buildings.
8. It causes a lot of harm to the environment.

Did you notice that all these collocations include negative nouns? With a partner, discuss what you think the pronouns **it** and **they** refer to in the sentences 1–8 above. For example:

1. 'It' could mean the police firing into the crowd or a speaker at a demonstration making very provocative comments.

Can you use any of the sentences 1–8 to talk about things you've seen on the news recently?

Liam Gillick's work of art entitled 'Mercatmercatmercatmercat' at the Tate.

Using grammar

1 | Relative clauses

When we talk about the things we've been doing, we usually follow facts with comments. For example:

I went to that new Matisse exhibition, which was really nice.
There was a riot in the city centre, which meant I couldn't get to the airport.

Try to think of comments for the following.

1. It was pouring with rain on Sunday, which meant . . . . .
   . . . .

2. I went to visit a whisky distillery, which was . . . .
   . . . .

3. Mieko and Keiko came over for a meal, which was . . .
   . . . .

4. I went to see *Tosca* at the opera last night, which was
   . . . .

5. I missed the train this morning, which meant . . . .
   . . . .

6. I failed my exam, which meant . . . .
   . . . .

2 | Speaking

Think of two things you've done recently, and tell your partner about them. Be sure to add comments starting with **which**.

▶ For more information on how to add extra comments using relative clauses, see G22.

Using vocabulary

1 | Oh, that reminds me!

When people are talking about what they have been doing, it often reminds us of things which we have thought of doing ourselves. Look at the highlighted expressions in these examples:

A: I went to see the Turner Prize exhibition the other day.
B: Oh, yeah. I keep meaning to go and see that myself. What was it like?
A: Oh, it was OK, but nothing special, really.

A: I went round to see my mum on Sunday.
B: Oh, that reminds me, I must phone my mum tonight. I always try to ring her once a week.
A: Yeah, parents get upset if you don't keep in touch, don't they?

Now make short dialogues by matching the statements 1–6 to the responses a–f.

1. I visited Alan in hospital last Friday to see how he was getting on. ☐

2. I spent all day Sunday catching up on all my mail. ☐

3. I went and saw that musical, *Chicago,* last week. ☐

4. I went round to Mike and Sue's the other day to see that new car they've been telling everyone about. ☐

5. I went down to Bristol for the weekend a couple of weeks ago. ☐

6. I just stayed in last night and watched TV. There's a great thing on on Fridays at the moment about Antarctica. ☐

a. Oh, that reminds me. I must record that new thing on Channel Four tonight. It's meant to be really funny.

b. Oh, really? I've been thinking about having a weekend away myself. Were you camping or what?

c. Oh, that reminds me. I must send in my passport application.

d. Oh, did you? I keep meaning to go and see him myself. How was he?

e. Oh, that reminds me. I must give them a call. I haven't spoken to them for ages.

f. Oh, I've been meaning to go and see that for ages. Was it as good as everybody says?

 **Now listen and check your answers.**

2 | Practice

Practise reading the dialogues in Exercise 1 aloud with your partner. Try to add a third response, as in this example.

A: I visited Alan in hospital last Friday to see how he was getting on.

B: Oh, did you? I keep meaning to go and see him myself. How was he?

A: Not bad. You should go and see him. I'm sure he'd love to see you.

With a partner, have similar conversations using these ideas.

1. buy a birthday card for my brother
2. phone my parents
3. pay my telephone bill
4. book my summer holiday
5. send in my application form
6. have my hair cut

3 | Speaking

Discuss these questions with a partner.

1. Here are six examples of things you might go and see. Do you find any of them morally offensive? Politically offensive?

   a. a display of Egyptian mummies

   b. an exhibition of the body of a man found frozen in the Alps after hundreds of years

   c. a zoo with lions and tigers in cages

   d. a museum in Britain displaying statues taken from Greece 200 years ago

   e. a science museum with human foetuses preserved in formaldehyde

   f. an exhibition about some of the most famous murderers in history

2. Would you ban any of them?

3. Would you be happy taking your children or your younger brothers or sisters to them all?

4. What do you think of the example of street art below?

It was absolutely brilliant! • But the acting was horrendous. • It's a bit like Paris, only smaller. • It's not exactly Shakespeare, is it
• That must've been lovely. • Didn't you find it a bit boring? • It looks far too violent for my taste. • What was it like? Any good?
• It wasn't bad – considering the price. • He's a bit like you, only better-looking. • Nothing special. • A bit over-the-top, if you
ask me. • Star fruit? I've never eaten one. • He's not exactly Superman, is he? • Loved the food. • Didn't you think it was a bi
bland? • It's a great city. • It's a great place to visit, although I wouldn't want to live there. • It was very disappointing, considering
how much it cost. • Sort of reddish with blond bits. • It look
more like a rat than a dog. • The style is rather art deco.

15 Describing things

Listening

1 Before you listen

Here are eighteen ways to describe something. Six of them mean **very good**; six mean **very bad**; six are mildly critical. Put them into groups.

terrific	horrible	awful
a bit bland	marvellous	nothing special
excellent	horrendous	on the dull side
very ordinary	dire	a bit over-the-top
dreadful	brilliant	superb
wonderful	terrible	a bit disappointing

Very good	Mildly critical	Very bad
. . . .	. . . .	. . . .
. . . .	. . . .	. . . .
. . . .	. . . .	. . . .
. . . .	. . . .	. . . .
. . . .	. . . .	. . . .
. . . .	. . . .	. . . .

Underline the main stressed syllable in each expression and practise saying them.

2 While you listen

You are going to hear three conversations where people describe what things are like. As you listen, take notes on what they are describing and which adjectives they use. Listen again if you need to.

3 Practice

Use some of the adjectives on this page to describe:

1. a film you've seen recently
2. the weather recently
3. a journey you've been on
4. a meal you've had recently

> **Real English:** over-the-top
>
> Over-the-top means 'exaggerated or extravagant in some way'. It could refer to someone's dress or behaviour or the amount of food or drink at a party. *Didn't you think their house was a bit over-the-top? I thought ten Rolls Royces at the wedding was a bit over-the-top.*
>
> Sometimes we say OTT instead.
> *It was a bit OTT!*

4 | Asking linked questions

We sometimes ask two questions at the same time. For example:

A: So what's that new film like? Any good?
B: Yes, it's great – if you like Hugh Grant.

A: What was Malta like? Was it hot?
B: Yes, it was really lovely. We were never out of the water.

Write similar questions to suggest these answers. The first one has been done for you.

1. A: *What's his house like? Is it big?*
   B: Yes, it's huge. It's got four bedrooms and an enormous garden.

2. A: . . . . ? . . . . ?
   B: No, it wasn't, actually. It was really boring. In fact, I didn't even finish reading it.

3. A: . . . . ? . . . . ?
   B: Yes, very much. My boss is really nice and it's quite well paid, really.

4. A: . . . . ? . . . . ?
   B: Yes, it *was* quite warm, but not as hot as the last time we went.

5. A: . . . . ? . . . . ?
   B: Yes, I think it's great. The third track is brilliant.

6. A: . . . . ? . . . . ?
   B: No, we lost three–one. It was just terrible. I can't believe it.

Check with a partner to see if you have similar questions. Then listen to the model questions and practise saying them.

5 | Practice

Now ask your partner two linked questions about the following.

1. the weather on their last holiday
2. their job
3. their house or flat
4. how they get on with their parents
5. how they are
6. their day yesterday

Using grammar

1 | Conjunctions

Look at these examples of sentences with although, considering and in spite of.

I quite like her new shoes – although I think the heels are just a bit too high.

I quite like her new shoes – considering how cheap they were.

I quite like her new shoes – in spite of the flashy designer label.

Now complete these sentences with although or considering.

1. **Talking about a new CD**

   a. I think the whole CD is really good – . . . . how many changes the band's had since their last one.

   b. I think the third track's the best – . . . . I quite like that song called 'Dolphins' too.

   c. I think it's a great CD – . . . . it's still not as good as their first album.

   d. I think it's really great – . . . . how different it is from what they usually do.

2. **Talking about a trip**

   a. The trip was great – . . . . the mosquitoes were a bit of a problem at night!

   b. I really enjoyed the flight in the end – . . . . how nervous I was before we took off.

   c. I had a really brilliant time – . . . . I probably wouldn't go back.

   d. We had a great trip, ... how little it cost!

Now complete these sentences with although or in spite of.

3. **Talking about buying a watch**

   a. I reckon this one's got to be the best buy, ... I know I shouldn't really spend more than £100 on a watch.

   b. I think this one just looks nicer – . . . . being a lot cheaper than the others.

   c. I'd go for that digital one, ... the strap. You can always get that changed later.

   d. I think the Rolex one's the nicest, ... it is going to nearly bankrupt me!

> For more information on how to use these conjunctions, see G23.

2 | Speaking

Make three questions you'd like to ask a partner with this pattern.

So what's ... like?

Now take turns asking and answering these questions. Try to describe things in as much detail as you can, using as much of the language from these pages as possible.

Listening

1 | While you listen

🎧 **Paul and Mick are two friends chatting over a coffee. Listen to them talking about the films they have seen recently.**

Cover the conversation. As you listen, try to answer these questions.

1. Which films are they talking about?
2. What do they think of them?

Listen again and try to fill in the gaps.

Real English:

It's not exactly Shakespeare.
This mildly sarcastic remark is typical in informal conversation between people who know each other. Do you understand what the following remarks refer to?
He's not exactly Superman, is he?
It's not exactly a Picasso, is it?

Do you say things like that in your language?

Not exactly Shakespeare!

Paul: Guess what I went and saw last night – *Titanic* – it's on again this week at the Duke of York's.

Mick: Oh, yeah. I saw that when it first came out. What did you think of it? (1) .... ?

Paul: Oh, it was great. I really enjoyed it. I thought the special effects were amazing, and the acting was brilliant. It's one of those films where, you know, when I first heard about how much money they'd spent on it, (2) .... , but it was really great. It was a bit like one of those old disaster movies, you know, like *Towering Inferno* or *Earthquake*, (3) ....

Mick: Really? I'm surprised. I thought the acting was a bit wooden myself, and the dialogue was just awful. (4) .... you actually thought it was worth the money they'd spent on it. I mean, (5) .... the whole thing just a little bit over-the-top?

Paul: Oh, no. (6) .... I thought it was brilliant.

Mick: But the acting was horrendous!

Paul: Well, I know it's (7) .... Shakespeare, but it's not meant to be, is it? I'll tell you something weird though, there was this guy sitting next to us who snored all the way through the film!

Mick: Really? That (8) .... really, annoying. How could anybody actually sleep through all that noise!

Paul: I don't know – just dead tired, I suppose.

Mick: Yeah, I guess so, but really, though, (9) .... it was all just a bit too sentimental?

Paul: (10) .... , but I honestly didn't. I really thought it was all done just right. It was so romantic.

Mick: Oh well, each to his own. Have you seen *Bomb Alert 2* yet?

Paul: No, I haven't even heard of it. (11) .... ?

Mick: Um, Jean-Paul van Klam, he's great in it and, um, that woman from *Kamikaze*, you know who I mean. Remember? She was Turtle-woman too, (12) .... I must (13) .... she wasn't very good in that.

Paul: Oh, her. So what's it like? (14) .... ?

Mick: Yeah, it's great – if you like blood all over the place and that sort of thing.

Paul: Oh, it doesn't really sound like (15) .... , actually. I think I'll give it a miss.

2 | Speaking

Discuss these questions with a partner.

1. Which film would you rather go to – *Titanic* or *Bomb Alert 2?*
2. What's the most over-the-top film you've ever seen?

Using grammar

1 | Negative questions

Mick asked: 'Didn't you think it was all just a bit too sentimental?' Negative questions can express an indirect opinion or surprise.

Do you like cheese? (normal question)
Don't you like cheese? (I'm surprised.)

What did you think of it? (normal question)
Didn't you think it was really boring? (I did.)

Negative questions are often followed by the verbs find and think.

1. *Don't/Didn't you find it + adjective*
   A: I really like living out here in the country.
   B: Oh, really. Don't you find it a bit boring?
   A: No, not at all. It's great.

2. *Don't/Didn't you think it + verb*
   A: I'm going to see *Dogs of War* tonight.
   B: Oh really. Don't you think it looks really violent?
   A: Yes, a bit, but then I like that kind of thing.

 Listen to these examples and practise them with a partner.

2 | Grammar in context

Complete these short dialogues with negative questions.

1. A: I really like watching films with subtitles.
   B: Really? . . . . them hard to read?

2. A: I really loved that Italian actress.
   B: Did you? . . . . she over-acted a bit?

3. A: Did you see that Chinese film last night?
   B: Yes, but . . . . it was a bit slow?

4. A: I thought that last scene was a bit slow.
   B: Yes, it was a bit, but . . . . it was really romantic?

5. A: I thought the plot was a bit too predictable.
   B: Did you? . . . . it quite funny, though?

6. A: I thought that lead actor was brilliant in it.
   B: Really? . . . . him a bit too much like Robert De Niro?

7. A: *Titanic* won loads of Oscars, didn't it?
   B: I know. it's a bit over-rated?

8. A: It was rubbish, but at least it was funny rubbish!
   B: Did you think so? . . . . it was just silly and typical of late-night cable TV?

With a partner, practise the conversations above.

3 | Grammar role play

Imagine your partner lives in the biggest city in the country. While you make a list of four or five negative things about living there, your partner should make a list of the positive things. Then have conversations like this:

A: Don't you find Tokyo just a bit too big and crazy?
B: Yes, I know what you mean, but I love the night life.
A: You must be mad! I can't stand it.

4 | Idioms focus

In the conversation, Paul said that the man who was snoring next to him must've been dead tired. There are many more idiomatic expressions which make common adjectives stronger.

Match 1–8 to a–h to make eight such idiomatic expressions.

1.	brand	a.	sharp	. . . .
2.	razor	b.	asleep	. . . .
3.	dirt	c.	hard	. . . .
4.	stark	d.	easy	. . . .
5.	dead	e.	cheap	. . . .
6.	fast	f.	awake	. . . .
7.	wide	g.	new	. . . .
8.	rock	h.	naked	. . . .

Now complete these sentences with the idiomatic expressions you formed above.

9. Be careful with that knife. It's . . . .

10. I got these shoes cheap in a second-hand shop, but they're almost . . . .

11. It was so embarrassing. He walked into the bathroom and saw me, ... !

12. I wish the kids would go to sleep. They're still . . . . and it's almost midnight!

13. I bought five bottles. They were . . . . I'll never see them at that price again!

14. Don't wake him. He's . . . .

15. I finished the crossword in a couple of minutes. It was . . . .

16. Throw that bread away! It's . . . .

5 | Comparing

One way of describing something is to compare it with something else. For example:

A: So, what was that fashion show you went to like?
B: Oh, all right, I suppose. It was a bit like last year's really, but not as good.

Here are some more common expressions for comparing.

It was a bit like . . .

but not as good/nice.
but there are a lot fewer people there.
only a lot louder/quieter/more beautiful.
only there are more/there aren't as many cars on the road there.

6 | Describing things

Complete these short dialogues with the expressions below.

1. A: What's Indonesian food like?
   B: Delicious. A bit like Thai food, I suppose,

2. A: What was Lizzie's party like, then?
   B: Oh, it was OK, a bit like her last one,

3. A: So, what's New Zealand like, then?
   B: A bit like Ireland, really,

4. A: So, what's Nick and Beth's flat like, then?
   B: I suppose it's a bit like ours, really,

5. A: What's snowboarding? I've never heard of it.
   B: Snowboarding? Well, it's a bit like skiing,

6. A: So, what's Graham's sister like, then?
   B: Well, actually, she's a bit like him,

7. A: What's your new laptop like?
   B: It's the same as my old one,

8. A: So, what're the Spiders like, then?
   B: They're OK, they're a bit like the Beatles,

a. only the kitchen's not as big.
b. but there's more sheep.
c. only a bit more modern-sounding.
d. only a lot faster.
e. but a little bit less spicy.
f. only a lot more difficult, really.
g. but there weren't as many people as I'd expected.
h. only she's easier to get along with, I suppose.

7 | Practice

Describe the things in these pictures.

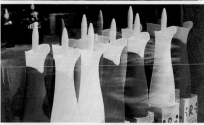

Now describe these things in a similar way.

1. a film you have seen
2. a big city you know
3. a café, restaurant or club you know
4. a drink
5. a band you like
6. a vegetable
7. a piece of furniture
8. a new television programme

Read your descriptions to a different partner. Can they guess what you are describing? For example:

A: OK. It's an alcoholic drink which is a bit like vodka, but it's made from rice.
B: Oh, it must be that stuff they drink in Japan. What do you call it? Oh yeah, sake.
A: That's it. Have you ever tried it?

▶ For more information on how to make comparisons like these, see G24.

8 *Must* for guessing

We often make guesses about something. Here are two ways of doing this using must:

must be

A: Have I told you yet? We've finally moved into our new house.
B: Oh really? It must be really nice to have a bit more space at last.

must've been

A: I grew up in a small village near Ludlow.
B: Oh, that must've been wonderful. It must've been a bit of a shock when you first moved to Birmingham, then.

Complete these sentences with must be or must've been.

1. Sally's new boyfriend has a foreign accent. I think he .... French.
2. The car won't start. The battery .... dead.
3. I'm not sure where Pete went to school. I think it .... somewhere in Wales, judging from something he said the other day about Cardiff.
4. Well, if this pen's not yours, it .... mine!
5. I'm tired. Surely it .... time to go home?
6. Bali .... wonderful! Are you planning to go back?
7. Just look at those poor people. It .... dreadful having no money and no food.
8. Two years ago we paid £30 a night. I should think it .... at least £40 now.
9. Did you see that police car? It .... doing over a hundred.

Real English: doing over a hundred
This means the car was going at over a hundred miles an hour. Look at these examples:
You can't do more than thirty in town.
We did an average of seventy on the motorway.

---

9 Grammar in context

Complete the responses in these dialogues using must or must've.

1. A: My brother and his wife have actually got eleven kids now.
   B: Eleven! ....
2. A: We stayed in this huge twenty-storey hotel.
   B: Oh, one of those places! ....
3. A: I usually cycle into work, if it's not raining.
   B: Oh really? ....
4. A: I got up at five, just as the sun was coming up, and went for a walk along by the river.
   B: Wonderful! ....
5. A: I like my job, but I have to work a six-day week every week!
   B: Every week? ....
6. A: The plane was delayed forty-eight hours! Can you imagine what it was like?
   B: Forty-eight hours! ....
7. A: Did you hear that over 200 people were killed in that crash?
   B: I know. ....
8. A: Every year we have our annual sales meeting at a beautiful castle in the Scottish Highlands.
   B: Really? ....

Compare your responses with a partner, then practise the conversations in pairs.

10 Practice

Tell a partner about two interesting things you have done or seen. Your partner should respond with a comment using must be or must've been. For example:

A: I spent a week in Hong Kong, which was great.
B: Wow! That must've been interesting. I've always wanted to go there. It sounds like an amazing place.

Where do you think the places in the pictures below are? Use must to make your guesses.

> For more information on how to use *must* for guessing, see G25.

16 Films and television

And then someone sat down right in front of me. • The ending was brilliant. • Pass the popcorn. • Ssshhh! • Has it g subtitles? • I loved every minute of it. • Where's the remote control? • I've heard it's really good. • Who's in it? • That wa rubbish! • Is there anything good on tonight? • Sport, sport and more sport! • Typical Hollywood stuff. • Surely you're nc going to watch *that*, are you? • You really must go and see it. • What's it about? • It's on cable. • They bleeped out all th f-words. • The special effects were amazing. • Leonardo who? • Turn it off. • There's too much sex and violence on TV thes days. • Have you seen his latest one? • I'd rathe watch the adverts! • 100 channels and nothing on!

Using vocabulary

1 | What kind of film is it?

Do you recognise any of the films shown in these pictures? Have you seen any of them? What were they like?

Which of these descriptions match the three films in the pictures?

1. It's a kind of sci-fi thing.
2. It's a costume drama.
3. It's a typical Hollywood blockbuster.
4. It's a romantic comedy.
5. It's a cult movie.
6. It's a real weepie.
7. It's an animated film.

Can you think of other examples for each kind of film?

What kind of films do you like most? Why?

Are there any kinds of films that you really can't stand?

2 Asking questions about films

Here are common questions to ask about films.

a. Who's in it?
b. What's it about?
c. Where's it on?
d. What's it like?
e. Who's it by?
f. When was it made?
g. Where's it from?
h. What kind of film is it?

Make short dialogues by matching the questions a–h above to the answers 1–8 below.

1. A: ....
   B: Two or three years ago.
2. A: ....
   B: Juliette Binoche and that guy who was in *Dimples*.
3. A: ....
   B: Japan, but it's subtitled.
4. A: ....
   B: At the Odeon in Queen Street.
5. A: ....
   B: This guy who has a mid-life crisis and drives across America looking for his parents.
6. A: ....
   B: Some Italian director.
7. A: ....
   B: It's a cross between a traditional cop movie and a more arty kind of movie.
8. A: ....
   B: It's silly. I mean, it was amusing for a while, but then I just got bored by it.

> **Real English:** some Italian director
> Using some in number 6 in Exercise 2 means that you don't know the person's name.
> *Some woman came to the door collecting for charity.*

3 And when you can't answer!

Put the words in order to make expressions that we use when we can't remember something.

1. Sorry, / completely / gone / mind's / blank / my
   ....

2. Wait, / minute / to / a / come / in / me / it'll
   ....

3. Wait, / it's / tongue / my / tip / the / on / of
   ....

4. Sorry, / my / top / the / head / can't / I / remember / off / of
   ....

🎧 **Now listen and practise saying the expressions above.**

a. Which expression means 'I'd need to look it up'?
b. Which two expressions mean 'I can almost – but not quite – remember'?
c. Which expression means 'I've forgotten'?

4 Pronunciation

🎧 **Practise saying the questions from Exercise 2. Listen, then say them again.**

With a partner, try to have your own conversations about films you have seen, using these questions.

Use the 'forgetting' expressions from Exercise 3 if you can't remember specific details.

5 Film vocabulary

Complete the sentences below with the words in the box below.

banned	stars	director
dubbed	cut	special effects

1. My favourite .... is Hitchcock. There's never been anyone else like him.
2. The government thought the film might corrupt people, so they .... it.
3. Have you ever seen *Mean Streets*? It .... Robert De Niro and Harvey Keitel.
4. I thought that the .... in *Jurassic Park* were amazing.
5. When they showed *Robocop* on TV, they .... about fifteen minutes out of it, because it was so violent.
6. I prefer to see foreign films in their original versions with subtitles, rather than ....

Now complete the sentences below with the words in the box.

soundtrack	set	scene
dialogue	plot	ending

7. The thing I love about that film is that the .... is just so sharp and witty. I laughed at almost every line.
8. I loved the .... so much that I went out and bought the CD the next day.
9. I loved all the twists and turns in the ...., and the way it only made sense right at the very end.
10. I liked most of it, although I did think that the .... was just a bit too sentimental.
11. It looks amazing. It's .... in New York in the year 2050.
12. My favourite .... in the whole film is the bit where the aliens finally come out of the spaceship.

6 Speaking

Discuss these questions with a partner.

1. Do you prefer foreign films to be dubbed or to have subtitles?
2. What are the best special effects you've ever seen in a film?
3. Do you have a favourite film soundtrack?

Reading

1 Before you read

Discuss these questions with a partner.

1. Do you think film censorship is a good thing? Give an example.
2. Did your parents ever stop you watching anything on TV? What? Why?
3. Have you ever seen *Robocop*? What did you think of it?

2 While you read

🎧 **Read this article about what happened when *Robocop* was shown on British TV. When you have read it, answer these questions.**

1. Why did the TV version of *Robocop* offend so many people?
2. What effect did censoring the film have?
3. Who was Mary Whitehouse and how does her organisation feel about the TV version of the film?

TV ROBOCOP
NOT VIOLENT ENOUGH FOR VIEWERS

The news that Mary Whitehouse has died at the age of ninety-one has brought the same kind of opposing reactions that she provoked when she was alive. For over thirty years she was the head of the National Viewers' and Listeners' Association, which she set up in the late sixties. She formed the organisation along with two other mothers in their mid-forties to 'protect children from the filth and violence that is flooding our TV screens and ruining our children's lives'. When it first started, the NVLA attracted hundreds of people to the meetings it held round the country, and the group forced the government and TV companies to create a nine o'clock watershed, before which programmes should not contain swearing, excessive violence or sexual behaviour. It also co-ordinated letter writing and phone campaigns to complain about certain films and programmes. A spokesman from the NVLA said, 'It's very sad that she has died, but she made a great contribution to this country. If it hadn't been for Mary Whitehouse, the quality of TV in this country would be much worse and the effect on our children would've been terrifying.'

One TV producer said in reply, 'I would say that's rubbish really. Mrs Whitehouse was just an ultra conservative who didn't understand art. She caused a lot of problems for producers of serious drama and, as a result, she might've persuaded some writers and TV executives not to show one or two things, but basically life moved on ahead of her. In the end, we're adults and we live in a democracy and we should be able to watch what we like.'

Paradoxically, a recent incident perhaps proves both sides of the argument. Following the showing of *Robocop*, the sci-fi movie best remembered for its comic-book violence, hundreds of people rang up to complain about it. However, what offended the audience was the polite language and the fact that it was not violent enough! Angry viewers called their local television stations saying that the TV version had been censored so much that the film had been ruined. All the f-words had been over-dubbed and the violence was so reduced that at times it was apparently hard to follow the plot. One man who complained said, 'This is a classic example of over-the-top censorship we constantly get on British TV because of people like Mary Whitehouse. When are you going to realise these people are dinosaurs and let us choose what we want to watch?'

The strong public reaction has actually led TV executives to consider putting back some of the bad language and violence when it is shown again. The film, shown last Saturday night at 10.05 pm, attracted more complaints than any other film this year. One executive commented that 'one can't help but notice we've maybe taken too much out of a film like *Robocop*. Maybe we've gone a bit too far this time.' Mrs Whitehouse must've been turning in her grave.

However, a spokesperson for the NVLA said, 'People who make these kinds of complaints are only concerned about their own interests rather than the good of society as a whole. Anybody who can't give up a little bit of film in order to reduce the current climate of violence should not be taken seriously.'

Real English: bad language and the f-word
Bad language is swearing. Saying the f-word is a common way of avoiding saying f**k itself. You should only use the word itself in very informal situations with people you know who are happy using it in conversation. Many people find the f-word very offensive.

3 Collocations

Complete the highlighted collocations in this summary of the article on page 112.

The TV version of *Robocop* caused a strong public (1) . . . . Many people rang their local (2) . . . . to complain that too much violence had been cut from the film. In fact, so much had been cut, it was difficult to (3) . . . . the plot. It was a classic (4) . . . . of over-the-top censorship. The NVLA, an organisation opposed to violence on television, was in favour of the cuts because they object strongly to the current (5) . . . . of (6) . . . . on television.

4 Speaking

Look at these statements about films. Decide how strongly you agree.

1 = strongly disagree
6 = totally agree

1. Violent films can be really offensive.
2. Cutting films ruins them.
3. Bad language should be cut out of films.
4. Very few people complain about violence.
5. Banning violent films will cut crime.
6. The TV version of a film should be censored more than the cinema version.

Discuss your opinions with a partner. See if the whole class can agree.

Do you agree more with the NVLA or the viewers who complained about *Robocop*? Why?

Using grammar

1 Past perfect simple

Look at these examples from the article.

The TV version had been censored.
The film had been ruined.

The past perfect is used to talk about an action or event which happened before another event in the past. For example:

I'd passed the turn-off for Leeds before I realised.
The house had burned to the ground by the time the fire brigade got there.

What sentence comes to mind in these situations? The first one is done for you.

1. I was terrified as I put on my parachute.
   I'd never jumped out of a plane before.
   . . . .
2. I was feeling sick at the thought of my speech.
   . . . . in my life before!
3. I was worried about meeting Mary's parents.
   . . . . before!
4. I wasn't sure if I'd like Korean food.
   . . . . before.
5. The woman in red was his first wife.
   . . . . once before.
6. The news said thousands were dead.
   . . . . an earthquake.
7. He left without saying goodbye to me.
   . . . . an argument.
8. I was terrified as I arrived at the airport.
   . . . . before!

2 Practice

Can you say something true about yourself using the past perfect and these ideas? For example:

I'd never eaten paella until I went to Spain.

1. . . . . until I went to a Chinese restaurant.
2. . . . . until I went abroad.
3. . . . . until I did my military service.
4. until I went to university.
5. . . . . until I went to Britain/America.
6. . . . . until I fell in love.

▶ For more information on using the past perfect simple, see G26.

Using vocabulary

1 | I've heard it's really good

Put the jumbled conversations about films into the correct order.

Conversation 1

a. No, I haven't actually, but I've heard it's really good. Friends have told me it's worth seeing.

b. Have you seen *Day of the Dogs* yet?

c. Really? Well, I must admit it looks a bit too violent for me.

d. Yes, I'm not sure if I want to see it myself.

Conversation 2

a. I'm thinking of going to see that new De Niro film.

b. Well, the reviews I've seen were very good.

c. Are you? I've heard that it's terrible. Just typically Hollywood.

d. Were they? I've heard the opposite.

Conversation 3

a. But it's meant to be one of the best horror films ever made!

b. Is it? You're not going to watch it, are you? It's supposed to be really horrible.

c. Excellent. It sounds right up my street, then.

d. *Thriller Killer* is on tonight.

e. Well, someone told me that it's the most disgusting thing they'd ever seen in their life.

2 | Speaking

With a partner, use the language highlighted in the conversations in Exercise 1 above to talk about a new film that you would really like to see.

3 | Television vocabulary

Complete the text below with the words in the box.

series	remote
channel	documentaries
digital	aerials
advertisements	cable

As I sit here today in front of my TV with my (1) .... control in my hand, it's easy to forget that when I was growing up in the fifties, there was only one (2) .... in the UK. It was BBC and it was years before we got ITV and BBC2. The main difference was that ITV had (3) .... and BBC didn't.

During the fifties, lots of houses had television (4) .... on their roofs, but nowadays they are becoming a thing of the past. Things have changed so much with the arrival of (5) ...., (6) .... and satellite TV.

At first, the idea in the UK was that TV should be educational, so there were lots of (7) ...., but today the channels seem to do nothing but fight to see which one gets the biggest audience for soaps such as *Neighbours, Eastenders* and *Coronation Street*.

The BBC is still one of the best companies when it comes to making serious drama (8) .... – *Pride and Prejudice* and things like that.

4 | Speaking

Discuss these questions with a partner.

1. Have you got satellite or cable TV? What about digital – is it really better?

2. Do you know anyone who doesn't have a television? Why don't they have one?

3. How much TV do you watch per week? What kind of thing do you normally watch? What makes you switch the television off?

5 | Audiences

Exercise 3 above talked about TV audiences. Complete the sentences below with the words in the box.

spectators	congregation	on-lookers
fans	audience	viewers

1. The .... gave the singers a standing ovation.

2. The .... were silent as the priest came in.

3. Boy bands usually have mostly girl ....!

4. Lots of .... object to violence on TV.

5. Some .... were injured when Hakkinen crashed.

6. The police couldn't get to the crash because of all the ....

Which of these different groups of people have you been part of? When?

Whitehouse.

Using grammar

1 | Mixed conditionals

In the text on page 112, the person from the NVLA said: 'If it hadn't been for Mary Whitehouse, the quality of TV in this country would be much worse and the effect on our children would've been terrifying.' The speaker thinks Mrs Whitehouse had a very positive effect on the country and we should be grateful to her. The speaker uses would be and would've been. What's the difference between them?

Look at sentences 1–6 about influential people. Decide which ones talk about an imaginary past result and which ones talk about an imaginary present result.

1. If it hadn't been for him, I would never have gone to university.
2. If it hadn't been for him, I'd probably be dead.
3. If it hadn't been for her, the country wouldn't be in such a terrible state.
4. If it hadn't been for him, animation would never have become so popular.
5. If it hadn't been for her, millions more people would be dying every year.
6. If it hadn't been for her, I probably wouldn't be doing what I'm doing now.

What kind of person do you think sentences 1–6 above are talking about?

Now complete sentences 7–12 by putting the verbs in brackets in the correct form.

7. If it hadn't been for my friend Reo, I .... to Japan last year. (never / go)
8. If it hadn't been for my mum, I .... anyone to babysit my daughter when she was growing up. (not have)
9. If it hadn't been for the unions, you .... a pension now, Joyce. (not get)
10. If it hadn't been for Federico Fellini, I .... foreign films as much as I have. (never / get into)
11. If it hadn't been for our first president, we .... in the Dark Ages. (still / live)
12. If it hadn't been for her parents, nothing .... wrong and we .... married! (go, still / be)

Now make five sentences about people who influenced your life – or your country. Use the same pattern as the examples above.

Tell your partner what you have written.

> For more information on how to use mixed conditionals, see G27.

2 | Speaking

Discuss these questions with a partner.

1. Do you know who the people in the pictures below are?
2. How do you think they have influenced the world?

Review: Units 13–16

1 | Tenses

Choose the correct form.

1. I've been / I went to China last year on holiday. It was great.

2. I've played tennis / I've been playing tennis twice this week.

3. Have you been staying in / Have you stayed in quite a lot lately? I haven't seen you about.

4. I've asked / I asked him five times now, and he still hasn't done anything about it!

5. A: It rained the whole time we were in Wales.
   B: Really? That must be / must've been horrible!

6. I've been trying / I've tried to do it all week, but I still haven't managed to get it done.

7. Did you speak / Have you spoken to him before he left to go home?

8. A: I'm working six days a week at the moment.
   B: Wow, that must be / must've been really exhausting!

9. What's happened to Mike? I haven't seen / I haven't been seeing him for ages.

10. I wish I hadn't done / I didn't do that! It was really stupid of me!

2 | Multiple choice

Choose the correct alternative.

1. I've worked here … .
   a. since five years   b. for five years

2. I've … .
   a. never been anywhere like Kos before
   b. never been somewhere like Kos before

3. a. Don't you think him a bit dull?
   b. Don't you find him a bit dull?

4. I do quite like life in central London, … !
   a. in spite of the fact it's so noisy
   b. considering it's so noisy

5. I've been trying to understand the present perfect … !
   a. since ages
   b. for ages

6. We spent a couple of weeks in Hawaii, … .
   a. that was nice
   b. which was nice

7. I didn't feel like going, because … that film before.
   a. I saw   b. I'd seen

8. Our train was late getting in, … .
   a. which meant a bit of a pain
   b. which was a bit of a pain

Compare your answers with a partner and discuss your choices.

3 | Mixed conditionals, *I wish I'd* …

Match the statements 1–6 to the follow-up comments a–f.

1. I wish I'd studied computing at school. ☐

2. I wish we'd done some shopping earlier. ☐

3. I sometimes wish I'd never married you! ☐

4. I wish I hadn't flogged my stamp collection when I did. ☐

5. I often wish I'd kept in touch. ☐

6. I wish I hadn't gone to that party. ☐

a. We wouldn't have to have rice again tonight if we had.

b. I'd probably get a much better price for it now.

c. It'd be easier to find a job now if I had.

d. I'd love to know what she's up to now.

e. It would've been more fun just staying in.

f. My life would be a lot easier now if I hadn't!

With a partner, try and think of another possible follow-up comment for statements 1–6 above.

4 | Speaking

Tell a partner five things you wish you had done or hadn't done. Try to use mixed conditionals to explain why you feel like this.

5 | Conversation

Put the jumbled conversation below into the correct order.

a. I bumped into Richard and Judy the other day. 1

b. I must admit, it doesn't really sound like my sort of thing, actually. ☐

c. No, they really enjoyed it, actually. They said it was a bit like Thailand, only wilder! ☐

d. Oh really? How are they? I haven't seen them for months. ☐

e. What did they think of it? Didn't they find it really difficult? ☐

f. They're great. They've been travelling around India and have just got back. ☐

6 | Look back and check: Recommending

Look back at Conversation 1, Conversation 2 and Recommending expressions on page 99. Underline any bits of language you have forgotten. Ask your partner about anything you have forgotten.

With another partner, do Exercise 4 on Page 99 again. This time you should begin:

I went and saw that film called … the other day/the other week.

7 | Expressions

Complete the sentences below with the expressions in the box. All the expressions are from units 13–16.

> he's not exactly
>
> get a life
>
> it's not worth the entrance fee
>
> that reminds me
>
> I haven't seen you for ages
>
> a sore point

1. A: I was thinking of going to see the new *Star Trek* movie tonight.
   B: Really? I wouldn't bother if I were you.
   . . . .

2. I can't believe you haven't been out anywhere since you arrived here! You really need to
   . . . .

3. A: What's your brother like? Is he good-looking?
   B: Well, let's just say . . . . the best-looking guy you've ever seen.

4. A: Whatever you do, don't mention cars to Andy.
   B: Why on earth not?
   A: His was pinched last month and it's still a bit of
   . . . .

5. A: I'd better just give my mum a call, to say I've arrived safely.
   B: Oh, ... I must remember to send *my* mum a birthday card this week.

6. Hi, how are you? . . . .

Can you think of three other situations where you might tell somebody to get a life?

Can you think of six words you could complete this sentence with?

He's not exactly the most … guy I've ever met.

8 | Collocations

Match the verbs 1–8 to the best collocations a–h.

1.	follow	a.	a point of doing something
2.	dub	b.	twenty minutes out of a movie
3.	cut	c.	and see an exhibition
4.	give	d.	to the point
5.	star	e.	the plot
6.	go	f.	in a movie
7.	make	g.	it a miss
8.	get	h.	a film into a foreign language

Now match 9–16 to i–p.

9.	get	i.	a mid-life crisis
10.	have	j.	the third track best
11.	object	k.	a lot of suffering
12.	cause	l.	for a meal
13.	send in	m.	the message
14.	give	n.	to violence on TV
15.	like	o.	your application form
16.	come over	p.	the performers a standing ovation

Now discuss these questions with a partner.

17. Have you ever seen a film you couldn't follow the plot of?
18. Do you object to anything on TV? Why?
19. What's your favourite album? Which tracks do you like best on it?

9 | Real English

Match the questions 1–7 to the responses a–g.

1. Hi, Dave. How are you?
2. How's things at work? OK?
3. What are his paintings like? Any good?
4. Did you see that car?
5. Don't you find him a bit on the slow side?
6. Who was that at the door?
7. Where's Nigel gone for his holiday? Anywhere good?

a. Well, we've actually been incredibly busy just lately.
b. Yeah. It must've been doing about a hundred and twenty!
c. Oh, just some guy asking if we wanted any work done in the garden.
d. Well, he's not exactly Picasso, if you know what I mean!
e. Lee! Hello. Long time, no see!
f. Oh, I can't really remember. Some Greek island or other, I think.
g. Well, he's not exactly Einstein, is he!

117

10 Idioms

Make idioms by matching the beginnings 1–8 to the endings a–h.

1. We got off
2. It drives
3. I'd give it
4. He was stark
5. He hates
6. They went their
7. You're pulling
8. I've got a bit of a soft

a. naked.
b. my guts.
c. spot for him.
d. on the wrong foot.
e. my leg.
f. separate ways.
g. a miss, if I were you.
h. me crazy!

11 What can you remember?

With a partner, note down as much as you can remember about the two texts you read in units 14 and 16.

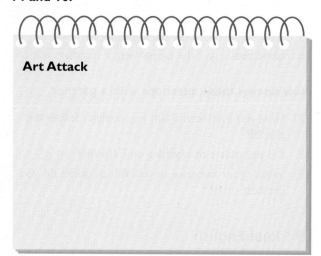

Art Attack

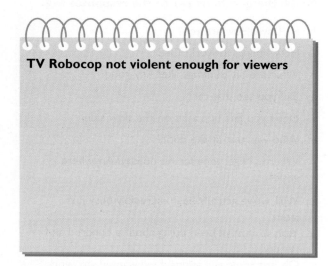

TV Robocop not violent enough for viewers

Now compare what you remember with another pair. Who remembers more?

Which text did you enjoy more? Why?

12 Vocabulary quiz

Answer these questions with a partner. Then compare your answers with another pair. Who got most answers right?

1. If you don't see the point of something, do you need glasses?
2. Do the police look for reasons or motives for crimes?
3. Does a weepie make you cry or laugh?
4. Can you think of three things that could be rock hard?
5. Can food be a bit bland?
6. Where are sci-fi films usually set?
7. What things might you need to get over?
8. Name two things you can pickle.
9. Do censors dub films into foreign languages?
10. Can you go and see a banned film at your local cinema?
11. What's the difference between a still life and a portrait?
12. What does OTT mean?
13. When are costume dramas usually set?
14. Does an old friend have to be old?
15. Complete this sentence in five different ways: It caused a(n) … .
16. Is a plot the same as a story?
17. Do you find turning points in the road or in your life?
18. If you give someone your consent, are you stopping them from doing something?
19. If two people hit it off immediately, are they friends?
20. Was the film *Titanic* set in Hollywood or made in Hollywood?

Learner advice: The authors speak!

Discuss these questions with a partner.

1. Are you happy with your English accent at the moment? Why/why not?
2. How much better do you think you can get?
3. What do you think the best way of improving your pronunciation is?

Now read this text and see what the authors of this book have to say about pronunciation.

Over the years I've been teaching, I've sometimes met students I really can't understand at all. I've tried getting them to repeat themselves or to speak slower, but it didn't make any difference. Eventually, once they wrote down what they were trying to say, I usually ended up realising that they actually knew quite a lot of English, but were just really bad at saying it. It's a shame when all the English you've learned is wasted because people can't understand you. Students like this need to work first on their pronunciation before learning new words. Most of you probably won't be this bad, but pronunciation may well still be an issue, and it can be quite a problematic one.

I personally find pronunciation the most difficult thing to give advice on. I've had several students come to me complaining that their accent is terrible when I could understand every single word! I want to tell them it's fine and advise them to spend their time on something else. However, when I think of my experience of learning Spanish, I know I really didn't want people to hear immediately that I was English. I wanted to feel I wasn't a complete foreigner. You simply have to decide what's most important to you and what you want to spend your time on.

When you work on your pronunciation, you may need someone to show you how to form new sounds. Sometimes words sound different when they're heard on their own, rather than in an expression. For example, when one word ends in a consonant and the next one starts in a vowel, we often join the words together. When one word ends in a 't' and the next word starts in a consonant sound, we don't usually say the 't'. Normally, we only stress the words which carry the meaning of a sentence. As a result, it's probably best to try and practise saying whole phrases. Ask your teacher to say new phrases so you can repeat them and mark the stressed words and other features of pronunciation when you record them in your notebook. There are several exercises asking you do things like this in this book.

A lot of textbooks and books for English language students have tapes or CDs with them. It's a good idea to listen and read at the same time and then try to repeat the sentences yourself.

Tell your partner which of the things above you already do. Are there any other things you'd like to start doing? What?

Oh no, look at the traffic. • Well, that's a difficult question. • When are they going to start doing something about it? • It's
major issue. • Personally, I think it's ridiculous. • I agree with you up to a point. • That would be far better. • What we need i
more policemen on the streets. • I know what you mean. • Things are just getting worse and worse. • What we need is mor
sleeping policemen. • This place gets crazy in the summer. • What sort of car have you got, then? • Stop! I thought this wa
supposed to be a one-way street. • Sorry, officer. • Was I really doing ninety? • Just ban all cars, full stop! • It's getting impossible
• They've introduced a congestion charge. • I couldn't find a parking spac
anywhere. • That's a case of road rage. • Slow down!

17 Cars and cities

Listening

1 | Traffic survey

You are doing a survey of traffic problems in the town where you live. Here are ten possible steps which could be taken to improve the situation.

1. install speed cameras at all accident black spots
2. increase parking fines
3. put more sleeping policemen in quiet streets
4. ban all on-street parking in the town centre
5. pedestrianise the main shopping area
6. set up more bicycle lanes
7. provide better and cheaper public transport
8. ban all cars from the town centre
9. double the number of traffic wardens
10. start a one-way system

In pairs, decide which four should have the highest priority, which three are of medium priority, and which three should have the lowest priority.

> **Real English:** sleeping policemen
>
> Sleeping policemen is the normal way in British English of referring to speed humps on the road, designed to slow cars down in town.

2 | While you listen

Chris and Claire are having coffee in a town centre café. Cover the conversation on page 121. As you listen, try to answer these questions.

1. What traffic problems do they mention?
2. What suggestions for solving these problems do they come up with?

Listen again and try to fill in the gaps in the conversation on the next page.

More sleeping policemen!

Chris: Did you hear about that kid who was knocked down on Junction Road the other day?

Claire: Yes, it was awful, wasn't it? Still, it's (1) .... , is it?

Chris: What do you mean?

Claire: Well, there are always accidents down there, aren't there, (2) .... with the speed cars go at. And, well, basically, the crossing's in the wrong place, isn't it? I don't know why they've never moved it. I mean, (3) .... it was exactly opposite the shops, wouldn't it?

Chris: Yes, (4) .... They could do something to slow the traffic down, couldn't they? Maybe they could put sleeping policemen there or something like that.

Claire: Yeah, maybe – maybe one every so often would help, but (5) .... really great is if they had one of those speed cameras.

Chris: Big Brother, you mean!

Claire: No, they really make a difference. You should see how they've slowed the traffic down where my parents live.

Chris: Yeah, (6) .... I'm only against them because I got caught by one last month.

Claire: You're kidding!

Chris: No. A hundred and fifty pounds it cost me! A fine *and* six penalty points!

Claire: Oh, that's terrible!

Chris: Yeah, but it was my own silly fault. I mean, I should've known better, but (7) .... to what you were saying about the crossing, you're right. It would be far safer if it was closer to the shops, because that's where everybody crosses, you know. That's where most kids cross, so (8) .... if it was moved down.

Claire: Yes, I think that's the root of the problem. I mean, it does seem a funny place for a crossing. And (9) .... the other problem with it is the fact that lots of cars park all round there.

Chris: Yes, that does make it difficult to see, I suppose. Apparently, the car that hit that kid had just driven off from there.

Claire: Oh, really? Had it? Well, you see what I mean, then.

Real English: I mean

I mean is very common in spoken English. It is used before we go on to make our meaning clearer.

A: *So, what was Iceland like?*
B: *Oh, I loved the place. I mean, I wouldn't want to live there, but it's a great place for a holiday.*

Real English: six penalty points

In Britain there is a system of penalty points. If you are caught speeding, for example, you could get four penalty points. If you get too many, you lose your driving licence.

Is the system the same in your country?

3 Driving vocabulary

Complete this story with the words in the box.

one-way	pull over	U-turn	headlights
petrol	turning	direction	brakes

Last Friday night, I was driving to a friend's when I suddenly realised I'd taken a wrong (1) .... and I was going in completely the wrong (2) .... So, I quickly did a (3) .... to get back to the main road. Unfortunately, I'd gone down a (4) .... street and all I could see were (5) .... coming straight towards me, so I quickly slammed on my (6) .... and tried to (7) .... so that I could wait till the road was clear. The car suddenly stalled and I realised that I'd run out of (8) .... ! What a nightmare!

Now complete these collocations with verbs from the text above.

1. .... a wrong turn
2. .... in the wrong direction
3. .... a U-turn
4. .... down a one-way street
5. .... on the brakes
6. .... out of petrol

4 Speaking

Discuss these questions with a partner.

1. Do you drive? Have you got a car? Do you use it in town?
2. Have you ever driven in Rome, Athens, London, or Paris?
3. What's the worst city you've ever driven in?
4. Have you ever been stopped by traffic police? What had you done?
5. Have you got any stupid/embarrassing/funny driving stories?

Using grammar

1 | Second conditionals for making suggestions

In the conversation on page 121, Chris and Claire talked about the pedestrian crossing. Chris said: 'It would be far safer if it was closer to the shops'. Make short dialogues by matching 1–4 to the responses a–d.

1. This town's dead at night, isn't it?
2. The traffic's impossible, isn't it?
3. They've made the main car park bigger.
4. So, what do you think they should do about all the homeless people sleeping rough?

a. Yes, but it'd be more useful if they built a multi-storey.
b. Absolute chaos! What would be really great is if buses were cheaper and there were more of them.
c. Well, I'm not an expert, but I think it'd be a really good idea if they spent more on trying to build flats for single people.
d. I know. It'd be far better if the shops stayed open a bit later in the evenings.

Now match 5–8 to the responses e–h.

5. It really annoys me that they close the library for the whole of August.
6. The pollution in the High Street is really bad. I wish they'd do something about it.
7. So, what do you think they should do about all the street crime?
8. I can't believe that people are still allowed to smoke on the buses.

e. I know. It'd be better if there was just a total ban on it in all public places.
f. Well, I think it'd be a really good idea if they had more police cameras around.
g. Me too! It'd be more useful if they kept it open all through the summer.
h. I know. What would be really great is if there were some way of importing fresh mountain air from Switzerland or somewhere like that!

2 | Sentence starters

In the responses a–h in Exercise 1, find four different if- sentence starters. Write them below.

1. .... 2. ....
3. .... 4. ....

3 | Practice

Practise reading out the dialogues in Exercise 1 with a partner. Then change partners and this time, use the four different sentence starters in Exercise 2 to make your own suggestions about the problems expressed in 1–8.

> For more information on how to use second conditionals for making suggestions, see G28.

Using vocabulary

1 | Collocations

Here are some useful expressions for talking about your views on things. Circle the word that collocates correctly in each.

1. Well, that's a difficult / big question to answer.
2. I don't really have any heavy / strong views on that. What do you think about it?
3. You would've thought they'd be able to tackle / put away that problem somehow, wouldn't you?
4. I know what you mean, but that also brings / raises the question of how you could do that, doesn't it?
5. Yes, but I think that that can cause / do problems as well as solve them.
6. You'd think that it was such a large / major issue that they'd do something about it.
7. Oh well, it seems that we've got completely different / unlike views on that.
8. I think you're trying to escape / avoid the issue by saying that.

Do you have any strong views on anything? What?

What are the major issues in your country/in the world at the moment? How do you think they should be tackled?

Real English: impersonal *they*

They is common in spoken English when, for some reason, we don't know, or don't need to name, the subject. In these examples, they refers to the local council or the police.
They could do something to slow the traffic down. They could create a pedestrian precinct.

With a partner, decide who they refers to in these sentences:
1. They're supposed to be getting tougher on car crime, aren't they?
2. They haven't taken the rubbish this week.
3. They're thinking of putting up income tax.
4. I only arrived five minutes after the flight closed, but they wouldn't let me through.

2 | Personal opinions

Here are some ways of giving your opinion.

Personally, I think it's As far as I'm concerned, I think it's	brilliant. a great idea. not a bad idea. outrageous. ridiculous. mad.

With a partner, use the expressions above and give your opinions on these topics.

1. shops staying open twenty-four hours a day
2. men in kilts
3. getting married at sixteen
4. legalising cannabis
5. one car per family
6. body piercing
7. free coffee during English lessons

3 | Role play

You and your colleagues have decided it's time to meet to discuss your working conditions. You work for a very old-fashioned bank, founded in 1748. The management don't like change. Suggest changes to the following – which you are not happy about. Use as much language from these two pages as you can.

- The computer system is ten years old and there is no network system.
- People can smoke wherever they want.
- There are no plants or pictures or anything on the walls.
- There is only one toilet for both men and women.
- Everybody has got to start at 8.30 and finish at 4.30.
- Women must wear skirts and men must wear ties.
- Private Internet use and telephone calls are not allowed.
- There is nowhere to relax during breaks or lunchtime.
- You have to buy your own tea and coffee. It is not provided by the bank.

Can you think of any changes you'd like to make to the place where you work or study?

4 | Disagreeing

Put the words in the correct order to make very common sentence starters which show you disagree.

1. Well, / a / agree / I / but / up / to / point
   ....
2. what / I / you / but / Yes, / know / mean
   ....
3. think / Yes, / don't / that / but / you
   ....
4. don't / Yes, / forget / that / but
   ....

Listen and check your answers. Practise saying them. Then in pairs, take turns putting forward and disagreeing with the views below. Try to continue the conversations.

1. There's too much sport on TV, isn't there?
2. The way I see it, most TV these days is just a load of rubbish.
3. I don't mind a bit of violence in films. It's more realistic, isn't it?
4. People like footballers get paid far too much. At least, that's what I think.
5. If you really want to improve your English, the only thing to do is go and live in Britain or America.

Now do this exercise again, but this time begin by saying: 'Oh yes, I know what you mean.' Then add why you agree.

5 | Talking about cities

Complete the sentences below with the words in the box. The words are commonly used when describing cities.

shanty towns	historic	overcrowded	inner city
capital	cosmopolitan	industrial	centre

1. Is Sydney the . . . . of Australia?

2. Sheffield used to be nothing but factories and steel works – very . . . . , but not any more.

3. New York's one of the most . . . . places I've lived in – every nationality under the sun!

4. There are a lot of slums in the . . . . You know, lots of tiny bedsits with no bathrooms.

5. York's a really . . . . city – Roman ruins and the medieval walls still in good condition.

6. Thousands of the poorest people live in . . . .

7. The city . . . . shopping mall is the place to go.

8. There's seventeen million people living in Jakarta. It's really . . . .

6 | Speaking

Discuss these questions with a partner.

1. What's the most historical city you've ever been to? And the most cosmopolitan?

2. Have you ever been to a very industrial city? A very overcrowded city?

> **Real English: inner city**
> When British people talk about the inner city, they usually mean the poor, overcrowded areas around the city centre. It's a negative expression. We sometimes talk about inner city crime and inner city problems. If this is different in your country, it's probably better to say I live near the city centre, not I live in the inner city.

Using grammar

1 | The passive

Look at these modern pictures of Brighton. Say what each place used to be and then make a passive sentence about each one. For example:

It used to be a bank.
It's been turned into a video shop.

1. estate agent's → restaurant

2. insurance office → trendy bar

3. bank → fish and chip restaurant

4. public toilet → sandwich bar

Now talk about your home town and tell other students how buildings have changed and what they have been turned into. You might also want to say:

There used to be a ... near my house/near where I work, but it was knocked down and they've built a ... there instead.

2 | Grammar check

The passive is often used to talk about things going on in our town or city. The passive can be used with most tenses.

How good are you at using this structure? Try to complete these sentences and find out.

Present perfect

1. They've found an old bomb in the town centre.
   An old bomb ....

2. They've closed the High Street.
   The High Street ....

Present continuous

3. They're cleaning the swimming pool today.
   The ....

4. They're building a multi-storey car park.
   A ....

Present simple

5. They collect the rubbish on Wednesdays.
   The ....

6. They never clean the streets round here.
   The ....

Past simple

7. They closed down that restaurant last year.
   That ....

8. They found rats in the kitchen.
   Rats ....

Past continuous

9. They were still cleaning the toilets when the Queen arrived.
   The toilets ....

10. They were repairing the road all last week.
    The ....

Going to

11. They're going to build a new airport.
    A ....

12. They're going to improve the street lighting.
    The ....

Should

13. They should do something about all the litter.
    Something ....

14. Maybe they should put a zebra crossing there.
    A ....

▶ For more information on how to use the passive, see G29.

3 | Idioms focus

A **zebra crossing** is a kind of pedestrian crossing where the road has black and white stripes. Complete the idiomatic expressions in the sentences below with the animal words in the box.

cat	dogs	fish	horse
cows	donkey	goose	sheep

1. That night club is dreadful now. It's usually half empty. It really has gone to the ....

2. A: I discovered Pascal's got a black belt in judo.
   B: Really? He's a bit of a dark ...., isn't he?

3. You've done absolutely nothing today! You can't expect to sit around while I do all the .... work.

4. It was really weird. I was the only Asian person there. I felt like a .... out of water.

5. Please don't tell mum that we're going to have a surprise party for her. And tell Jane not to let the .... out of the bag either!

6. Our daughter is always watching TV instead of doing her homework. She could watch soap operas till the .... come home.

7. I suppose I'm the black .... of the family. I mean, I went away to New Zealand and didn't get in touch for twenty years.

8. No wonder we couldn't find the right house! You sent us on a wild .... chase! You gave us the wrong address.

Can you translate the idioms above into your language?

Oh no, I don't believe it! • Dogs shouldn't be allowed in this park. • It really bugs me. • Calm down. • I wish he wouldn't d
that. • I thought it was going to be free. • It's a free country. • Just look at that. • It doesn't really bother me. • Whose ide
was it, anyway? • BMW drivers! • It really annoys me. • Not again! • You're a bit late, aren't you? • Stop going on about it.
People who're always whistling. • That's the last thing I need. • How was the journey? • Don't ask! • Mobile phones ringing o
trains. • There's nothing you can do about it. • I suppose you think that's funny. • It makes my blood boil. • That's the secon
time this week that's happened. • Does she do that all the time
then? • I find it really irritating. • He just gets on my nerves.

18 Annoying things

Reading

1 Before you read

Discuss these questions with a partner.

1. What problem can you see in this picture?
2. Do you have this problem in your town/city?
3. Can you think of some ways of tackling it?

2 While you read

🎧 **Now read this article about ways of trying to solve the chewing gum problem in two different places.**

Which idea do you prefer? Why?

A sticky problem

You can imagine the scene. You're walking down the street of an old English town. You decide to sit on a bench to admire the fine buildings and beautiful flowers a little bit longer. Then as you stand up, you feel that nasty pull on your dress or trousers and turn round to see the remains of a lump of chewing gum, half of which is now stuck to your behind! A wonderful moment is destroyed and your mood changes for the rest of the day, or however long it takes you to remove the awful stuff from your clothing. Well, one town has finally had enough of all the complaints it receives each year and is not going to put up with it any more. Darlington, which last year won a 'Beautiful Britain' competition, has decided to act by providing special boards where people can stick their gum once it has been used.

Up to thirty chewing gum 'parking boards' are to be put up in an area in the town centre, which recently underwent a a one-million-pound facelift. They will cost £3,000 to provide, are aimed at the thirteen-to-twenty-three age group, regarded as the worst offenders, and will bear the messages 'Don't Gum Up Darlington', 'Chew It, Bin It' and 'Park Your Gum Here.' The town council believes boards will help save some of the £6,000 a year it spends on cleaning up gum from the streets.

The boards, to be situated at places such as sports centres and cinemas, will have a bull's-eye target so youngsters can aim at them. Keith Atkinson, head of Darlington's environmental and consumer protection department, said, 'Most people don't see chewing gum as litter, but we are hoping the boards will help people to start thinking that way. We've been flooded with complaints, mainly from visitors, who say gum on the streets, sticking to pavements and shoes, is both unpleasant and makes Darlington look untidy.'

Darlington isn't the first place in the world to try to tackle the sticky issue of chewing gum. In 1992, the Asian city state of Singapore banned all eating and importing of chewing gum after it was claimed trains had been delayed because trapped chewing gum caused the automatic doors to stick. The ban came with severe penalties for breaking the law. Smugglers bringing gum into the country could get a jail sentence of one year plus an eight-thousand-dollar fine. The government also tried to reinforce its message with advertising campaigns, which included slogans such as: 'If you can't think because you can't chew, try a banana.'

The policy has been a great success as even its critics admit. 'The whole ban idea was not a good idea to start with, but it did help to educate Singaporeans about the nuisance effects of chewing gum. Now Singaporeans, including kids, are more mature about their civic responsibilities,' said one man we spoke to. And certainly, Singapore is acknowledged to be perhaps the cleanest city in the world.

However, it now looks as if the ban will at least be partially lifted. This is not the result of thousands of frustrated Singaporean gum chewers, but instead it's come about because of pressure from the American government. They see the policy as a restriction on free trade – particularly of the big American gum manufacturers. As part of the negotiations on the new trade deal, the Singapore government has agreed to allow sugar-free gum prescribed by doctors and dentists to be sold by pharmacists. The relaxation of the law will only apply to smokers who are trying to give up by using nicotine gum and sufferers of dental and gum diseases for whom chewing offers therapeutic benefits.

3 | Comprehension check

Without looking back at the article, try to correct the following false sentences, using the exact words from 'A sticky problem'.

1. The town centre hasn't been improved recently.
2. The council haven't had many complaints about chewing gum.
3. In 1992, Singapore banned the export of chewing gum.
4. There's only a small punishment for breaking the anti-chewing gum laws in Singapore.
5. The Singaporean policy has been a failure.
6. They're going to legalise chewing gum completely in Singapore.

Now go back and see if you remembered the words correctly.

4 | Speaking

Discuss these questions with a partner.

1. What are the litter laws in your country? How do you feel about them? Do you ever break them?
2. Do you think the Singapore government should have to lift its ban on chewing gum? Why/why not?
3. Do you think free trade is a good thing or not? Why?
4. Has your country had any trade problems? Who with? Why?
5. Which of the slogans mentioned in the article do you like the best? Why?

Using vocabulary

1 | Phrasal verbs

In the article, you read that Darlington isn't going to put up with chewing gum on its streets any more. Here are some more phrasal verbs often used when complaining. Make sentences by matching the beginnings 1–5 to the endings a–e. Use a dictionary to check the meaning of any of the highlighted phrasal verbs if you need to.

1. If work carries on like this, I'm going to end up
2. I don't know how they can get away with
3. It drives me mad the way she goes on about
4. The dry-cleaners have completely messed up
5. I just can't put up with

a. these people any longer. I'm calling the police.
b. my shirt! Just look at the state of it!
c. her silly little problems all the time.
d. having a nervous breakdown.
e. such awful service. It should be illegal!

Now complete the pairs of sentences 6–10 with the correct form of one of the phrasal verbs above.

6a. If this weather doesn't get better, I'm going to .... going mad!
6b. If they don't do something about all these cats, the place is going to .... smelling awful!
7a. I really don't think I can .... the flat being in such a state any more!
7b. I don't know how you can .... him treating you like that. I'd resign if I were you.
8a. If I thought I could .... it, I wouldn't pay tax at all.
8b. She's the office golden girl. They let her .... murder!
9a. I somehow spilt my coffee and managed to totally .... that essay I've been working on.
9b. I don't trust them, personally. I'm sure they'll .... the economy, just like the last government did.
10a. She's always .... how hard life is and how little money she has to live on.
10b. I hate the way he's always .... how much money he's earning and how rich he is.

Look again at the sentences above. What follows the phrasal verbs – a verb or a noun? Pay close attention to the context of each example.

Does anywhere you know get away with really bad service – a restaurant, petrol station, shop?

Have you ever messed up anything really important? What was the last thing you really messed up?

2 | Speaking

Are you a complainer or do you just tend to put up with things? Which of these situations would you complain about? What would you say?

1. You get to your hotel room and discover they have given you a room at the back. You had booked a room at the front with a balcony overlooking the beach.

2. Your hotel room has a shower and you wanted one with a bath and shower.

3. Your soup has arrived at your table. It is warm, but not hot.

4. Your bill has arrived for your meal. They have overcharged you by £10.

5. Your bill has arrived for your meal. They have undercharged you by £10.

6. It is 2 am. You're trying to get to sleep. Your neighbour's dog is barking. You like your neighbours.

7. It is 2 am. You're trying to get to sleep. Your neighbour's dog is barking. You don't like your neighbours.

8. Someone has just lit a cigarette on the train. Smoking is not allowed in any part of the train.

Using grammar

1 | Was/were going to

We often complain about things that have happened to us using was/were going to. For example:

I thought it was going to be the holiday of a lifetime, but it was a nightmare from start to finish.

I thought the hotel was going to be really romantic, but it was horrible.

The advert said we were going to have a sea view, but we had a tiny room at the back of the hotel.

With a partner, imagine you were on this holiday. Complete these sentences using was/were going to and the verb in brackets.

1. I thought we . . . . in a five-star hotel, but it turned out to be only a three-star. (stay)

2. It said there . . . . a drinks party on arrival, but there was nothing. (be)

3. It said the new swimming pool . . . . ready, but it wasn't. (be)

4. I thought the hotel . . . . a five-minute walk from the beach, but it was more like twenty! (be)

5. They said every room . . . . fresh flowers every day, but we didn't see any. (have)

6. The brochure said that we . . . . new towels every day, but we only got one! (have)

Now complete these sentences using was/were going to and a passive form of the verb in brackets.

7. I thought we . . . . at the airport and taken to the hotel in a taxi, but we weren't. (meet)

8. I thought our towels . . . . every day, but they were only changed once. (change)

9. It said we . . . . on a moonlight cruise round the bay, but we never were. (take)

2 | Your complaints

Now take a minute or two to think of things from your own experience which you thought were going to be better than they actually were. Tell a partner about them.

With a partner, take it in turns to moan about these things.

1. a bad haircut/hairdo you've just had
   I thought it was going to be ... , but ...

2. a diet someone told you about
   I thought I was going to lose ... , but ...

3. a second-hand car you bought
   I thought it was going to ... , but ...

4. a film you went to see
   I thought ... , but ...

5. your favourite TV show not being on
   I thought ... , but ...

> For more information on how to use *was/were going to*, see G30.

Real English: a haircut/a hairdo
Both men and women can have their hair cut. It is usually only women who have their hair done. A hairdo implies more than just cutting. What other things might having your hair done involve?

What's the worst hairdo you've ever seen?

Using vocabulary

1 | Complaining about things

Complete these dialogues with the correct expressions.

1. Complaining about a meal

- they made it sound as if
- And then, to top the whole thing off
- It would've been OK if that was the only problem, but

Joan: How was the meal last night?
Mike: Oh, it was awful! The food wasn't very good.
        (1) . . . .
        the waiters were really rude as well. (2) . . . .
        . . . . ,
        they tried to overcharge us. Then when we
        complained about it (3) . . . .
        . . . . it was
        our fault!

2. Complaining about a situation

- I wish they wouldn't
- I've got a bit of a problem with
- I mean, the last thing I need

Terry: How's college going?
Julie: Not very well, actually. (1) . . . .
         . . . . my timetable this term. (2) . . . .
         . . . . is three lectures on
         a Friday. (3) . . . .
         change the timetable every term. Last term was
         much better.

🎧 **Listen and check your answers. Then with a partner, practise reading the conversations. Take turns being the first and second speaker. Make sure you try to sound annoyed when you're complaining.**

2 | Practice

With a partner, take turns complaining about these situations, using expressions from Exercise 1. Spend a few minutes preparing what you will say before you start.

Student A

1. a terrible English course
2. the trouble you had trying to find a friend's house using the map they gave you
3. roadworks going on right outside your house

Student B

1. a horrible hotel you stayed in
2. the trouble you had trying to work out how to use a new video recorder
3. a doctor who you don't feel is treating an injury you have properly

Now think of two really annoying situations from your own life that you'd like to complain about. Spend a couple of minutes planning what you're going to say. Then get things off your chest by telling your partner about these things. Use as many expressions from this unit as possible.

> **Real English:** get it off your chest
> This is a common idiom which means 'to tell somebody about something that is annoying or irritating you'.

3 | It really drives me mad

Put the words in brackets in order, to make expressions that are typical responses when people are complaining to us.

1. A: Doesn't it bug you the way shops always charge £9.99 when you know it's really £10?

    B: I must admit, ...
       (like / me / things / that / really / bother / don't)

2. A: Look, I'm really sorry. There's no way I can come to your party tomorrow night. I've got to work late.

    B: Oh, well, don't worry ....
       (world / not / end / the / the / it's / of)

3. A: I really thought I'd got the job. I mean, my interview went really well, and then they tell me I'm not even short-listed!

    B: Oh, well. ....
       (let / you / get / down / it / don't)

4. A: I've got about five bills I'm supposed to pay by the end of the month. What do they think I am? Made of money?

    B: Oh well, ...
       (you / do / nothing / can / about / there's / it)

Listen and check your answers, then practise the conversations with a partner. Try to keep the conversations going by adding further comments of your own.

4 | Practice

Tell a partner which of the things in the list below really annoy you. They should respond using some of the expressions from Exercise 3.

1. finding public telephones always out of order when you need to use them
2. chewing gum on the pavement sticking to your shoes
3. people letting their dogs foul the pavement
4. people talking loudly in public on their mobiles
5. finding out before breakfast that you've run out of milk
6. discovering that a pair of trousers you bought have shrunk in the first wash
7. uncollected rubbish in the street

Choose the three most annoying things and discuss how to prevent them from happening. Can you use some of the if- sentence starters on page 122 to make suggestions?

5 | Free practice

Use these sentence starters to make statements that are true for you.

1. One thing that really drives me mad is . . .
2. Doesn't it really bug you the way . . .
3. It really annoys me when people . . .
4. I don't know about you, but personally I can't stand . . .

Now walk around the class talking to some other students about the things that really annoy you.

> **Real English: it really bugs me**
> If something bugs you, it annoys you.
> *It really bugs me when people don't return my pen after they've borrowed it.*

6 | More expressions with *bother*

Make short dialogues by matching 1–8 to the responses a–h. Then underline all the expressions with bother.

1. Do you fancy coming out for a quick jog?
2. I'm going to complain about that guy smoking.
3. That was really delicious. Let me wash up.
4. I think I'll try that new bar tonight.

5. Sorry to bother you, but have you got the time?
6. I was really upset by her letter.
7. I can't stand mobile phones going off in public!
8. Are you sure you don't mind giving me a lift?

a. No, it's OK. You needn't bother! I'll do it later.
b. Really? Things like that don't bother me.
c. Oh, it's no bother at all. I'm going your way.
d. Sorry, no, I haven't.
e. Oh, don't let it bother you. She didn't mean it.
f. No, I can't be bothered. I'm too tired.
g. Why bother! You'll only start an argument.
h. I wouldn't bother if I were you. It's dead.

Spend two minutes trying to memorise the responses a–h. Then cover Exercise 6 while your partner reads out 1–8. Can you remember all the responses?

Translate the eight expressions with bother into your language. You will almost certainly need to use more than one verb. How many verbs do you need?

7 | Idioms focus

Complete the short dialogues below with the idiomatic expressions in the box.

> It's a Catch 22 situation, isn't it?
> Yes, and that's just the tip of the iceberg.
> It's a bit of a mixed blessing, isn't it?
> Yes, poor guy. It's a vicious circle, isn't it?

1. A: John drinks to stop himself worrying about money, and the more he drinks, the more he spends, and so on and so on.
   B: . . . .

2. A: The thing is, I can't get a work permit unless I've got a job and I can't get a job till I've got a work permit.
   B: . . . .

3. A: One hundred people have already lost their jobs.
   B: . . . .
   I think there's worse to come.

4. A: Our neighbours won half a million on the National Lottery last year, but six months later they separated and now they're divorced.
   B: . . . .

8 | Speaking

Can you think of any other examples where the four idiomatic expressions in Exercise 7 above could apply?

What I'd really like to do is marry a millionaire. • It all depends, really. • I'm happy doing what I'm doing. • Basically, I just wa[nt] to be happy. • I haven't got a clue. • I wish I knew. • Let's just go to Australia. • He knows what he wants and he knows ho[w] to get it. • I might try and learn another language. • Money's always a problem. • Have I got a future? • I really need a chang[e] • I'm sick of my job. • Just do it! • I just take things as they come. • If all else fails, then yes! • I'm looking all the time. • Th[e] minute I've finished this course, I'm going to change the world. • A safe job, a nice house, two or three kids. • I'm stuck in a r[ut] • Who cares? • Sometime in the not-too-distant future. • I'm too young to set[tle] down. • I'd like to do something like that. • I'm not ready to buy a house.

19 Your future

Listening

1 | Optimistic about the future?

Do you agree with these statements?

1. The world is a better place than it was twenty years ago.

2. You aren't even safe in your own home today.

3. Young people today have got a good chance of getting a well-paid job when they leave school.

4. There's no such thing as a safe job today.

5. Pollution is getting worse.

6. I feel much more confident than I used to.

7. The world is becoming a less tolerant place.

8. People are more aware of environmental issues than they used to be.

Complete this sentence by adding a pessimist and an optimist.

. . . . is someone who always thinks the glass is half-full, while . . . . always thinks it's half-empty.

Now mark the eight statements with an O or a P depending on whether you think they are optimistic or pessimistic.

2 | Speaking

Tell your partner how optimistic you feel about your own future, the future of your country, or the future of the world.

The young person in this picture is protesting against the cutting down of trees. Would you? Is there anything else you feel strongly enough about to protest against?

3 | While you listen

Rachel and Nick, two friends both in their last year at university, are chatting over coffee. Listen to them talking about what they see themselves doing in the future.

Cover the conversation. As you listen, try to complete these sentences.

1. Nick's thinking about . . . . , but it depends on . . . .

2. He'd like to . . . . , but he probably won't have . . . .

3. Rachel wants to . . . . and . . . .

4. If she . . . . , then she'll . . . . Otherwise, she'll probably go . . . .

Listen again and try to fill in the gaps in the conversation.

Now you're talking!

Rachel: So, have you had any more thoughts about what you're going to do next year, then?

Nick: Mm. I don't know, really. I mean, (1) .... that it might be a good idea to do that art course I was telling you about, but it all depends on my results.

Rachel: So what about France? (2) .... going to Paris a while back?

Nick: Oh, for that French course? Well, I would still like to do it, but I just don't know if I can afford it.

Rachel: Oh, I know what you mean. Money's always a problem, isn't it? I mean, (3) .... next year is to learn to drive and buy a car, but I'm not sure if I'll have the cash. (4) ...., I'm just so sick of having to get buses everywhere.

Nick: Dreadful, aren't they? You wait half an hour and then three come along at the same time. So, you're (5) .... just going to be staying around here, just trying to save up some money, then?

Rachel: Yes, I suppose so. It depends, really. I mean, if I can find a good job, then I'll stick around, but otherwise (6) .... eventually is going back to Glasgow.

Nick: Oh right, because you grew up there, didn't you?

Rachel: Yes, that's right, yes, so I suppose I do see myself ending up there eventually.

Nick: Yeah.

Rachel: So, (7) .... you do this art course, what do you see yourself doing after that, in the long term?

Nick: Oh, I don't know. No idea really. I haven't thought that far ahead. I'll just (8) .... and see what happens.

Rachel: Just listen to us, Nick! We just sound so boring! (9) .... go off somewhere together this summer, you know, maybe – I don't know – work abroad for six months?

Nick: What? You mean picking grapes in France? That kind of thing?

Rachel: Yeah, or, I don't know – working in a hotel in Spain, or –

Nick: Or going to Australia. If the Aussies can work over here, (10) .... go and get a job over there?

Rachel: Yeah, I'd love to do that. Where's the paper? What's the cheapest flight to Sydney?

Nick: Now you're talking!

4 | Speaking

Discuss these questions with a partner.

1. Are you the kind of person who could just suddenly go abroad for six months, on the spur of the moment? Have you ever done anything like that?
2. Have any of your friends ever gone off to work in another country? Where did they go?
3. Is it possible to plan too much for the future?

> **Real English: the Aussies**
> This is an affectionate term used by British people for Australians.
> New Zealanders are known as Kiwis while Australians call British people poms or pommies.

5 | Phrasal verbs with *up*

In the conversation, you met save up, end up and grew up. Complete the sentences below with the verbs in the box. Then go back and underline the phrasal verbs.

do	cheer	put	turned
beat	hung	come	bottling

1. This really strange thing happened last night. An old friend from school just .... up on my doorstep, totally out of the blue!
2. That was weird. Whoever it was on the phone just .... up as soon as they heard my voice!
3. Once we've saved up enough money, we're going to .... up our flat a bit.
4. A: Why don't I cook tonight, if you're not feeling up to it?
   B: Wow! That's the best idea you've .... up with all week!
5. I wish you'd .... up a bit! It's really starting to get me down, seeing you like that!
6. I got mugged last year, and when I wouldn't give them my watch, they .... me up really badly.
7. It's not healthy, you know, ... up all your negative emotions like this. It's much better to just get things off your chest.
8. If you're stuck for somewhere to stay, we could always .... you up on our sofa.

6 | Speaking

Discuss these questions with a partner.

1. Do you ever bottle things up?
2. How do you usually cheer yourself up?
3. Have you ever been beaten up?

Using grammar

1 | Starting with *what*

Rachel said 'What I'd really like to do next year is learn to drive'. What can be placed at the beginning of a sentence to give special emphasis to what follows. It means 'the thing that'.

What I really need to do is get away for a break.
What I'd really like to do is learn to drive.
What I was thinking of doing is going abroad.

Rewrite these sentences using the expressions with what above.

1. Your company is sending you to Japan, so you have to start learning the language.
What . . . .

2. You think it would be a great idea to buy a flat in the next couple of years.
What . . . .

3. You have no money and desperately need to start saving.
What . . . .

4. You think you would quite like to travel round India in the not-too-distant future.
What . . . .

5. You've always wanted to start a family as soon as you get married.
What . . . .

6. You've had an idea – maybe go abroad for Christmas this year rather than stay at home.
What . . . .

2 | Speaking

Complete these sentences in ways that are true for you.

1. What I really need to do before the end of the week is . . . .

2. What I'd really like to do this/next summer is . . . .
. . . .

3. What I was thinking of trying to do next year, if I get the chance, is . . . .

4. What I'd really like to be doing in a few years' time is . . . .

Now tell a partner about what you have thought of, giving more details if you can.

▶ For more information on how to use sentences starting with what, see G31.

Using vocabulary

1 | Plans for the future

Complete the sentences below with the words in the box. The sentences are all common answers to the question: 'What are your plans for the future?'

wait and see	perfectly happy
can't really	take things
change	see myself

a. I'm . . . . doing what I'm doing.

b. My plans . . . . fairly often.

c. I can't . . . . staying there for much longer.

d. I'll just have to . . . . what happens.

e. I just . . . . as they come.

f. I . . . . say yet. It all depends.

Now complete 1–6 using a–f above.

1. I'm a fairly laid-back kind of person. I mean, ... and only worry about things if and when they happen.

2. A: So, what are you going to do once you get back to Madrid?
B: Well, I might try and get a job as a chef, but yesterday I was thinking about maybe going back to college. Ask me again in a week! . . . . , you know.

3. A: So, how's it all going?
B: Well, to be honest, I'm really fed up at work. . . . .
A: It sounds to me like it's time to move on.

4. A: So, what are your plans for the future?
B: Well, right now, life's great. Maybe in a couple of years I might change my mind, but at the moment . . . .

5. A: So, are you still off to Kenya in the spring?
B: Well, I'm not 100% sure just now, because my dad's still very ill, so . . . .

6. A: So, how long are you going to be staying here for?
B: . . . . on my girlfriend. If things work out between us, we might think of getting married and settling down.

Do any of the expressions a–f apply to you in your present situation? For example:

I wouldn't say, 'I just take things as they come' now, but I might've done when I was eighteen or nineteen because I didn't have a job then, and I didn't really know what I wanted to do in the future.

2 | Collocations

Complete each of the sentences 1–4 in two different ways, using two different endings from the box below to make some common collocations about the future.

my own country	back to university
abroad	with my girlfriend
a new job	somewhere nicer to live
studying	where I grew up

1. I might try and find
   ..../................... .

2. I can see myself going
   ..../................... .

3. I'd really like to spend a bit more time
   ..../................... .

4. I really want to go back to
   ..../................... .

Now complete sentences 5–9 in the same way.

reading	south
a better laptop	my family
to buy a flat	for a DVD player
house	sport
the world	a new car

5. It'd be good to see a bit more of
   ..../................... .

6. I'm thinking of moving
   ..../................... .

7. I'd like to start doing a bit more
   ..../................... .

8. If I can, I'll probably save up
   ..../................... .

9. I think I'm going to buy
   ..../................... .

How many of the sentences above are true for you?

3 | Speaking

In the conversation on page 133, Rachel and Nick talked about going to Australia. If you had a year free, what would you do? Do any of these appeal to you?

1. building a primary school in Bangladesh
2. working for an aid agency in Ethiopia
3. going on an expedition to the North Pole
4. working with homeless people in Manchester
5. sailing round the world
6. writing a book

It's a perk of the job, isn't it? • A proper contract? • He's a real slave-driver. • So what do you do exactly? • I'm usually hom by four. • What's the pay like? • I'm a model in my spare time. • If you pay peanuts, you get monkeys. • What a nice uniform • Does it come with the job? • I've got that Monday morning feeling. • Anyone for coffee? • What's your boss like? • Coul we possibly discuss my salary sometime? • It's enough to live on. • Stress? You don't know the meaning of the word. • I've bee rushed off my feet all day. • Only two weeks' paternity leave? • We get a bonus at Christmas, which is always nice. • Th recession isn't helping. • I've got my boss breathing down m neck. • It must be great, being your own boss.

20 The world of work

Reading

1 What do you look for in a job?

Mark each of these ideas from 1 (not important) to 5 (very important), depending on how important they are for you when you're looking for a job.

- being able to work flexi-time
- getting holiday pay and sick pay
- earning a good salary
- doing a really interesting job
- knowing your job is secure
- not being stuck behind a desk all day
- doing something useful for society
- being able to work from home
- getting a company car
- getting maternity or paternity leave

Compare your answers with a partner. What else would you add to this list?

2 Before you read

Complete the sentences below with the words and expressions in the box.

full-time	lots of benefits	paid holiday
unfairly treated	sick pay	income tax
maternity leave	contract	

1. When my son was born, I took . . . . for three months and then went back to work part-time.
2. I can't go away much, because I only get three weeks' . . . . a year.
3. When I broke my leg, I managed to get two months' . . . .
4. . . . . starts at 20% and goes up to a maximum of 40%.
5. I appealed to a tribunal because I felt I'd been . . . .
6. I used to do only two days a week, but I work . . . . now.
7. I've been there six years now, but I've never been . . . . ber . . . .
. . . . ing about my job is that I get . . . . . – a company pension, private . . . rance and things like that.

3 While you read

A **casual worker** normally works for a company, but without a contract of employment. He or she is not permanently employed and in many countries has few rights. Read the article on page 139 about two casual workers who had a problem with their employer. When you have read it, answer these questions.

1. Why did Mrs Carmichael and Mrs Leese take their employers to court?
2. What was the judge's decision?
3. What are the implications of this decision for other casual workers?

We can work it out.

Getting a good job in Britain today is far from easy. More and more young people are going to university, so a degree has become the minimum qualification required, whereas once it was a magical door-opening piece of paper. If your CV does catch a potential employer's eye and you're lucky enough to get called in for an interview, you then encounter the next hurdle: you find yourself in a Catch-22 situation where you can't get a job unless you've got work experience and, of course, there's no way you can get any work experience until someone feels like giving you a job! If and when you do finally manage to land a job, you then realise that your troubles have only just begun.

The last twenty years have seen radical changes in employment laws, very few of which have benefited young workers in any way. Full-time contracts seem to have become a thing of the past, and instead you'll probably be offered a short-term casual contract – even if they're talking about employing you full-time! I've heard of people who've worked full-time for six or seven years and who are still being paid by the hour! One good thing that has changed recently, though, is that at least you're now entitled to the national minimum wage. Living on less than five pounds an hour isn't easy, but at least you can't be totally ripped off by your bosses anymore.

Because of all these changes, there's not much job security anymore. Companies have learned how to dress up mass redundancies in media-friendly language, calling huge job cuts 'down-sizing' or 'corporate restructuring'! If you do end up out of work, don't expect your union to be much help. The power of trade unions was cut dramatically in the 1980s after the endless industrial action of the 70s and today they've become a little bit toothless. However, as a recent landmark legal case has shown, it's not all doom and gloom, and there is still hope for the workers.

Last month two casual workers, who were never offered proper contracts of employment, won the right to the same benefits as full-time workers. A judge said that because Mrs Carmichael, 35, and Mrs Leese, 36, had signed letters accepting jobs at Blyth Power Station, they should have been treated the same as any other full-time employee of National Power. However, the two women had been denied holiday and sick pay and many other benefits normally given to full-time staff.

Despite taking income tax from their pay, making the women wear company uniforms, and giving them the use of company cars, National Power tried to insist that Mrs Carmichael and Mrs Leese never worked directly for the company. They were, therefore, refused a proper contract, and were not given any employment protection or benefits.

The judge's decision means that casual workers all over the country can now fight for the right to sick pay, holiday pay, maternity leave and other benefits. The judgement also means that casual workers can appeal against unfair dismissal by their employer if they are sacked without reason. A solicitor acting on behalf of the two women said it was a major breakthrough in employment law, which was likely to have a very positive effect on the working lives of thousands of men and women employed on a casual basis.

4 | Speaking

Discuss these questions with a partner.

1. Does the situation in Britain sound similar to the situation in your country? In what way? What's different?
2. Have you ever done any casual work? How were you treated? What was the money like?
3. Who's the worst employer you've ever worked for?
4. Have you heard of any companies which have a good/bad reputation for the way they treat their workers?

5 | Vocabulary work

Discuss these questions with a partner.

1. What is the difference between a full-time worker, a part-time worker and a casual worker?
2. What are the usual reasons people get sacked?
3. What's the difference between getting sacked and being made redundant?
4. What kind of things do you put in your CV?
5. What are the names of the biggest trade unions in your country? What do they do?

Using vocabulary

1 | *Work* or *job*?

Complete these sentences with work or job.

1. He's never done a day's .... in his life!
2. Are you still looking for a ...., then?
3. It's quite hard .... finding a flat in a big city like Milan.
4. It's a dirty ...., but someone's got to do it!
5. I know the money's not very good, but at least you're getting some good .... experience.
6. Oh, the kitchen looks lovely now. You've made a really good .... of it.
7. I'm sorry, but I can't let you use the phone to ring Australia. It's more than my ....'s worth!
8. I've been up to my eyes in .... all week!

2 | Speaking

Discuss these questions with a partner.

1. Do you know anyone who's never done a day's work in their life? How do they get by?
2. Can you think of three other things that are quite hard work?

Listening

1 | Before you listen

With a partner, decide what the people in the pictures on these pages do for a living.

Which of the jobs in the pictures would you most/least like to do? Why?

What do you think these jobs would involve? Could you or would you do any of them?

2 | While you listen

Now listen to three of the people in the pictures talking about their jobs. As you listen, try to decide what their job is. Then compare answers.

1. ....
2. ....
3. ....

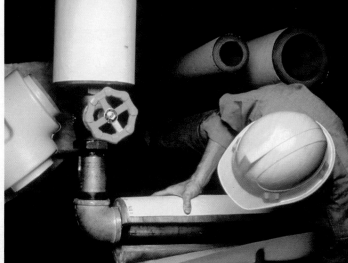

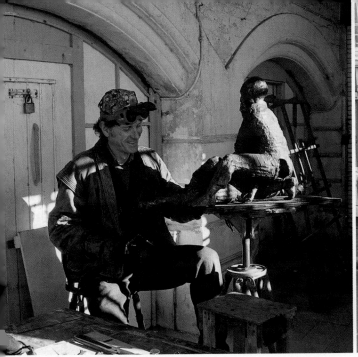

Using vocabulary

1 | How are things at work?

Match the common questions about work 1–5 with typical answers a–e.

1. How are things at work?

   a. • It's OK. It's enough to live on.
      • It's not very good – more like slave-labour!
      • Well, actually, I don't think it's any of your business!

2. So, what exactly does your job involve, then?

   b. • They're OK, the usual nine to five.
      • Awful. I don't usually get home until ten!
      • Great. I'm usually home by two or three.

3. Have you been doing it long?

   c. • Crazy! I've been rushed off my feet all week!
      • Oh, we've been pretty quiet, actually.
      • Oh, it's OK, the same as ever.

4. What are the hours like?

   d. • Well, I'm in charge of Accounts.
      • I do all the marketing.
      • I deal with all the complaints that we get.

5. What's the money like?

   e. • Yes, it's about ten years now, I suppose.
      • No, I've only just started, actually.
      • Yes, too long!

In your country is it acceptable to ask someone how much they earn?
Are you happy to talk about how much you earn?

2 | Role play

Imagine you are one of the people in the pictures on these pages. Spend two minutes thinking about how you would answer the questions in Exercise 1 above, using the typical answers if necessary. Your partner should then ask you the questions and try to guess which job you do.

3 | Boss jokes

Below are three joke answers to the question: 'So what's your boss like?' Discuss with your partner which one you find the funniest and why.

1. He's really flexible. He lets me come in any time I want before nine, and then lets me leave whenever I want after five!

2. He's so mean that if you're three minutes late for work, he fines you, and if you turn up five minutes early he actually starts charging you rent!

3. He's really hard on late-comers. Actually, one day one of his assistants turned up over an hour late, covered in blood, and as he staggered over to his desk, my boss went up to him and asked him where he'd been. The assistant apologised and said he'd fallen down three flights of stairs.
'What?' said my boss, 'that took you a whole hour, did it!'

Listen to the jokes. Mark the stresses and pauses. Then tell the jokes to each other in pairs with one student asking: 'So what's your boss like, then?'

4 | The ideal boss

Make answers to the question: 'What's your boss like?' by matching the beginnings 1–8 to the endings a–h.

1. Well, he's not exactly the most

2. He's awful, a real

3. Dreadful! All he ever does is

4. Oh, he's great, he's a really

5. Oh, she spends the whole time

6. Terrible, she's really

7. Oh, she's brilliant, really

8. He's always getting on to

a. • sit at his desk and give orders!
 • talk to the other guys about football.

b. • domineering.
 • bossy and dictatorial.

c. • on the phone to her boyfriend!
 • jetting off to Paris and Rome on business trips!

d. • easy-going and easy to talk to.
 • nice and friendly.

e. • me about things that aren't my fault.
 • everyone about spending too much money.

f. • approachable person I've ever met, but he's OK, I guess.
 • intelligent bloke I've ever worked for, but I guess he's OK.

g. • dictator!
 • slave-driver!

h. • nice guy.
 • good person to work for.

5 | Speaking

Discuss these questions with a partner.

1. Do any of the comments in Exercise 4 above remind
   ... boss or one you have known?

   ... er what kind of a boss you think you'd

   ... your class do you think would make
   ... hy?

4. Is it important for a boss to be friendly and approachable or is it OK if they're a bit distant from their staff?

5. Are there other qualities which are important?

6. What do you call the boss of a school? A department? A football team?

7. How many other words can you think of with a similar meaning to 'boss'? For example: head, employer, manager, supervisor, superior, etc. Which do you prefer?

Using grammar

1 | Future continuous

Notice the highlighted words in these sentences.

I'll be meeting my boss next week, so I'll talk to her about my chances of promotion then.

The twins will be starting school this autumn, so I'll have a lot more free time.

Both situations are about the future ('ll and will). In both cases the verb is extended in time (meeting and starting). It is common for the future continuous form to be followed by a clause that begins with so.

Make sentences by matching the beginnings 1–6 to the endings a–f.

1. I'll be doing some work in your area tomorrow,
2. I'll be going back to Japan in the autumn,
3. I'll be passing your front door,
4. I'll be doing a computer course in April,
5. I'll be writing my MA thesis all summer,
6. I'll be going down to my dad's next Saturday,

a. so it's no trouble giving you a lift.
b. so then I'll be an expert on the Internet.
c. so don't try and call me until Sunday night.
d. so I'll be working in the library a lot.
e. so I'll pop in and say hello if I get a chance.
f. so I'll try and get you a cheap Walkman, shall I?

2 | Grammar in context

Make short dialogues by adding sentences from Exercise 1 above.

1. A: Well, I really like this Sony, but it's just too expensive really.
   B: Well, look, ...
   A: Oh, that'd be great if you could. I'd pay you for it, of course.

2. A: So, John, when are we going to see you next, then?
   B: Well, ...
   A: Oh great. Try and make it around twelve or so and then maybe we could have lunch.

3. A: So, are you looking forward to the holidays, then?
   B: Well, no actually. . . . .
   A: Oh well, I'll be thinking of you while I'm lying on the beach.

4. A: So, are you still having problems getting online?
   B: Well, actually, things are looking up.
   . . . .

5. A: I'll give you a call over the weekend about the following week.
   B: Yeah, that's OK, but . . . .
   A: Sure. I probably won't know what I'm doing until then anyway.

6. A: Thanks to this rail strike, I don't know how I'll get home.
   B: You're in luck. I drove today.
   . . . .

3 | Career plans

Walk around the class and chat to some other students about the kind of work you see yourself doing in the future, where you see your career going in the short term, any long-term career plans you've got, and so on. Try to use as much of the new language from this unit as you possibly can. For example:

If we meet in ten years' time, if everything goes according to plan, I'll have my own company. I'll be driving a top-of-the-range Mercedes. I'll be living in a huge house with my own private plane. I'll own an island somewhere hot.

> For more information on how to use the future continuous, see G32.

Review: Units 17–20

1 Tenses

Choose the correct form.

1. They still haven't been fixing / haven't fixed our TV yet.
2. The restaurant was redecorated / was being redecorated, so we had to find somewhere else.
3. Bills have to pay / have to be paid within a month, or else they cut your electricity off.
4. I wish they'll / they'd do something about all the stray dogs in the park.
5. I see / I'll be seeing Bill later, so I'll ask him if he got your e-mail.
6. I thought the film will be / was going to be great, but it wasn't as good as the book.
7. A new stadium is being built / is going to be built sometime in the next four or five years.
8. If everything goes / went according to plan, we should be able to move by the end of the month.
9. That bridge should've been widened / should've been being widened years ago.
10. I'll be back / I'm back at university quite soon, touch wood!

2 Multiple choice

Choose the correct alternative.

1. What would be really great is if my parents … !
   a. will buy me a car   b. bought me a car
2. I've applied for a job in Stockholm, but … , I might try Denmark.
   a. if that falls through
   b. if nothing goes wrong
3. If it doesn't stop raining, I'm going to end up … !
   a. going mad   b. to go mad
4. … is get other people to do her job for her!
   a. All Kate ever does   b. All Kate is ever doing
5. I'd like to end up with my own business, but … , I'll probably have to work in the family shop.
   a. basically   b. hopefully   c. realistically
6. What I'd really like … the guitar.
   a. to do this year is learn to play
   b. doing this year is learning to play
7. … to wait outside till he was ready.
   a. ?   b. He said me
   … re nine. … .
   … ng dinner   b. We'll have dinner

… swers with a partner and discuss

3 Second conditionals

Complete these sentences by putting the verbs in brackets into the correct form.

1. A: Have you heard? They're going to knock the cinema down and turn it into a car park.
   B: Really? It . . . . (be) much better if they just . . . . (leave) it as it is.
2. A: They're going to charge people to drive into the city centre, aren't they?
   B: Yeah, but if you ask me, it . . . . (be) far better if they just . . . . (ban) cars altogether and . . . . (pedestrianise) the whole area.
3. A: There's so much litter everywhere.
   B: I know. What . . . . (be) really great is if they . . . . (collect) it daily instead of weekly.
4. A: This bus is hardly moving! The traffic's awful.
   B: I know! I think it . . . . (be) a really good idea if they . . . . (bring) back the trams.
5. I think it . . . . (be) a really good idea if they . . . . (not charge) people to get into museums. You . . . . (get) a lot more people going.
6. A: They're going to open another coffee shop there.
   B: Really? It . . . . (be) far more useful if we . . . . (have) a decent supermarket instead.

4 Speaking

Make a list of things that annoy you about your town/city. Tell your partner your ideas and suggest alternatives using the second conditional structures above.

5 Conversation

Put the jumbled conversation into the correct order.

a. So, how are things at work? `1`
b. I think of nothing else, actually! I've got an appointment with Personnel tomorrow, so that might make a difference.
c. Dreadful, to be honest! I feel as if I'm going to end up having a nervous breakdown!
d. How will that help?
e. Well, I'll have the chance to talk about the problems in my department. They might listen. On the other hand, they might not!
f. Is it as bad as that? Have you had any more thoughts about leaving them?

6 Look back and check: More expressions with *bother*

Look back at 'More expressions with *bother*' on page 131. Tick any of the expressions you can remember. Ask your partner about anything you have forgotten.

With a partner, write eight new sentences that would produce the responses a–h. Compare what you have written with another pair. Did you have any similar ideas?

Now cover Exercise 6 on page 131. Your partner will read out your eight new sentences. Can you remember all the responses?

7 Expressions

Complete the short dialogues below with the expressions in the box. All the expressions are from units 17–20.

> just doing what I'm doing
>
> don't let it get you down
>
> wait and see
>
> if everything goes according to plan
>
> I know what you mean

1. A: I'm getting tired of Mr Owens complaining about our department all the time.
   B: Look, ... There's nothing you can do about it. Forget him!

2. A: I just can't believe that all the banks here shut at four! How can I get to one if I'm working!
   B: Yes, ... It'd be far better if they were open in the evening.

3. A: So, what exciting plans have you got?
   B: Nothing, really. To be honest, I'm quite happy . . . . for the time being.

4. A: So, you're going to be in Nepal next year, then, James?
   B: Yes, ... !

5. A: So, did you get that job you applied for?
   B: I haven't heard yet. I'll just have to . . . .

Can you think of three other situations when you might say: 'Don't let it get you down' to someone?

Can you think of three other questions you could answer by saying: 'I'll just have to wait and see'?

8 Collocations

Match the verbs 1–10 to the best collocations a–j.

1.	deny	a.	a flat nearer where I work
2.	see	b.	house
3.	move	c.	with all the complaints
4.	buy	d.	a problem
5.	take	e.	about her problems all the time
6.	deal	f.	a bit more of my wife and kids
7.	tackle	g.	things as they come
8.	go on	h.	a casual worker his holiday pay
9.	do	i.	the brakes
10.	slam on	j.	a U-turn

Now match the verbs 11–18 to the best collocations k–r.

11.	get	k.	in the wash
12.	mess up	l.	my flat
13.	shrink	m.	myself living abroad
14.	do up	n.	made redundant
15.	bottle up	o.	the issue
16.	see	p.	going to the dentist's
17.	dread	q.	my exam
18.	avoid	r.	your feelings

Now discuss these questions with a partner.

19. Have you ever messed up any exams? What happened?
20. Do you know anyone who really bottles up their feelings?
21. Do you know anyone who's always going on about how awful their life is?

9 Real English

Match the questions 1–6 to the responses a–f.

1. So, when will you be able to go back to work? ☐
2. Have you seen Emma's new hairdo? ☐
3. I wish he'd stop coughing! It's really bugging me. ☐
4. Have you tried talking about working in Wales with your girlfriend? ☐
5. I'm sorry to bore you with my problems. ☐
6. So, what happened next? Did they fine you? ☐

a. Really? Things like that don't really bother me.
b. That's OK. It's good to get these things off your chest, isn't it.
c. Yeah, five hundred pounds – and six penalty points on my licence as well!
d. No, not yet, but I heard she's had it bleached blonde.
e. In a week or two, I think – touch wood!
f. Of course I have. I mean, that was the first thing I actually did. But she just won't talk about it. Whenever I mention it, she changes the subject!

10 | Idioms

Make sentences with idioms by matching the beginnings 1–10 to the endings a–j.

1. That bar has gone
2. He let the cat
3. I'm the black sheep
4. It's a vicious
5. I've been rushed
6. It's good to get things
7. ... and to top
8. I changed
9. It's a bit of a mixed
10. That's just the tip

a. of the family.
b. off my feet all week!
c. off your chest.
d. my mind.
e. out of the bag!
f. blessing.
g. to the dogs.
h. the whole thing off ...
i. of the iceberg.
j. circle.

11 | What can you remember?

With a partner, note down as much as you can remember about the two texts you read in units 18 and 20.

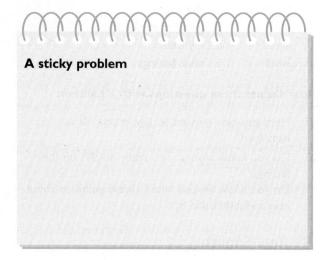

A sticky problem

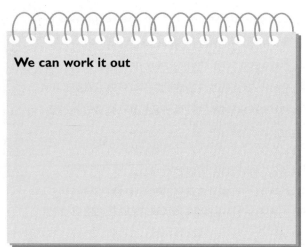

We can work it out

Now compare what you remember with another pair. Who remembers more?

Which text did you enjoy more? Why?

12 | Vocabulary quiz

Answer these questions with a partner. Then compare your answers with another pair. Who got most answers right?

1. If I send you on a wild goose chase, what do you come back with?
2. Apart from people, what else might need a facelift?
3. Are shanty towns nice places to live or not?
4. What is the difference between working flexi-time, full-time and part-time?
5. If you find your boss domineering, does it mean you get on with him/her or not?
6. Is an optimist afraid of the future?
7. Is it only bosses who can be bossy?
8. When would a woman get maternity leave?
9. If women get maternity leave, what do men get?
10. If you find your boss approachable, does it mean you get on with him/her or not?
11. Name one other thing apart from water that an office can be flooded with.
12. If someone is in charge of all the complaints, do they make complaints or deal with them?
13. What is the capital of the country you're studying in? And what's the capital of Australia? Bulgaria? Chile? South Africa?
14. Give an example of a vicious circle.
15. Give one reason why you might appeal to a tribunal.
16. Where might you pull over? Why?
17. If you do most of the hard work on a job, does this mean you have done the rat work, the dog work, or the donkey work?
18. If I tell you that they've banned all on-street parking, who are 'they'?
19. Can you think of two things you sometimes just have to put up with?
20. What's the difference between the inner city and the city centre?

Learner advice: The authors speak!

Discuss these questions with a partner.

1. Are you happy with your English at the moment? Why/why not?
2. How much better do you think you can get?
3. How are you going to improve your English after this course?

Now read this text and underline anything you strongly agree or disagree with.

Students often ask me how they can improve their English, and sometimes I really don't know the answer. I've taught students who seem to remain permanently at intermediate level. They keep coming to class, they buy coursebooks and dictionaries and grammar books, but never really improve. Sometimes they're the kind of student we've already talked about. They are perhaps spending time doing the wrong things. However, I've also noticed that a lot of them work – they're doctors, teachers, chefs – they have families or are doing degrees; they have social lives. Basically, they're busy adults! They also actually speak quite well. Upper-intermediate is a good level. Just think of the things you have talked about in this book! So my first piece of advice would be to recognise the limitations on your time, relax and enjoy being a good speaker of English. Secondly, set yourself reasonable goals which you can meet in the short term – learn these ten expressions by next week – rather than speak like a native by next year. Thirdly, think about *why* you're doing things and if it's good for your English. So if you read an English newspaper because you are interested in British news and you enjoy it, fine. However, if you're reading it to learn new words which will help you speak, then it's probably not a good idea. That's because newspapers are full of specific expressions and cultural references which aren't often spoken. You'd be better off reading a book written for language learners or doing vocabulary exercises from something like the 'Keywords for Fluency' series or 'English Vocabulary Organiser'.

However, even then, just doing exercises isn't going to improve your English that much. There must come a point when you put your learning into practice. Fluent speakers spend time with other fluent speakers – through work or study or friendship. It's easier said than done, I know, but why not try one of these ways of doing it?

- Find native speakers at your language school or local university who'll do a language exchange.
- Join an English-speaking club. Many cities have them. If there's a British Council in your town, they may have information.
- Start your own club with the people from your school. Go out for a meal and only talk in English.
- Chat through the Internet. There are some useful links on the 'Innovations' website.

In any of these situations, you could use the topics in this book as a starting point for conversations. Good luck!

Compare what you've underlined with a partner. Are there any other ways of improving your English in the future that you can think of?

Tapescript

Unit 1

Who's who? (page 8)

Kirsty

Kirsty? She's really interesting. She's quite sporty and musical as well. She plays the piano a lot. She's actually quite good. She's in her twenties and has got lovely shoulder-length blonde hair.

Nick

You'd like Nick. He's really nice. He's very easy-going. He's got a great sense of humour. He's only thirty-five. He's got really short hair – shaved, I think. He's very interested in photography and arty things.

Jenny

Jenny is in her forties. She's a really energetic sort of person – always doing things. She's got a very warm personality and enjoys helping other people. She has short, dark hair and dark eyes.

Matt

Matt is still at university. He's really friendly and is one of the most popular people I know. He's very hard-working and serious, but he's also a lot of fun. He's got fair hair and he wears glasses.

The Brother from Hell! (page 10)

Melanie: I can't remember. Do you take milk?
Simon: Please, but no sugar. Thanks. It's weird, you know, but I've been to your house three times now, and I still haven't met your parents.
Melanie: Yes, they're out a lot. My dad works for the BBC and my mum's a, she does sort of temping work for a company. You know, like an advertising agency. They're both really busy.
Simon: Oh, they sound really interesting.
Melanie: Do you think so? I find my dad a bit dull, to be honest. He works late every day, even works some weekends, doesn't read, doesn't go out. I mean, don't get me wrong, he's quite nice, but I don't know, I just don't have anything to say to him. I think the thing is, we just don't spend enough time together.
Simon: How old is he, then?
Melanie: About fifty-five, I think. I can never really remember.
Simon: Oh, yeah.
Melanie: But my mum's lovely. She's really nice, a bit too nice though, sometimes, always trying to look after me. She worries about me leaving home. She's a bit over-protective, if you know what I mean. I'm an only child, so …
Simon: Oh, I didn't know that.
Melanie: What? You mean you can't tell!

Simon: I don't know. I've never thought about it, I suppose.
Melanie: So, what about you? Have you got any brothers or sisters yourself?
Simon: Yes, I've got one of each, actually.
Melanie: Oh right. Older or younger?
Simon: My sister's two or three years younger than me, but my brother's quite a lot older. He's about forty now.
Melanie: Do you get on with them all right? You haven't really talked about them very much.
Simon: Well, my brother, not that well, actually. He's different from me, a bit old-fashioned, a bit traditional. Well, actually, he's a bit, how can I put it, right-wing. You know – things aren't what they used to be, more police, death penalty – that kind of thing. He's a bit of a fool, actually.
Melanie: Oh, well, it takes all sorts, I suppose.
Simon: But my sister, she's great. We get on really well. We've got the same kind of sense of humour.
Melanie: Just a pity about the brother from hell, eh?
Simon: Yes. Oh, but he's not that bad. We get on all right, as long as you steer clear of certain topics. Anyway, you were telling me about your parents.
Melanie: Oh, there's not much to tell, actually.

Unit 2

Giving bad news (page 19)

1. A: Can you give me a lift home?
   B: I'm sorry, I'm afraid I can't. I lost my licence last week – had a bit too much to drink and got stopped by the police!

2. A: Do you think I could get that camera back off you sometime soon?
   B: I don't know how to put this, but I think I lost it last night while I was out. I'm really sorry, but I've searched everywhere and I can't find it. I'll get you another one. I'm extremely sorry.

3. A: Have you heard from Jan recently?
   B: Well, actually, I haven't – not for about six months – we had a bit of an argument last year.

4. A: Is your grandfather any better?
   B: I'm afraid not. We're very worried about him. But then, he is ninety.

5. A: So, has Peter had his results yet?
   B: Well, yes, I'm afraid he has. He didn't pass – so he's got to re-sit part of his exams in July.

6. A: Are you feeling all right, Steve?
   B: Well, actually, no. I've just had some very bad news.

7. A: Hello, how are you?
    B: Oh, fine thanks. Well, actually, I think I'm getting the flu, so I'd stay away if I were you.

8. A: I thought you had a dog.
    B: We did. But unfortunately, it ran out into the street and was run over. I'm afraid we had to have it put down.

Unit 3

Not as often as I used to (page 21)

Interview with June, the bus driver.

1. A: How often do you work in the evenings?
    B: Not all that often, actually, just when I have to. Some people like the extra money, but I prefer to be at home with my kids.

2. A: How often do you get up early on Saturdays?
    B: Oh, all the time! My boys play football every Saturday morning, so I've got to be up by eight.

3. A: How often do you see your parents?
    B: Well, they live in Wales, so, not as often as I'd like to. I suppose I see mum and dad two or three times a year.

4. A: How often do you have your hair done?
    B: Oh, about every fortnight. It depends really. If I'm going out somewhere, I might have it done specially.

5. A: How often do you see your best friend?
    B: Whenever I can. She lives quite near me, but she's a nurse, so she's got to work at weekends quite a lot.

6. A: How often do you go away for the weekend?
    B: Oh, only a couple of times a year. It's difficult when you've got children.

7. A: How often do you go to the cinema?
    B: Oh, hardly ever. I usually wait till films come out on video and then get them for an evening.

8. A: How often do you go clubbing?
    B: Not as often as I used to. Before I got married, I used to go out every weekend.

So what shall we do tonight? (page 22)

Dan: So what do you feel like doing tonight? Any ideas?
Helena: Well, I'd quite like to see a film, or, I don't know, see if there's any good bands around, if you're into bands.
Dan: Yes, that's an idea. What kind of music do you like, then?
Helena: Oh, all sorts, really, you know, a lot of pop and I quite like blues and jazz and things like that.
Dan: Oh, really? I'm more into dance music myself, so maybe …

Helena: Well, if you'd rather, we could always go and see a film. I like really scary things.
Dan: What? You mean like *Halloween?*
Helena: Yes, that kind of thing, and I also quite like action movies, you know, car chases, guns, bombs, anything that's fast and exciting.
Dan: Oh, right. To be honest with you, I'm not really that keen on violent films.
Helena: You're kidding! And I thought this was going to be the perfect relationship!
Dan: So did I! But it doesn't sound like we've got all that much in common, really, does it?
Helena: Oh come on, there must be something we can do!
Dan: Let me think. Well, I suppose we could always go clubbing.
Helena: What? Somewhere like Paradox?
Dan: Is that the new place that's just opened?
Helena: Yes, just last week. Right, so how about going clubbing, then?
Dan: OK. Why not? Do you go much yourself?
Helena: No, not all that often, actually. A couple of times a year, I guess.
Dan: Oh, me too now, but I used to go a lot more when I was younger – almost every weekend. The thing was, though, it just got to me after a while, staying out dancing all night and then having to go to work first thing in the morning. I'm getting a bit too old for it now.
Helena: Oh, well, that's that off the menu, then! So, what shall we do then?
Dan: I don't know. Couldn't we just get a video, and a curry, and have a nice quiet evening in in front of the telly?
Helena: Oh, you've got to be joking! We're not in our graves yet. I mean, that's the kind of thing my parents are probably doing right now! Look, it's not what I'd normally do on a Monday night, but let's give clubbing a go! It might be a laugh.

Not really keen (page 23)

1. A: I love nearly all winter sports.
    B: Really? I'm not really very keen on them, myself. I once broke my leg skiing and it put me off – for life!

2. A: Going out with a crowd of friends and having fun, that's what I really like doing.
    B: Do you? It's not really my kind of thing, I'm afraid. I prefer to go out with just one or maybe two people. I hate crowds.

3. A: I'm really interested in politics.
    B: Oh, it's not really my kind of thing, I'm afraid. I don't really understand what makes all the parties different. They all seem the same to me!

4. A: I'm really into older music, you know, before 1967.
    B: Are you? I'm not really that keen on anything before 1980.

5. A: My favourite kind of things are comics and cartoons.
   B: I don't really like things like that myself. I don't see the point of them. I prefer a good novel – the longer the better!
6. A: I'm really into roller-blading. It's a bit like roller-skating.
   B: Are you? It's not really my kind of thing. I'm always worried I might get hurt.

Unit 5

Who did what? (page 36)

Speaker 1: It was total chaos. We had all our things lying around all over the place, making it impossible to get in or out of the house. It took forever to get everything all boxed up and into the van. We had to make five trips just to shift everything – and then there was the unpacking! What a nightmare!

Speaker 2: It was a real weight off my shoulders. Things had been bad for a while and I'd just got to the point where I just couldn't stand it any more. Every day there was hell, but then once I'd handed in my notice, I felt free again, and the future suddenly looked a lot brighter.

Speaker 3: I had my last one and stubbed it out, and then I felt really pleased with myself, but a couple of hours later the craving really started and I found myself absolutely dying for one. I was so tempted during the lunchbreak, but I managed to get through the whole day without one, and after that it was plain sailing.

Forty a day! (page 40)

Phil: Just time for a quick smoke. Oh sorry, do you want one?
Jason: No, thanks. I gave up years ago.
Phil: Good for you! I've given up even trying to give up!
Jason: Yeah, it's a nightmare, isn't it?
Phil: Tell me about it! I don't know how you managed it.
Jason: Well, it's funny, but it was my job that did it. I mean, I'd been smoking for years, and you know it's destroying your lungs, don't you, and I knew I wouldn't be able to become a fireman if I didn't give up.
Phil: So, what's becoming a fireman got to do with it? Is it the fire risk or something?
Jason: No, it's just that I knew I'd have to pass a physical to get in, and I wouldn't be able to do that if I was smoking forty a day.
Phil: Forty a day! Just as well you gave up! So, how come you decided to become a fireman anyway?
Jason: Mm, I'd have to think about that. I suppose it all goes back to when I got out of college. I wanted to do something exciting and different, you know, and a friend of my dad's was in the local fire brigade.

Phil: Oh, right. So, he helped you, did he?
Jason: Yes, he helped me get the job. I mean, I knew I didn't want to spend my life sitting in an office pushing bits of paper round a desk or stuck in front of a computer screen!
Phil: Yeah, I know exactly what you mean. I'm half-blind already! So, why did you decide to move to London, then? Was it for work or because of a relationship or what?
Jason: Well, it was mainly work, but also because I was just really fed up with where I was living at the time.
Phil: It was down in Crawley, wasn't it? It's pretty quiet down there, isn't it?
Jason: Quiet? Yeah, it's dead. There's absolutely nothing to do there.
Phil: So, was it the right decision, then?
Jason: What? Becoming a fireman?
Phil: No, no, moving to London, I mean.
Jason: Oh yeah, definitely. I love it. I don't think I could live anywhere else now.
Phil: No, it's the same for me. It gets you after a while, doesn't it? It's like a drug.

Jokes (page 41)

1. A: How come you drive with your brakes on?
   B: I want to be ready in case there's an accident!
2. A: How come you were born in New Zealand?
   B: I wanted to be near my mum!
3. A: I wish I'd brought the piano with me.
   B: How come?
   A: Because I left the plane tickets on it!
4. A: When I was a kid, I ran away from home. It took them six months to find me.
   B: Six months! How come it took them so long?
   A: They didn't look!

Unit 6

Flying joke (page 44)

Alfred had never flown before and was extremely nervous. He was flying across the Atlantic to visit his sister, who had emigrated to Canada. When he got on the plane he found he was sitting in a window seat. After a few minutes, the person next to him arrived – an enormously fat American. Not long after the plane took off, the American fell asleep and began to snore loudly. It was obvious to Alfred there was no way he could get out, even to get to the toilet, without waking the man up.

After the in-flight meal had been served, the plane entered an area of severe turbulence. The American continued to snore. Alfred, however, started to feel sick. He was desperate to get to the toilet. Finally, he was sick – all over the man's trousers. The American didn't wake up, but he just continued to snore. Alfred didn't know what to do.

As the plane touched down, the American finally woke up and saw his trousers. Alfred turned to him and said, 'Are you feeling better now?'

Strong adjectives (page 45)

1. A: It must've been really hot in Greece.
   B: Hot? It was boiling! That's why we made sure the hotel had air-conditioning.

2. A: Oh, you're from São Paulo originally, are you? It's a pretty big city, right?
   B: Big? It's enormous! That's why I moved to a small town out in the country.

3. A: How's your flat? It must be a bit cold with all this snow we're having.
   B: Cold? It's freezing! That's why I've decided to have central heating put in.

4. A: It's pretty quiet down in Devon, isn't it?
   B: Quiet? It's dead! That's why I decided to move to the city!

5. A: You must've been pretty surprised when you read the report in the papers.
   B: Surprised? I was shocked! That's why I contacted my solicitor straightaway.

6. A: It's a bit small in here, isn't it?
   B: Small? It's tiny! You can hardly swing a cat in here!

7. A: So, is he good-looking, then, your new boyfriend?
   B: Good-looking? He's gorgeous! You'll die when you see him!

8. A: It must've been a bit scary, going so high up like that.
   B: Scary? It was terrifying! There's no way you'll catch me doing that again!

Unit 7

Planning expressions (page 48)

Gavin: Well, tonight I guess I'll probably just stay in and have a quiet night in front of the telly. I'm a bit too tired to do anything really. Then on Saturday morning, I'm going to try to get up really early and go off and play football with some mates of mine in the park, which should be fun. Then Saturday afternoon, unfortunately, I've got to do some things around the house, because the place is a tip at the moment. Then, Saturday night, I've got a big night because a friend's having a party at her place and Karen's going to be there. And Sunday morning I imagine I'll need to have a lie-in just to recover, really, and then in the afternoon, I've got a friend coming over. And then, finally, Sunday night, I guess I'll probably just stay in and have an early night.

Thank goodness it's Friday! (page 50)

Steve: Thank goodness it's Friday! This week's been dragging on forever.
Ken: Tell me about it! So, what are you up to this weekend?
Steve: Oh, nothing special, really. This evening, I'm just going out for dinner with my parents.
Ken: Oh, that should be nice.

Steve: Yes, we're going to this little French place near where I live. The food's great there, and then tomorrow I've got to get up really early – at least for me! – and do some cooking, because I've got some people coming over in the afternoon. And I'll have to give the place a really good clean as well. And, I'm not sure, but I think we'll probably be going out after that – to see a film or something. We haven't really planned anything. What about yourself?
Ken: Well, tonight I'm supposed to be going out with some people from my old job, but I don't really feel like it any more. I'm feeling really tired.
Steve: So, you're just going to stay in, then?
Ken: Yes, because tomorrow night I've got a big night. I'm going to my friends Pete and Rachel's party. It's on a boat.
Steve: Oh, that sounds great. Whereabouts?
Ken: Down by the river. You know, in the docks.
Steve: Oh yes, I know where you mean. I went to a party there myself a while ago.
Ken: Right. Is it OK down there?
Steve: Yes, it's great, but it's not all that big. There's not that much room on the boat.
Ken: Mm, sounds cosy!
Steve: Oh, yes, you can get really close to people! Lots of sweaty bodies!
Ken: I don't think it's going to be that sort of party!
Steve: Well, you never know. If you're lucky, it might become one! No, I'm only joking, it's actually a great place for a party.
Ken: Good. I'm really looking forward to it. But then on Sunday, unfortunately, I've got to do some things for work.
Steve: No rest for the wicked! Well, listen, I might give you a ring on Sunday, then, just to hear all about your quiet night out down on the river!

Unit 9

Lifestyle (page 64)

1. I hate going there, but I'd run out of things to wear and, to be honest, some of my clothes were a bit – well, you know, so I thought I'd better have some clean shirts before work on Monday.

2. It's not something I normally do but I just felt like a bit of fresh air and it was a nice summer's evening and quite a few shops were open so, yes, it was really nice.

3. Not much really. I was quite tired when I got in from work, so I just got myself something to eat and then wrote a couple of letters, read a bit, watched a bit of TV and before I knew it, it was nearly midnight.

4. Sorry I couldn't ring you last night, but Wednesdays are my evenings for Art History. It's something I've always been interested in, so I thought I'd try this ten-week course that the university's running this autumn.

The Worst Disco in Town! (page 66)

Lucy: Hey, Rose, there's a letter for you.

Rose: Thanks. You must've got in late last night. I didn't even hear you come in – and I went to bed after one.

Lucy: I did, actually, yes. I went and met some old friends from college that I hadn't seen for ages.

Rose: Oh, did you? That must've been nice.

Lucy: Yes, we had a drink and a chat and caught up with all the gossip. You know what it's like.

Rose: Uh-huh.

Lucy: Then we had something to eat and then another drink and then we ended up going on to this awful disco in town.

Rose: Oh, did you? Which one? Not Stardust. No, surely not Stardust?

Lucy: I'm afraid it was, actually – and it was really terrible, just full of kids and the music was so loud I could hardly hear myself think. It was like being back at school all over again. Kids of fourteen acting as if they were eighteen!

Rose: I could've told you that!

Lucy: This boy came up to me – you know, bottle of beer in his hand, acting all macho, and asked me to dance! I bet he hadn't even started shaving!

Rose: And did you?

Lucy: What? Dance with him? Of course I did! Then I told him I was thirty-five!

Rose: You're so cruel.

Lucy: Well, I just figured it was better he found out sooner rather than later that I was old enough to be his mum!

Rose: I thought you were supposed to be there talking to old friends.

Lucy: I was, but there was so much noise, you couldn't really have a proper conversation. And then to top it all, I missed the last train home and had to get a cab and didn't get in until three!

Rose: Didn't you? You must be feeling exhausted this morning, then.

Lucy: Yeah, I could do with another hour or two in bed, that's for sure. Anyway, what about you? How was your night?

Rose: Oh, it was OK. I just did a bit of shopping on my way home, cooked myself some ramen noodles.

Lucy: Cooked yourself some what?

Rose: Ramen noodles, you know, just Japanese noodles.

Lucy: Oh, OK.

Rose: They're really quick and easy, and then I just did a bit of tidying-up, you know, nothing amazing or anything, read for a bit, watched a bit of telly – some film – you know the kind of thing that's on late on Channel 4. Actually, I was so tired, I fell asleep in the middle of it!

Lucy: Oh, don't! You're making me feel even more exhausted!

Linking ideas (page 69)

1. It was so cold, my hands felt like they were going to fall off.

2. I was so exhausted, I just went straight to bed as soon as I got in.

3. I was so hungry, I could've carried on eating all night!

4. It was so hot, I could hardly breathe.

5. His conversation was so dull, I could hardly stop myself from yawning.

6. I was so angry, I could've killed him!

7. I was so worried, I rang the police.

8. The film was so bad, I walked out halfway through.

Unit 11

Hair today, gone tomorrow! (page 76)

Cathy: So, we've got to take this one and then change at Cannon Street, right?

Diane: Yes, that's it. Hey, did I tell you about what happened with me and my dad on the underground last year?

Cathy: No, go on, what?

Diane: Well, about a year and a half ago, I decided to get all my hair cut off, right? I always used to have really, really long hair – ever since I was about fourteen or fifteen, you know – way down past my shoulders – parted in the middle like curtains. So, anyway, about a week after I had it all cut off, you know – really short – and I looked quite different.

Cathy: Yeah, I bet.

Diane: So, anyway, I was going home on the tube, and I was half asleep because it was five or six o'clock and I was just standing there, minding my own business – and little did I know that my dad was actually coming back from a business trip abroad, passing through London on the underground to get his train back to Durham. And guess what? He got into the same carriage as me! The doors closed behind him. So there I am, standing there face-to-face with my own father! I don't recognise him at first, but then I think, 'Ah, that's my dad,' and, of course, he's obviously only seen me with really long hair for the last ten years, and so I'm standing there, staring at him and he keeps on glancing at me nervously, thinking, 'Who's this lunatic staring at me?' and I'm thinking – you know, it's the strangest feeling not being recognised by your own dad – so I just stood there thinking, 'Well, shall I just get off at the next stop without telling him, or shall I risk giving him a nervous breakdown and a heart attack by saying, 'Hello dad'? But, anyway, eventually I went, 'Hello dad' and he went, 'Diane!' and then said how he was getting really worried because he thought I was a pick-pocket or a drug addict or something who'd been getting ready to pinch his wallet or something – and, um, yeah, that was a pretty strange and funny thing.

Cathy: Yeah, really strange.

Story-telling expressions (page 78)

A: Did I tell you about what happened to me in France last year?

B: No, I don't think you did. Go on.

A: Well, I was on holiday with my parents in this little village near the sea, and we ran out of money.

B: Really? That's awful.

A: Yes, so we went into town to find a cash machine – which we did, no trouble. Anyway, when we put the card in the machine, it just started spitting out loads and loads of money.

B: You're joking! So did you keep it?

A: Of course we did! Wouldn't you?

Unit 13

Long time, no see! (page 93)

Sharon: Barry! Hi, how are you? I haven't seen you for ages.

Barry: Hello, Sharon. Long time, no see.

Sharon: I know. So how're you doing?

Barry: I'm all right, thanks. And you?

Sharon: Yeah, not too bad. So, what've you been up to since I last saw you?

Barry: Not a lot – working mostly – I've been working really long hours this week, getting really fed up with it, you know.

Sharon: Really?

Barry: Yeah, but I went down to Kent last weekend, for my grandma's birthday party.

Sharon: Oh, how old was she?

Barry: Eighty-five. It was really great. We went for this lovely meal and then we went for a walk along the beach. It was good to get out of the city.

Sharon: I bet. I keep meaning to have a weekend away myself.

Barry: I know. You get to the point where you really need it, don't you? If you don't get out of London from time to time, it starts driving you crazy, you know. Anyway, what about you? What've you been up to?

Sharon: Well, on Sunday morning I went and saw that exhibition at the Royal Academy.

Barry: Oh yes, the one there's been all that fuss about – dead sheep and pictures of toilet rolls and things.

Sharon: Yeah, my friend Angela – she's at art school – she kept nagging me to go and see it, so I went.

Barry: And what did you think of it? Was it any good?

Sharon: Oh, I actually thought it was excellent, really good and challenging. There's only one thing that made you go 'yuk!' – the dead sheep. I think it's meant to shock you, though. Anyway, after that, I popped round and saw a friend of mine, Richard, for a bit and then we went up to Camden market to do a bit of shopping.

Barry: Oh yeah, it's nice up there on a Sunday, isn't it?

Sharon: Yeah, it's great. And then I spent the evening at my mum's, which was nice.

Barry: Oh, that sounds good.

Sharon: Yeah, and apart from that, I've been doing things for college, really.

Barry: Uh-huh, still being a good student, then. Oh look, there's my bus into town. I'd best be off. I'll see you soon, then. Bye.

Sharon: Yeah, OK, bye.

I wish (page 97)

1. I sometimes wish I'd known my grandfather on my mum's side. He was supposed to have been a really interesting guy.

2. I wish I hadn't eaten so much earlier. I feel really sick!

3. I often wish I had travelled more when I was younger. I just don't have the time to do it now.

4. I really wish I had gone to see the doctor about it earlier. It wouldn't have got so bad if I had.

5. I sometimes wish I hadn't wasted so much time when I was at university. I wouldn't be working here if I'd got a better degree.

6. I wish I hadn't spent so much money while I was on holiday. I wouldn't be so badly in debt if I hadn't.

7. I wish I'd met her earlier. I wouldn't have had to spend so many years of my life on my own!

8. I really wish I hadn't lost my address book. I'm going to lose touch with loads of people now.

Unit 14

Recommending (page 99)

Conversation 1

A: I went and saw an exhibition at the Hayward Gallery earlier in the week.

B: Oh, did you? What was it?

A: It was a collection of photos from the first lunar landing.

B: Oh, really? It sounds quite interesting. What was it like?

A: Quite good, actually, the photos were really great, quite amazing – some of them.

B: So, you'd recommend it, then?

A: Yes, you should go and see it.

Conversation 2

A: I went and saw that new exhibition at the National Gallery the other day.

B: Oh, did you? Which one's that again?

A: Oh, it was this collection of Flemish paintings from the seventeenth century.

B: Oh really? What was it like?

A: Well, I didn't think much of it myself. It was all a bit dull, you know.

B: So, you wouldn't recommend it, then?

A: No, I'd give it a miss, if I were you – unless you really like that sort of thing, of course.

Recommending expressions (page 99)

1. It's OK if you're into that sort of thing.
2. It's a must.
3. I really recommend it.
4. I'd give it a miss if I were you.
5. It's well worth a visit.
6. It's not worth the entrance fee.
7. It's not really my cup of tea.

Oh, that reminds me! (page 102)

1. A: I visited Alan in hospital last Friday to see how he was getting on.
   B: Oh, did you? I keep meaning to go and see him myself. How was he?

2. A: I spent all day Sunday catching up on all my mail.
   B: Oh, that reminds me. I must send in my passport application.

3. A: I went and saw that musical, *Chicago*, last week.
   B: Oh, I've been meaning to go and see that for ages. Was it as good as everybody says?

4. A: I went round to Mike and Sue's the other day to see that new car they've been telling everyone about.
   B: Oh, that reminds me. I must give them a call. I haven't spoken to them for ages.

5. A: I went down to Bristol for the weekend a couple of weeks ago.
   B: Oh, really. I've been thinking about having a weekend away myself. Were you camping or what?

6. A: I just stayed in last night and watched TV. There's a great thing on on Fridays at the moment about Antarctica.
   B: Oh, that reminds me. I must record that new thing on Channel Four tonight. It's meant to be really funny.

Unit 15

So what was it like? (page 104)

Conversation 1

A: Mm, this fish is really nice. What's yours like?
B: Well, I'm beginning to wish I'd had the same as you. I usually love chicken, but, to be honest, this is a bit bland. The waiter said it was in a delicious mushroom sauce, but it doesn't taste of anything.

Conversation 2

A: So, is the wine all right?
B: Mm, yeah, it's all right, but it's nothing special.
A: I see what you mean. £15 for this! It really is very ordinary.
B: Yes, it's a bit disappointing, to say the least. Shall we send it back?
A: No, I can't be bothered. It's not that bad.

Conversation 3

A: Didn't you go to see *Macbeth* last week?
B: Yeah, it was brilliant. I've been to it a few times before, but I think this was the best production I've ever seen.
A: Yeah, someone I work with went and said it was wonderful. I wish I'd been able to get a ticket.

Asking linked questions (page 105)

1. A: What's his house like? Is it big?
   B: Yes, it's huge. It's got four bedrooms and an enormous garden.

2. A: What was that book like? Was it interesting?
   B: No, it wasn't, actually. It was really boring. In fact, I didn't even finish reading it.

3. A: What's your new job like? Are you enjoying it?
   B: Yes, very much. My boss is really nice and it's quite well paid, really.

4. A: What was Tunisia like? Was it warm?
   B: Yes, it *was* quite warm, but not as hot as the last time we went.

5. A: What's this CD like? Is it any good?
   B: Yes, I think it's great. The third track is brilliant.

6. A: How was the match? Did you win?
   B: No, we lost three – one. It was just terrible. I can't believe it.

Not exactly Shakespeare (page 111)

Paul: Guess what I went and saw last night – *Titanic* – it's on again this week at the Duke of York's.

Mick: Oh, yeah. I saw that when it first came out. What did you think of it? Did you like it?

Paul: Oh, it was great. I really enjoyed it. I thought the special effects were amazing, and the acting was brilliant. It's one of those films where, you know, when I first heard about how much money they'd spent on it, I just couldn't believe it, but it was really great. It was a bit like one of those old disaster movies, you know, like *Towering Inferno* or *Earthquake*, only better.

Mick: Really? I'm surprised. I thought the acting was a bit wooden myself, and the dialogue was just awful. I can't believe you actually thought it was worth the money they'd spent on it. I mean, didn't you find the whole thing just a little bit over-the-top?

Paul: Oh, no. Not at all. I thought it was brilliant.

Mick: But the acting was horrendous!

Paul: Well, I know it's not exactly Shakespeare, but it's not meant to be, is it? I'll tell you something weird though, there was this guy sitting next to us who snored all the way through the film!

Mick: Really? That must've been really annoying. How could anybody actually sleep through all that noise!

Paul: I don't know – just dead tired, I suppose.

Mick: Yeah, I guess so, but really, though, didn't you think it was all just a bit too sentimental?

Paul: I know what you mean, but I honestly didn't. I really thought it was all done just right. It was so romantic.

Mick: Oh well, each to his own. Have you seen *Bomb Alert 2* yet?

Paul: No, I haven't even heard of it. Who's in it?

Mick: Um, Jean-Paul van Klam, he's great in it and, um, that woman from *Kamikaze*, you know who I mean. Remember? She was Turtle-woman too, although I must admit she wasn't very good in that.

Paul: Oh, her. So what's it like? Any good?

Mick: Yeah, it's great – if you like blood all over the place and that sort of thing.

Paul: Oh, it doesn't really sound like my sort of thing, actually. I think I'll give it a miss.

Unit 16

And when you can't answer (page 111)

1. Sorry, my mind's gone completely blank.
2. Wait, it'll come to me in a minute.
3. Wait, it's on the tip of my tongue.
4. Sorry, I can't remember off the top of my head.

Unit 17

More sleeping policemen! (page 121)

Chris: Did you hear about that kid who was knocked down on Junction Road the other day?

Claire: Yes, it was awful, wasn't it? Still, it's hardly surprising, is it?

Chris: What do you mean?

Claire: Well, there are always accidents down there, aren't there, especially with the speed cars go at. And, well, basically, the crossing's in the wrong place, isn't it? I don't know why they've never moved it. I mean, it'd be better if it was exactly opposite the shops, wouldn't it?

Chris: Yes, I know what you mean. They could do something to slow the traffic down, couldn't they? Maybe they could put sleeping policemen there or something like that.

Claire: Yeah, maybe – maybe one every so often would help, but what would be really great is if they had one of those speed cameras.

Chris: Big Brother, you mean!

Claire: No, they really make a difference. You should see how they've slowed the traffic down where my parents live.

Chris: Yeah, I suppose you're right. I'm only against them because I got caught by one last month.

Claire: You're kidding!

Chris: No. A hundred and fifty pounds it cost me! A fine *and* six penalty points!

Claire: Oh, that's terrible!

Chris: Yeah, but it was my own silly fault. I mean, I should've known better, but going back to what you were saying about the crossing, you're right. It would be far safer if it was closer to the shops, because that's where everybody crosses, you know. That's where most kids cross, so it'd be more sensible if it was moved down.

Claire: Yes, I think that's the root of the problem. I mean, it does seem a funny place for a crossing. And I would've said the other problem with it is the fact that lots of cars park all round there.

Chris: Yes, that does make it difficult to see, I suppose. Apparently, the car that hit that kid had just driven off from there.

Claire: Oh, really? Had it? Well, you see what I mean, then.

Disagreeing (page 123)

a. Well, I agree up to a point, but *(it's not as simple as you think.)*

b. Yes, I know what you mean, but *(it's time we did something about it.)*

c. Yes, but don't you think that *(we should wait till later?)*

d. Yes, but don't forget that *(everything costs money.)*

Unit 18

Complaining about things (page 129)

Complaining about a meal

Joan: How was the meal last night?

Mike: Oh, it was awful! The food wasn't very good. It would've been OK if that was the only problem, but the waiters were really rude as well. And then, to top the whole thing off, they tried to overcharge us. Then when we complained about it, they made it sound as if it was our fault!

Complaining about a situation

Terry: How's college going?

Julie: Not very well, actually. I've got a bit of a problem with my timetable this term. I mean, the last thing I need is three lectures on a Friday. I wish they wouldn't change the timetable every term. Last term was much better.

It really drives me mad (page 130)

1. A: Doesn't it bug you the way shops always charge £9.99 when you know it's really £10?

   B: I must admit, things like that don't really bother me.

2. A: Look, I'm really sorry. There's no way I can come to your party tomorrow night. I've got to work late.

B: Oh, well, don't worry. It's not the end of the world.

3. A: I really thought I'd got the job. I mean, my interview went really well, and then they tell me I'm not even short-listed!

B: Oh. well. Don't let it get you down.

4. A: I've got about five bills I'm supposed to pay by the end of the month. What do they think I am? Made of money?

B: Oh well, there's nothing you can do about it.

Unit 19

Now you're talking! (page 133)

Rachel: So, have you had any more thoughts about what you're going to do next year, then?

Nick: Mm. I don't know, really. I mean, I was thinking that it might be a good idea to do that art course I was telling you about, but it all depends on my results.

Rachel: So what about France? Weren't you talking about going to Paris a while back?

Nick: Oh, for that French course? Well, I would still like to do it, but I just don't know if I can afford it.

Rachel: Oh, I know what you mean. Money's always a problem, isn't it? I mean, what I'd really like to do next year is learn to drive and buy a car, but I'm not sure if I'll have the cash. The thing is, I'm just so sick of having to get buses everywhere.

Nick: Dreadful, aren't they? You wait half an hour and then three come along at the same time. So, you're basically just going to be staying around here, just trying to save up some money, then?

Rachel: Yes, I suppose so. It depends, really. I mean, if I can find a good job, then I'll stick around, but otherwise what I was thinking of doing eventually is going back to Glasgow.

Nick: Oh right, because you grew up there, didn't you?

Rachel: Yes, that's right, yes, so I suppose I do see myself ending up there eventually.

Nick: Yeah.

Rachel: So, assuming you do this art course, what do you see yourself doing after that, in the long term?

Nick: Oh, I don't know. No idea really. I haven't thought that far ahead. I'll just take it as it comes and see what happens.

Rachel: Just listen to us, Nick! We just sound so boring! Why don't we go off somewhere together this summer, you know, maybe – I don't know – work abroad for six months?

Nick: What? You mean picking grapes in France? That kind of thing?

Rachel: Yeah, or, I don't know – working in a hotel in Spain, or …

Nick: Or going to Australia. If the Aussies can work over here, why can't we go and get a job over there?

Rachel: Yeah, I'd love to do that. Where's the paper? What's the cheapest flight to Sydney?

Nick: Now, you're talking!

Unit 20

What's the job? (page 140)

First job

A: So, what exactly does your job involve then?

B: Well, basically, I prepare all the prescriptions and keep a check on all the drugs we have in stock. I also give advice to people who come in with minor problems. You know the sort of thing – what cream to use for a rash, what to take for an upset tummy – that sort of thing. Sometimes, I'm just like a shop assistant, selling things over the counter; other times I feel like I'm a doctor.

Second job

A: So, how long have you been doing this, then?

B: All my life – since I left school. I worked with my father, and now I've got my son working with me. I really enjoy working with wood. I love taking a piece of wood and turning it into something useful. I learned everything I know from watching my father and the older men at work. Now, it's great passing on my skills to younger guys.

Third job

A: So, do you enjoy doing what you're doing?

B: Yeah, well, I mean, somebody's got to do it, haven't they? Just think, if nobody did it, what would the place be like? I mean, when I was a boy, if you dropped something, the police would be after you, but these days people don't care. They just drop everything – coke cans, cigarette packets, newspapers, everything, you name it, I've picked it up. Mind you, I've found the odd £20 note. I'd never work indoors. I just couldn't stand it.

Grammar introduction

Vocabulary: words and collocations

You already know a lot of English grammar, and you probably keep a vocabulary notebook, so it is easy to think that the two best ways to improve your English are to improve your grammar and learn new words. But there is another thing you can do which is even more helpful, especially now you already know quite a lot of English. You need to notice **collocations** and record them in your notebooks. So, what are collocations?

We hardly ever use one word on its own. You will usually meet a new word in a text, where it is used with other words. So, it is always better to learn **groups of words which are often used together.** These groups of words are called **collocations**.

Complete each sentence with one word.

I must've . . . . a mistake.
Have you . . . . your homework?
He's a really . . . . smoker – at least twenty a day.
Shall we . . . . a . . . . break?

You already know 'chunks' of language. For example:

make a mistake   do your homework
heavy smoker   have a short break

These are all collocations.

If you learn words one by one, it is easy to make mistakes when you use the words later. You might, for example, say: *I think I did a mistake,* or *I haven't made my homework.* If you learn words in groups, you will not make as many mistakes.

There are lots of different kinds of collocations. It is a good idea to have a different section in your notebook for collocations of different kinds. Here are some of the most important kinds:

curly hair	(adjective + noun)
pay the bill	(verb + noun)
theme park	(noun + noun)
highly offensive	(adverb + adjective)
on either side of	(prepositional phrase)
on the other hand	(adverb phrase)
talking to some old friends	(verb + adjective + noun)

The most important kind of collocation you need to learn is *verb + (adjective) + noun.* For example:

apply for a new job

Notice that you may know all the words in a phrase, but not recognise the phrase **as a single chunk. Learning it as a chunk is very important.** Notice the opposite of *a light colour* is *a dark colour,* but the opposite of *a light*

meal is *a heavy meal.* You cannot translate *light* into your own language until you know what word is used with it. That is why collocation is so important. If you write collocations in your notebook, make sure you translate the collocation **as a single chunk.**

Grammar: the verb

You have met lots of English tenses – the present continuous, the present perfect, the present perfect continuous and so on. You might think the system is very complicated. In fact, it is fairly simple. There are only three really important patterns that you need to understand.

Continuous forms

Here are some examples:

The present continuous:
Oh no, it's raining again.

The past continuous:
I was working all last weekend.

The present perfect continuous:
There you are! – I've been trying to ring you all morning.

In every example the speaker sees the action as extended between two points in time, so a continuous form is used. This is also true for events organised before now which will happen after now:

We're having a few friends round on Friday. Would you like to come?

The game is being played next Tuesday.

The continuous always emphasises that the speaker thinks the event is extended over a period:

Next week I'll be lying on the beach in the sun.

Perfect forms

The present perfect:
Oh, you've changed your hair. I prefer it that way.

The past perfect:
Steve told me, but I'd already heard from Amanda.

The present perfect continuous:
There it is! I've been looking for that everywhere.

In every case the speaker is looking back on an earlier event. In spoken English we often notice something now which makes us comment on what happened earlier. The sentence often links the cause of the present situation, or the result of what happened earlier:

The journey only takes me twenty minutes now because they've opened the new road at last.

We've moved, you know, so I have to come on the train nowadays.

Simple forms

These are used if the speaker is giving a summary, or overview of the whole situation. Different kinds of overview all use the simple form:

> I see what you mean.
> I never eat meat.
> I promise I won't say a word to anybody.
> I play tennis at least once a week all year round.
> It takes about two hours, depending on the traffic.

If you use another form, it adds extra meaning, so the simple form is the basic form. It is the most common form of the verb in English.

Grammar: the noun

There is only one really important grammar pattern with English nouns – the difference between *countable* and *uncountable* nouns.

Countable nouns are things which exist in units:

> books, days, children

or which we think of in units:

> ideas, plans, opportunities

Because countable nouns are about units, you can have one – a book, an opportunity *(the singular)*. Or you can have more than one – six days, three children *(the plural)*.

Uncountable nouns are things which we do not usually think of in units:

> luck, happiness, water, sand

Some words have two different meanings, one countable, and one uncountable:

> 1. Do you think there is life out there in space?
> 2. There's a free space next to that red Volvo.

In (1) space = the single, great cosmos.

In (2) space = the marked area where you can leave a car in the car park. You can count the spaces in the car park.

So, it is not words which are countable or uncountable – it is the particular **meaning** of the word. Some words have two very similar meanings, but the grammar is different:

> 1. I've only played two or three times before.
> 2. Hurry up – we haven't much time. The train leaves at twenty past.

In (1) times = occasions. You can count how many times you have done something.

In (2) time = the abstract idea of time. You can measure it, but you can't count it.

> 1. I'm very fond of cheese.
> 2. France is sometimes described as the land of 200 cheeses.
> 3. You need a very strong cheese for this recipe.

In (1) you are talking about cheese in general.

In (2) cheese = different kinds of cheese. You can count Camembert, Roquefort, Brie, etc.

In (3) you are contrasting one kind of cheese – strong – with another.

Learning rules and noticing examples

Two things are very important if you want to improve. Firstly, you need to hear and read a lot of English. It doesn't matter if you don't understand everything; if you understand part of what you hear or read, that is enough to help you improve. Secondly, you need to *notice* the language you meet. If your teacher says, *'You made a mistake,'* you need to notice that the expression is *made a mistake*, not *did a mistake*. If you do not notice something, you will not remember it.

With grammar, it is also very important to notice the examples you meet. Again, you need to notice whole expressions, and record them in your notebook **exactly as you find them.** Record examples you meet like this:

> It's time you stood on your own two feet.
> I searched high and low for it.
> OK, I can take a hint.

Not like this:

> to stand on your own two feet
> high and low
> take the hint

Do not change them so that they look like a dictionary. Changing them makes them more difficult to remember, and when you use them later, there is more chance that you will make a mistake. If you write a translation, translate the phrase as a single expression.

Slowly, you will begin to see groups of examples which are similar in some way. If you can see a pattern, and you can describe it, the description is a 'rule'. A 'rule' is nothing more than a description of some examples which are similar in some way.

But remember that examples which are similar in one way may be different in other ways, so your 'rule' may be only partly true. Even the rules in grammar books are often only partly true.

The real examples come first; rules come later, so the examples are more important.

With vocabulary, notice and record words in chunks – collocations and expressions.

With grammar, notice and record the examples in context, exactly as you find them.

Noticing and recording language in chunks will help you learn more quickly, and make fewer mistakes when you use English yourself.

Grammar commentary

Unit by unit grammar notes

G1 | Modifiers (page 9)

Modifiers are words such as *very, really,* and *quite*. They are used to 'modify' – strengthen or weaken – adjectives.

Really, very

> She's very nice.   He's really bossy.

These two modifiers are used to make positive or negative adjectives stronger. However, with 'extreme' adjectives – *boiling, fantastic, delicious, huge, tiny, freezing,* etc. – you can only use *really*. *It's very huge* or *It was very fantastic* sound very strange.

> It's really boiling today, isn't it?
> It's really delicious, this soup.

Quite

The meaning of *quite* depends both on the way it is stressed and on the context you hear it in.

> John's quite creative – he paints and draws.

In the sentence above, *creative* would be stressed and the sentence means you think that John really *is* creative. However, in the sentence below, *quite* would be stressed and the sentence now means you think Pete is creative, but not particularly creative.

> Pete's quite creative, but he's not Van Gogh!

a bit too

> She's a bit too nice, if you know what I mean.

The structure *a bit too + positive adjective* is usually used either to disagree slightly with what has just been said, as in this example:

> A: She's very good-looking, don't you think?
> B: Yes, a bit too good-looking, if you ask me. I mean, she's very big-headed about it.

or to add an extra comment to a statement we have already made. For example:

> She's really talkative . . . actually, she can sometimes be a bit too talkative, now I come to think of it! I mean, she just never shuts up once she gets going!

G2 | Present simple and present continuous (page 13)

The present simple is the most common tense in English. The present simple here is used to talk about things that the speaker sees as facts about life – things that are always, normally or usually true:

> I find my dad a bit dull.
> (always, not just at the moment)

> Do you get on with them all right?
> (generally)

The present continuous, however, is used when the speaker sees the action or event described as only being temporary, as something already in the process of being completed.

> She's being really nice at the moment.
> (This is strange, because normally she's horrible!)
> He's working this weekend.
> (But he doesn't usually, it's only a temporary arrangement.)

Remember that the difference between the present simple and present continuous is about how we see an event. Both forms can be used about the same event, for example:

> Jane's living in Greece.
> Marie lives in Greece.

The difference is probably that Jane has a job in Greece for a year, but Marie is married and has a family there. The fact that the two people live there is the same, but the way the speaker sees the situation is different.

G3 | Comparatives (page 17)

You probably know the basic rules for how to make comparisons using adjectives already: we generally use *adjective + -er* or *more + adjective*. For example:

> A: Shall we take the bus?
> B: No, let's walk. It'll be nicer.

> Everything's so much cheaper here than it is in the UK.
> Most of the other people there seemed a lot more experienced than I was.
> I found this book a lot more interesting than the other things I've had to read for the course.

Note: In conversation, the two things you are comparing are usually obvious to the person you're talking to. As a result, we tend not to compare them both within the same sentence. This is why we **don't** say: *No, let's walk. It'll be nicer than taking the bus* in the first example above.

The rules for when to add *–er* and when to add *more* are quite complex. Generally, words of three syllables take *more*, and most shorter adjectives of one or two syllables take *–er*, but this is not always true. Participle adjectives (ones which end in *–ing* and *–ed*), for example, always take *more* – even if they have a short sound (e.g., *bored, crowded*) – and so do adjectives ending in *–ful* and *–less* (e.g. *helpful*). There are also two very common irregulars: *better* and *worse*.

Remember that as well as making adjectives into comparatives, we can also use adverbs and adverb phrases to compare how things are done. For example:

He finished it much more quickly than I thought he would.

I get on with him, much, much better than I used to.

To compare the first thing we are talking about negatively with the second thing we are talking about, we use *not as … as* for adjectives:

He's not as old as most people think he is.

It's not as expensive here as it is back home.

To do the same with adverbs, we use *don't + verb + as + adverb + as*.

I don't like this as much as I thought I would.

She doesn't come over as often as she used to.

I don't get on with him as well as I did when we were younger.

There are lots of common fixed phrases for making comparisons. We often use them when we are answering questions. It's a good idea to keep a record of these every time you meet a new one. Here are some typical examples:

not as often as I used to
not as often as I'd like to
not as much as I used to
not as good as I thought it would be
not as difficult as I thought it would be

G4 | Using auxiliaries (page 23)

If an auxiliary verb is used in the initial statement, the response will use the same auxiliary:

So + auxiliary + I

A: I'm going to stay in tonight and do nothing.
B: Oh, so am I.
A: I've just booked my summer holidays.
B: Oh, that's funny, because so have I.

If we want to agree with a negative statement, however, the pattern is:

Neither + positive form of the auxiliary + I

A: I don't like things that are too sweet.
B: No, neither do I.

A: I can't stand sea water.
B: Oh no, neither can I.

If no auxiliary verb is present in the initial comment, we agree by adding a 'dummy auxiliary' *do*:

So + do + I

A: I prefer coffee without milk.
B: Oh, so do I.

A: I never go abroad.
B: No, neither do I.

Notice, that if the initial comment has more than one auxiliary verb, we agree by using the *first* of the two auxiliaries:

A: I've been thinking about moving house.
B: Oh, that's strange, because so have I.
A: I haven't been feeling all that well just lately.
B: There must be something going round, because neither have I.

Finally, note that it is very common in spoken English to simply use *Oh, me too* to agree to a positive statement and *No, me neither* to agree with a negative one.

A: I love fish and chips. / I've been there loads of times now. / I can speak a bit of Japanese.
B: Oh, me too.
A: I don't like him much. / I can't stand this kind of music. / I haven't seen her for ages.
B: No, me neither.

G5 | Would (page 31)

Would (or *'d*) is used when the speaker wants to make a statement sound more tentative or hypothetical:

Would you mind if I left a bit early today? I've got a doctor's appointment.
(I understand it might not be possible.)

It'd be great if you *did* come and stay in the summer.
(though, of course, I realise you might not be able to)

I'd quite like the green one, if you can find it.
(but don't worry if you can't)

However, there are also lots of useful expressions using *would* which you should just try and learn to use as whole chunks:

That'd be great.
I wouldn't mind.
I would if I could.
I'd quite like to.
It'd be nice if you could.
I wouldn't do that if I were you.

It is a good idea to listen for and collect other expressions using *would*.

G6 | Past perfect continuous (page 37)

The past perfect continuous is generally used to talk about the background to an event in the past or to explain why this event happened. It usually describes the events or actions leading up to something which is the main focus of our story or description.

We hadn't been getting on for a long time, so we decided to go our separate ways.

A: So how come you didn't have any money?
B: Well, I hadn't been working much, and I'd been having a lot of problems with my car.

This contrasts with the past perfect simple, which is used to describe a single event which then had a result in the past. Look at these examples:

He looked really weird and then I suddenly realised he'd shaved his beard off! (just once!)

I wasn't feeling well . . . I'd had a cold for months.
(not 'I'd been having a cold' – having a cold is not something you can *do* over and over again)
Remember that the past perfect is always connected to other events in the more recent past.

G7 | Second conditionals (page 39)

Second conditionals are used to talk about situations which the speaker sees as unlikely or hypothetical.

There are several very frequently used second conditionals. For example:

I wouldn't do that if I were you.
I wouldn't bother if I were you.
I would if I could, but I can't.
It'd be great if you could.
It'd be terrible if they did.
I'd die if that happened to me!

One thing to remember is that when we report first conditionals, they then have the same verb forms as second conditionals:

He told me that I could if I wanted to.
(His actual words: *You can if you want to.*)

I always used to think that if I needed her, she'd be there for me.
(My actual thought: *If I need her, she'll be there for me.*)

We also use the same grammatical structure to talk about typical things that happened a lot in the past. For example:

When I was a kid, if it snowed, we'd all go out and have huge snowball fights.

If my dad ever got really angry with me, I'd run upstairs and then I'd hide under my bed.

Note that in these examples, *if* means *every time* or *whenever*.

Whether you use a second conditional or not is very much a matter of choice. For example, logically, you would expect people to use one when talking about winning the lottery, but actually you often hear people saying things like this:

If I win this week, you won't see me back at work next Monday! or – even more optimistically! – When I win, I'm going to tell my boss what he can do with his job!

G8 | Gerund and infinitive (page 46)

Sadly, there is no easy way to learn which verbs are followed by gerunds and which by infinitives. The best thing to do is to try to learn useful chunks that you can use a lot.

I'll try to do it later.
I managed to do it in the end.
I must remember to call her.

I love living here.
I've finally stopped smoking.
I started doing it years ago.

It is also worth remembering that there are lots of adjective expressions which are followed by a preposition plus gerund:

I'm not very <u>keen on cooking</u>.
You must be <u>tired of people always asking</u> you where you're from.

There are two or three common verbs which can be followed by gerunds and infinitives. Look at these examples:

I clearly <u>remember swimming</u> in the sea near our house.
(it happened in the past)

I must <u>remember to call</u> my mum tonight.
(in the future)

Have you <u>tried asking</u> the guy next door?
(Have you already tried this method of solving your problem?)

Just <u>try to forget</u> about it.
(in the future)

I just totally <u>forgot to pay</u> the phone bill.
(I should've done it, but didn't.)

I'll never <u>forget climbing</u> that mountain in Peru.
(I still remember it and I expect to remember it in the future.)

G9 | Talking about the future (page 49)

When you are trying to decide which form to use to talk about the future, the most important thing to think about is *why* you think the actions you're talking about are going to happen. Here are some guidelines to help you:

'll - the normal, everyday, contracted form of *will*

That's the phone. I'll get it.
I think I'll have the chicken.

'll describes a decision made at the moment of speaking.

Going to + verb

Ugh! I think my tooth's going to fall out.
I'm going to hand in my notice at work next week.

Going to is used when there is evidence now for the future event – something you can see or feel – or to talk about a decision you have already made on your own.

Present continuous

They're leaving next week sometime.
I'm seeing her for lunch tomorrow.

The present continuous is used to describe events that have already been arranged with other people.

Present simple

My class finishes around nine.
She arrives on 2nd March.

These events are seen as facts, particularly facts connected to timetables – of movies, lessons, trains, boats, planes, etc.

G10 | More ways of talking about the future (page 51)

I've got (somebody) (coming round).

This structure is mainly used with the verbs *arriving*, *visiting* and *coming*. Here are the most normal uses:

> I've got my mum arriving tomorrow.
> I've got some friends coming round later on.

I've got to + verb (or I have to + verb).

This structure is used to talk about things you don't want to do, but feel are necessary.

> I've got to do some things for work.
> I've got to take my kids to school tomorrow.

It is also used to explain why you can't do something. For example:

> A: Hey, we were wondering if you wanted to come out with us tonight?
> B: Oh, I'd love to, but I'm afraid I've got to work late today. Maybe next time.

I'm supposed to be -ing, but . . .

Supposed to be is used to describe arrangements you have already made with other people and which you haven't changed yet, but which you now feel could be changed.

The structure is often used with a *but*-clause explaining that you no longer feel like keeping to this plan.

> I'm supposed to be meeting some friends tonight, but I don't really feel like it any more.

It is also used with a *but*-clause saying that you haven't definitely decided yet.

> I'm supposed to be going round to see him later, but I'm not entirely sure.

You can also say *I might go round to see him later,* or *I might be going round to see him later.*

G11 | Responding with auxiliary verbs (page 67)

Notice that when no auxiliary verb is present in the initial statement, we respond using the dummy auxiliary *do*. It is also very common to add a follow-up question or comment. For example:

> A: I went off to Margate for the weekend.
> B: Oh, did you? That must've been nice.
> A: Yes, it was lovely.

> A: I speak pretty good Russian.
> B: Oh, do you? Where did you learn that then?
> A: At university. I did French, Russian and Polish.

Be careful not to confuse *had* as a past tense verb with the auxiliary verb *have*. For example:

> A: We had (main verb) a great meal over at Jim's.
> B: Oh, did you? What did he cook?

> A: I've (auxiliary verb) got my new stereo at last!
> B: Oh, have you? I'd better come over tonight, then.

G12 | not ... until ... (page 68)

We use the structure *not . . . until* when we want to emphasise that we did something later than usual. For example:

> I overslept this morning. I didn't wake up until ten!
> I didn't start learning English until last year, so I'm quite pleased with how well I'm doing.

G13 | Linking ideas (page 69)

Look at these two ideas:
> It was very cold.
> We needed two pullovers!

We can link these two ideas in one sentence using a *so*-clause. For example:
> It was so cold, we needed two pullovers!

In spoken English, this is a very common way of expressing cause and result, with the *so*-clause explaining the cause. The *so*-clause may come first or second:

> It was so hot, (that) I was sweating like a pig!
> I was sweating like a pig (because) it was so hot!

> It was so quiet in there, (that) you could've heard a pin drop.
> You could've heard a pin drop (because) it was so quiet in there.

Notice that in normal spoken English, you do not need to use the linking words in brackets, as they are implicitly understood.

G14 | Judging by appearances (page 70)

He/She looks is always followed by an adjective:
> She looks really nice and friendly.
> He looks a bit stressed-out to me.

He/She looks like is followed by a noun or a noun phrase:
> He looks like a dentist or a doctor or something.
> He looks like the kind of person who'll help.

He/She looks as if he/she is followed by a verb clause:
> He looks as if he's about to cry.
> She looks as if she's been running.

Note that in everyday spoken English, *as if* is often substituted by *like*:
> She looks as if/like she's been working all day.

If someone *seems* a bit depressed, it is something you feel through knowing them, not just seeing them.
> Dave seems a bit down at the moment. Is he OK?

G15 | Expressions with modals (page 74)

There is a fine line between what is grammar and what is vocabulary. The expressions here are probably best treated as bits of vocabulary and just learned as whole, fixed expressions. These kinds of expressions are very useful in everyday English. Learning them will help you understand the meanings of the different modals.

However, here are a few things to bear in mind:

1. *Must* is used to make guesses which the listener feels fairly sure are true, because of the evidence available.

   You must be joking! £100 for that?
   You must be American with an accent like that.

2. Similarly, *must've* is used to make guesses about the past, based on the evidence available.

   It must've been nice getting out of the city for a bit.
   You must've been really pleased to see her again.

3. *Could've* is used to talk about things you now feel were possible in the past, even if they didn't actually happen.

   I could've told you that!
   I could've helped you if you'd asked.

4. *Should've* is used to talk about what we think would have been a good idea in the past. It can be used to express regret or retrospective advice.

   You should've known better.
   You should've tried to get the price down.

G16 | Telling a story (page 78)

Notice that when we give background details to our stories, we usually use the past continuous or *used to* + verb.

A few years ago, when this friend of mine <u>was coming</u> home from work, . . .

<u>I used to live</u> in this flat in down-town New York, and one day I <u>was taking</u> the subway uptown . . .

Last Thursday I <u>was riding</u> home on my bike . . .

When we introduce the problem in a story, it is very common to switch to present tenses. This makes this part of the story sound more dramatic and immediate.

When all of a sudden, this big, scary-looking guy <u>runs</u> up to me and <u>tries</u> to pinch my bag.

Then suddenly this girl <u>appears</u> from nowhere, and she<u>'s crying</u> and <u>screaming</u>, so I <u>ask</u> her what's up.

G17 | Present participles (page 79)

It is very common to join two ideas together by using clauses using the present participle (-*ing* clauses). It is possible to add more than one clause, but we do not normally add more than three clauses at any one time:

I was just standing there, <u>waiting</u> for my bus, <u>minding</u> my own business.
She was driving along quite normally, <u>singing</u> along to this song on the radio, <u>feeling</u> pretty good, when all of a sudden . . .

G18 | Past simple and past continuous (page 84)

The past continuous is only used if the speaker wishes to emphasise that the action described was extended over a period of time. As a result, the past continuous is often used to describe an action which was already in progress when it was in some way 'interrupted':

I was driving through town when I got stopped by this police car.

I was just getting ready to leave when this brick came flying through my window!

I met my first wife while I was living in Paris.

Notice that the clauses here are linked using *when* or *while*. In certain contexts, verbs do not get extended in time – they just happen once. For example, it is correct to say:

I was finding the lecture really interesting until he started talking about bio-physics!

but not:

~~I was finding~~ the diamond when we were cleaning the flat.

You can only find a diamond once! The difference in grammar is because the meaning of *find* changes slightly in these different contexts.

The past simple is used to talk about things the speaker sees as complete, finished facts. These might be things that only happened once:

I found the diamond on the floor!
I crashed straight through the newsagent's window.
I broke my leg playing football.

Or they might be things that happened over a long period of time but which the speaker wants to talk about by giving an overview of the facts.

I lived in Nicaragua for six years in the eighties.
I worked on a farm for a few years after I left school.

G19 | or something / or anything (page 86)

Or something is added to positive sentences and questions to mean *or something else like that*. *Or anything* is added to negative sentences or negative questions.

I think he's a lawyer or a judge or something.
Have you got a screwdriver or something?
I didn't even kiss her or anything!
Didn't he even phone you or anything?

This feature of spoken English is not slang or 'bad English'. It is one of the ways we express 'vagueness' when we do not know precise details.

G20 | Present perfect simple and present perfect continuous (page 95)

The present perfect simple is a bit like the past simple in that both tenses are used to talk about things that happened in the past. The difference is, however, that we use the present perfect simple if we see these events as somehow connected to the present; perhaps we see a present result of these actions, as in the examples.

Oh, you've had your hair cut! It looks great, much better than it did.

I can't play basketball today. I've twisted my ankle.
Is black tea OK? We've run out of milk.

We can also use the present perfect simple to stress that we have had an experience and can talk about it now if the listener wants us to.

Well, I've worked in pubs before, and I've done plenty of washing up in restaurants and things.
Oh, you play the piano! I've just started learning myself!

Note: When we use a finished time reference, e.g. *last Friday, in 1991, two weeks ago, when I was at high school,* the present perfect is never used.

The present perfect continuous is used when we want to show that an action that started in the past is continuing now.

I've been trying t find a job for months now!
(And I still haven't found one.)

My leg's been feeling weird for the last few days now.
(And it's still feeling painful.)

The present perfect continuous is also used when we want to stress that we see the past action described as having been extended over a period of time, that we see it as having happened again and again and again. Notice that there is a present result.

I've been waiting here for you for hours – you could at least say you're sorry or something!
Have you been drinking? Your breath smells very odd!

With certain verbs, there's often only a very subtle difference between the present perfect simple and present perfect continuous.

I've been working here for about twenty years now.
(But maybe I'm ready for a change now. I see my job as only temporary.)

I've worked here for twenty years now.
(It's just a fact about my life. I se my job as permanent.)

Notice that lots of verbs don't work well with the present perfect continuous.

I've always liked this kind of food. ✓
I've always been liking this kind of food. ✗

You either like something or you don't. You can't like it over and over.

G21 Wish (page 97)

We usually use *wish* to talk about things we regret doing – or not doing – in the past or to talk about ways in which we would like the present to be different. When we are talking about things we regret about the past, we use *wish + the past perfect.* We often add a reason explaining why we feel like this.

I wish I hadn't eaten so much earlier. I feel dreadful now.

I wish you hadn't told me about it. I can't stop thinking about it now.
I wish I'd seen it while it was out. I'll have to wait till it comes out on DVD now.
I wish I'd been a bit more honest about things. Things might've worked out between us if I had been.

When we talk about things we feel bad about or disappointed about in the present, we use *wish + past simple verb.*

I wish I could drive. I hate having to rely on my mum and dad to take me everywhere.
I wish I was a bit slimmer. I can't get into my old summer clothes anymore.
I wish I didn't have to get up so early every day. I could really do with a lie-in!

We also use *wish + you/he/she + would/wouldn't* to complain about other people's annoying habits.

I wish you wouldn't smoke in here!
(You do it a lot and you're doing it now and it's driving me mad!)
I wish it'd stop raining!
(It rains a lot and it's raining now and I hate it!)

Note : Don't get *wish* mixed up with *hope.* We usually use *hope* to talk about things we would like to happen – or that we don't want to happen – in the future. It's also got different word grammar. Usually it's followed by the present simple, even if we're talking about the future.

I hope it stops raining later.
I hope she comes to the game tomorrow.
I hope the exam next week isn't too hard.

G22 Relatives clauses (page 102)

It is common to comment on the events described in a sentence by adding *which was + a descriptive noun/adjective:*

It was freezing in Chile, <u>which was a bit unexpected</u>.
I finally managed to ask for a pay rise, <u>which was a real weight off my shoulders</u>.

We can also add *which meant + subject + verb + object:*
It rained the whole time we were in Thailand, <u>which meant I didn't get much chance to go sunbathing</u>.
I failed three out of four of my tests that year, <u>which meant I had to re-take the whole year's courses</u>.

G23 Conjunctions (page 105)

Although

In spoken English, *although* is followed by a main clause and usually introduces a clause that reduces the strength of the statement which comes before it.

I do like vegetables, although I must admit that I'm really more of a meat person myself.
It was lovely in Saudi, although the heat did get a bit much sometimes.
I really like my job, although a little bit more money wouldn't go amiss!

Considering

Considering is often followed by a *how*-clause and adds the meaning *which is strange when you think about it*:

The food there was really great, considering how cheap it was!

The party was pretty good, actually, considering there were only about twenty people there!

In spite of

In spite of is followed by a gerund or a noun clause and introduces an idea which has been thought about, but which doesn't affect the statement that comes before or after it.

She got great grades all through college, in spite of having to deal with all kinds of family problems.
Pete's Spanish accent is almost unintelligible, in spite of having lived in Madrid for three years!

G24 Comparing (page 108)

Notice that in everyday spoken English, it is now very common to hear plural nouns and plural uncountable nouns preceded by *there's* instead of *there are*. Even well-educated, careful speakers will say things like:

It's a bit like Cairo or somewhere, only <u>there's a lot more cars</u> on the road there.

<u>There's hundreds</u> of sheep blocking the road down by the farm.

Business is OK, but <u>there's not as many tourists</u> coming this year as there were last year.

There are is also correct in these situations.

G25 *Must* for guessing (page 109)

We often make guesses about things we think are true based on the evidence available to us, and use *must* to show we are fairly sure, but not 100% certain that what we are saying is true.

It <u>must be</u> nice having a bit more space now that you've moved house.

It <u>must've been</u> really great in New York.

Remember that the opposite of *must* for guessing is not *mustn't* but *can't*:

You can't be serious!

You can't earn much working in a burger bar.

It can't have been very well made if it only lasted three weeks before falling to bits! (See also G15.)

G26 Past perfect simple (page 113)

The past perfect simple is generally used to talk about the background to an event in the past or to explain why this event happened.

It is usually used with other past tenses, and allows us to jump further back into the past from the main point in time that we're talking about.

My leg was killing me, because <u>I'd twisted</u> it at the gym the day before.
I had a dreadful headache, because <u>I'd had</u> a bit too much to drink the night before.
<u>I'd never done</u> anything like that before so I was really nervous about it. (See also G6.)

G27 Mixed conditionals (page 115)

We use second conditionals to talk about ways in which we imagine the present or future could be different.

If I had a bit more time, I'd start going to the gym more often.
If I were you, I'd just tell her what happened and hope she understands!

We use third conditionals to talk about imaginary pasts – ways in which the past could have been different, if the situation had been different.

If I'd known, I would've tried to talk to him about it.
(But I didn't know, so I didn't talk to him.)
If she hadn't been there, I might've died!
(But she was there and she helped me.)

However, past events don't only have past results; they also often have present results. If we want to talk about the imaginary present results of a past event, we have to use a mixed conditional. Often, this is half of a third conditional – to talk about the past – and half a second conditional – to talk about the imaginary present:

If she hadn't encouraged me, I wouldn't be a teacher now.
If my mum hadn't been hitch-hiking that day, she and my dad wouldn't be married now.
If I hadn't moved to Brighton when I did, I'd probably still be working in that factory.
If it hadn't been for him, we'd still be living under military rule today.

Did you notice that in the second conditional part of the sentence, we often use the continuous form? We do this when we want to talk about an imaginary action that we think might already be in progress if the first half of the sentence had actually been true.

Mixed conditionals are very common in both spoken and written English. The best way to deal with them when you meet them in future is to try to understand when each half of the sentence is referring to and to try and work out if it's talking about an imaginary or a real condition. (See also G7.)

G28 Second conditionals for making suggestions (page 122)

Notice that the *if-* sentence starters here are all second conditionals – the structure we use to talk about things we see as being hypothetical or imaginary at the time of speaking:

It'd be great <u>if the shops stayed open a bit longer.</u>
It'd be much better <u>if there was a gym.</u>
It'd be lovely <u>if I didn't have to get up so early!</u>

It is very common to find second conditionals beginning with the sentence starters given here, so try and remember the whole phrase in each case.

G29 The passive (page 125)

It is not helpful to think of the passive as being 'the opposite' of the active. We always use the passive for a very specific reason. Either we don't know who the doer of the action was:

My brother was killed during the civil war.
My car was stolen from right outside my house!

or the action was done by a large group of people:

The stadium was built in the thirties.
(obviously by workmen)

At least three versions of this song have been recorded.
(obviously by musicians and singers)

Note that the active equivalents of these sentences use *they* as a 'dummy subject':

They built this stadium back in the thirties.
They've recorded at least three versions of this song.

We also use the passive when the doer of the action is known, but not relevant or important at the moment of speaking:

My car's being repaired at the moment.

Three of my teeth were knocked out last year when I was playing rugby.

This model was developed in our Seoul team.

Passives are more common in formal, written English.

G30 Was/were going to (page 128)

This structure is often thought of as the 'future in the past' and is commonly used to report our past thoughts or words, particularly when they proved to be inaccurate in some way:

I thought <u>it was going to rain,</u> so I brought the washing in – just in case.

They'd told me <u>I was going to be transferred</u> to Mexico, but nothing ever came of it.

However, it doesn't always have to have a past time reference. It can be used to talk about things in the future that we've already decided to do, but now suddenly decide we might not do after all.

A: Do you want to come over later and eat something?
B: Well, <u>I was going to stay in</u> and try and get some work done, but I guess I could always do that tomorrow instead.

Oh, it's funny you should call! <u>I was going to call</u> you later, but you beat me to it!

One of the most common uses of this structure is when you phone someone and they answer:

Oh, I was just going to ring you.

Have you noticed that certain people always say this?

G31 Starting with *what* (page 134)

When we want to emphasise what we are going to say by adding *what* at the beginning of a sentence, the grammar of the statement changes. We often use *do* as a dummy auxiliary and we also add the verb *is/was*.

I really need to take a holiday soon.
What I really need to do is take a holiday soon.

I was thinking of going to China next year, if I can afford it.
What I was thinking of doing next year is going to China, if I can afford it.

There are lots of quite common sentence starters that use this structure. Try to learn them and use them as whole phrases.

What I found really interesting about it was . . .
What really annoys me about him is the way . . .
What worries me most about the idea is . . .
What I still don't understand is why . . .

G32 Future continuous (page 143)

This structure is often used to talk about an event in the future that we see as already arranged but which now, because of what has come up in the conversation, we also see as the background to another newer event, described in the *so*-clause:

A: We've run out of milk.
B: Oh well, look, I'll be going shopping later (I've already decided this), so I'll get some, if you want. (new decision/offer)

A: I really love proper pesto sauce.
B: Oh, do you? Well, look, I'll be going back to Italy for a week in March (I've already decided this), so I'll bring you back some of my mum's special! (new decision/offer)

Expression organiser

This section helps you to record and translate some of the most important expressions from each unit. It is always best to record words in phrases, rather than individual words. Sometimes you can translate very easily. Sometimes you will need to think of the equivalent expression in your own language. In each section, there is space for you to add any connected expressions or collocations you want to remember.

Unit 1

He's got a really good sense of humour. ....

He's quite conservative. ....

He's a bit of a workaholic. ....

She's a bit on the plump side. ....

He's quite elderly now. ....

She can be a bit too nice sometimes. ....

He looks really interesting. ....

He's a total pain in the neck. ....

She's extremely ambitious. ....

He runs his own business. ....

She works in advertising. ....

He's unemployed at the moment. ....

My brother works in IT. ....

She's a retired doctor. ....

I do a bit of temping work sometimes. ....

....

....

....

....

....

Unit 2

He's infamous. ....

It cost me an arm and a leg. ....

We just don't see eye to eye. ....

I'm up to my eyes in work. ....

It's on its last legs. ....

not as often as I'd like to ....

not as much as I used to ....

It's better than my last one. ....

It wasn't as good as I remembered. ....

Cheer up! It's not the end of the world. ....

Haven't you heard? ....

It's done a lot of damage. ....

Oh, I am sorry to hear that. ....

I'm afraid not. ....

smashed to pieces. ....

....

....

....

....

....

Unit 3

I work out a lot.	....
I really love going round junk shops.	....
A couple of times a year.	....
How long did it take you to learn?	....
How much does it usually cost you?	....
The thing is, ...	....
pop and R'n'B and that kind of thing	....
It's not really my cup of tea.	....
I'm not really that keen on clubbing.	....
What do you feel like doing tonight?	....
She's really into keeping fit.	....
I used to, but I grew out of it.	....
I just lost interest in it after a while.	....
Oh well, each to their own.	....
It's just one of those things.	....

....
....
....
....
....

Unit 4

I spend my weekends mountaineering.	....
She spends a lot of time helping the homeless.	....
Is everything all right?	....
I go riding whenever I can.	....
He committed suicide.	....
There's still a lot of discrimination.	....
It's male-dominated.	....
You're taking a real risk.	....
There's a lot of opposition to the plan.	....
I would if I could, but I can't.	....
I'd quite like to go to the cinema tonight.	....
If you'd rather, we could always ...	....
I can give you a lift, if you want.	....
I wouldn't do that, if you paid me!	....
That'd be great.	....

....
....
....
....
....

Unit 5

Why did you decide to do that, then? ....

How come you decided to go there, then? ....

It was a real weight off my shoulders. ....

It was total chaos. ....

I'd been thinking about it for ages. ....

Why on earth did he say that? ....

It's a piece of cake. ....

It's like getting blood out of a stone. ....

It's easier said than done. ....

I work as a bouncer at weekends. ....

It's a very demanding job. ....

It was a mutual decision. ....

It was a very unpopular decision. ....

A friend of mine recommended it. ....

Good for you! ....

....

....

....

....

....

Unit 6

It's not allowed. ....

He was fined a thousand dollars. ....

He can't handle the pressure. ....

I'm expecting a phone call. ....

I didn't want to make a fuss. ....

It looks fine to me. ....

Can you watch my bag for a minute? ....

I can't see it anywhere. ....

It was great, much better than I'd expected. ....

Quiet? It's dead! ....

That's a good question. ....

I haven't really thought about it. ....

I'd have to think about that. ....

He's finally given up smoking. ....

I fed up with doing the same thing every day. ....

....

....

....

....

....

Unit 7

What're you up to this weekend?	....
I will if I get the chance.	....
I've got to do some things for school.	....
It'll be nice to have a lie-in.	....
I've got to catch up with my e-mails.	....
I'll do it later, I promise.	....
Tell me about it!	....
I'm supposed to be going out tonight, but I don't really feel like it.	....
I've got some friends coming over tonight.	....
He's staying at a friend's.	....
I'm going away for the weekend.	....
I'm going on a guided walk.	....
Rather you than me!	....
Oh well, beggars can't be choosers!	....

....
....
....
....
....

Unit 8

We're having a house-warming party this Friday.	....
I went to a rave last weekend.	....
They tried to gatecrash our party.	....
I'll sort out the music if you sort out the food.	....
Did you have a hen night?	....
It really ruined the night.	....
It led to calls for tighter laws.	....
I just couldn't believe my eyes.	....
I just couldn't make up my mind.	....
It nearly ended in tragedy.	....
They're very right-wing.	....
They came to power in the last election.	....
They ought to ban it.	....
They really need to crack down on it.	....
They've relaxed the laws a bit.	....

....
....
....
....
....

Unit 9

I just had an early night. ....

I didn't know a single person there. ....

We had absolutely nothing in common. ....

I was on the edge of my seat. ....

I fell asleep halfway through. ....

She gets very well-paid. ....

I'll have to have a word with my boss. ....

I bet he doesn't. ....

Oh, did you? That must've been nice. ....

Oh, are you? Anywhere particular in mind? ....

I was so angry, I could've killed him! ....

I was so bored, I walked out! ....

You did *what* last night? ....

You went *where* last night? ....

I didn't get in until three last night. ....

....

....

....

....

....

Unit 10

He looks like a bit of a nerd. ....

She looks a bit dull. ....

You look a bit down. Are you OK? ....

He's a macho idiot! ....

I bet he still lives with his mum. ....

She can be quite unpredictable. ....

That's the worst chat-up line ever. ....

My parents don't really approve of her. ....

How long've you two been going out? ....

Are you pulling my leg? ....

It took me ages to come to terms with it. ....

Their marriage is on the rocks. ....

I tend to eat out most nights. ....

I could've told you that. ....

You should've known better. ....

....

....

....

....

....

Unit 11

Did I ever tell you about the time I ...   .

I was just minding my own business, ...

when all of a sudden   ....

Well, what happened in the end was ...   .

It seems funny now, but it wasn't at the time.   ....

Sorry. I didn't recognise you.   ....

I think it's dyed.   ....

He seems like a really nice bloke.   ....

It's another one of his tall stories.   ....

He smokes like a chimney.   ....

He was driving like a lunatic.   ....

I was so tired, I slept like a log.   ....

I'm dying for a coffee.   ....

I'm sick to death of it.   ....

She gets away with murder.   ....

....

....

....

....

....

Unit 12

What was I thinking of?   ....

They must have money to burn.   ....

My dad grounded me for a week.   ....

We stopped off to get something to eat.   ....

We broke down on the way there.   ....

We took a wrong turn.   ....

I bumped into an old friend of mine.   ....

What a horrible journey!   ....

I went travelling round India for a year.   ....

I like to travel light.   ....

She looks about thirty-ish.   ....

It's just an urban myth.   ....

She's got reddish-brown hair.   ....

He was sort of smiling at me.   ....

a hammer or something like that.   ....

....

....

....

....

....

Unit 13

Hello. Long time, no see! ....

I haven't seen you for ages. ....

You haven't changed a bit. ....

What've you been up to since I last saw you. ....

He just doesn't get the message. ....

It was a very controversial film. ....

I've completely forgotten your name. ....

I've just had an idea. ....

Get to the point! ....

I just don't see the point. ....

It was the high point of our trip. ....

I wish you'd told me earlier. ....

I wish I hadn't said that. ....

They hate each other's guts. ....

We just hit it off at once. ....

....

....

....

....

....

Unit 14

I went and saw this great exhibition. ....

I prefer sculpture to paintings. ....

It's OK if you're into that kind of thing. ....

It's not worth the entrance fee. ....

It's a bit too abstract for me. ....

I prefer his portraits to his landscapes. ....

Would you recommend it? ....

It causes a lot of problems. ....

I went to the opera, which was nice. ....

I've been meaning to see that for ages. ....

Oh, that reminds me. ....

I'd like to do that myself. ....

It's well worth a visit. ....

I think it's really offensive. ....

It caused outrage in the media. ....

....

....

....

....

....

Unit 15

What did you think of it? Was it any good? ....

It was horrendous! ....

It was a bit disappointing, to be honest. ....

It was nothing special. ....

Didn't you find it a bit over the top? ....

I found it a bit bland. ....

It was really good, considering how cheap it was. ....

He's not exactly Einstein, is he? ....

Don't you think it's a bit over-rated? ....

I was just dead tired. ....

It's a bit like skiing, only not as difficult. ....

It was a bit like his other book, only better. ....

That must've been dreadful. ....

You must've been really annoyed. ....

You must be exhausted. ....

....

....

....

....

....

Unit 16

It's a cult movie. ....

It's a typical Hollywood blockbuster. ....

some Italian guy ....

I can't remember off the top of my head. ....

It's on the tip of my tongue. ....

It'll come to me in a minute. ....

It's got subtitles. ....

They dubbed it into French. ....

The dialogue was brilliant. ....

Who's in it? ....

The special effects were amazing! ....

I'd never been there before. ....

It was the first time I'd seen that kind of thing. ....

It's meant to be incredible. ....

I wouldn't have, if it hadn't been for you. ....

....

....

....

....

....

Unit 17

It'd be really good if they . . .   .

What would be really great is if they . . .   .

I don't really have any strong views on that.   . . . .

That's a difficult question to answer.   . . . .

Well, I agree up to a point, but . . .   .

It's hardly surprising, is it?   . . . .

They've pedestrianised the town centre.   . . . .

There's a one-way system.   . . . .

I had to do a U-turn.   . . . .

The traffic is a nightmare.   . . . .

Personally, I think it's ridiculous.   . . . .

It's really gone to the dogs.   . . . .

He's the black sheep of the family.   . . . .

It's a very industrial place.   . . . .

The shanty towns are awful!   . . . .

. . . .

. . . .

. . . .

. . . .

. . . .

Unit 18

I don't know how you put up with it.   . . . .

They completely messed it up.   . . . .

I wish you'd stop going on about it!   . . . .

It's a really awful hairdo.   . . . .

and then to top the whole thing off   . . . .

That's the last thing I need!   . . . .

It's good to get things off your chest.   . . . .

Things like that don't really bother me.   . . . .

Oh well, don't let it get you down.   . . . .

It really bugs me.   . . . .

It's a Catch 22 situation.   . . . .

It's just the tip of the iceberg.   . . . .

It's a bit of a mixed blessing.   . . . .

I can't be bothered.   . . . .

It's no bother at all. Honestly.   . . . .

. . . .

. . . .

. . . .

. . . .

. . . .

Unit 19

You're such a pessimist! ....

That's a bit optimistic, isn't it? ....

on the spur of the moment ....

We're doing our flat up at the moment. ....

He got really badly beaten up. ....

It's bad to bottle up your feelings. ....

What I'd really like to do next year is... ....

What I was thinking of doing is... ....

I'm happy doing what I'm doing. ....

I just take things as they come. ....

I can't really say yet. It all depends. ....

I can see myself going abroad one day. ....

They've got really high expectations. ....

I'm really dreading it. ....

I wish I didn't have to, but I do. ....

....

....

....

....

....

Unit 20

I'd hate to be stuck behind a desk all day. ....

I get a company car. ....

I got six months' maternity leave. ....

I haven't had a proper contract yet. ....

At least you know your job is secure. ....

Do you belong to a trade union? ....

They've made a really good job of it. ....

It's been really hard work. ....

I've been rushed off my feet all week. ....

It's slave-labour! ....

He's awful, a real slave-driver. ....

She's very domineering. ....

He's not the most intelligent guy I've ever met. ....

She's a really good person to work for. ....

He's always on the phone to his girlfriend.. ....

....

....

....

....

....